Teaching Elementary Mathematics:

A Resource for Field Experiences

Fourth Edition

Nancy L. Smith
Emporia State University

Diana V. Lambdin
Indiana University

Mary M. Lindquist
Columbus State University

Robert E. Reys
University of Missouri

WILEY

John Wiley & Sons

To order books or for customer service, please call 1-800-CALL-WILEY (225-5945).

ISBN-13   978- 0-470-41984-7

Printed in the United States of America

10 9 8 7 6 5 4 3 2 1

Printed and bound by Bind-Rite Graphics, Inc.

Table of Contents

Contents by Topic and Experience   ix
Preface to Prospective Elementary Teachers   x
Preface to Instructors of Prospective Elementary Teachers   xi
Professionalism and Confidentiality Agreement   xii
Field Experience Cover Page   xiii
Individual Learning Plan Template   xv
Field Experience Rubric   xvi

IN THE SCHOOL

Learning about the School and its Resources Content   1

Curriculum Guide   3
Mathematics in the School   4
Classroom Manipulatives—Finding Them   5
Classroom Manipulatives—Using Them   6
Classroom Sketch   7
Children's Literature in the Mathematics Classroom   8
Mathematics Textbook Lesson   9
Mathematics Textbook Unit   10
Testing   11
Connections in the Textbook and Classroom   12
Problem Solving in the Textbook and Classroom   13
Counting in the Textbook and Classroom: Grades K–2   14
Place Value in the Textbook and Classroom   15
Operation Meaning in the Textbook and Classroom   16
Basic Facts in the Textbook and Classroom   17
Computation in the Textbook and Classroom   18
Fractions in the Textbook and Curriculum Guide   19
Patterns in the Textbook and Classroom   20
Measurement Tools   21
Probability Models in the Classroom   22

Observing the Teacher and Students Content   23

Children's Development   25
Equity for Gender in Whole Class Lessons   26
Equity in Single-Gender Group Work   27

Equity in Mixed-Gender Group Work   28

Equity for Students with Special Needs   29

Equity for English Language Learners   30

The Learning Environment Observation Sheet   31

The Learning Environment   32

Teaching a Mathematics Lesson   33

Checking on Technology   34

Analyzing Classroom Discourse Observation Sheet   35

Analyzing Classroom Discourse   36

Focusing on Individuals Observation Sheet   37

Focusing on Individuals   38

Analyzing Textbook Use   39

Proctoring a Test or a Classroom Assignment   41

Analytic Scoring Scale   42

Holistic Scoring Rubric   42

Analytic/Holistic Problem Solving Scoring   43

Analytic Scoring Reflection   44

Performance Task Template   45

Performance Task   46

Mathematical Processes Observation Sheet   47

Mathematical Processes   48

Focusing on Counting and Number Recognition   49

Timed Tests   50

Focusing on Computation   51

Focusing on Geometry   52

Focusing on Measurement   53

Focusing on Probability and Data   54

Interviewing the Teacher and Students Content   55

Interviews by Topic   56

Resources for Teaching Mathematics   58

Equity   59

Teaching, Learning   60

Attitudes about Mathematics   61

Teaching a Topic   62

Grouping in the Classroom   63

Teaching with Technology   64

Assessment   65

Primary Interview on Place Value   67

Doing Math   69

Problem Solving Strategies   70

Conservation and Counting   71

Counting   72

Early Number Sense   73

Place Value   74

Developing Place Value Concepts   75

Basic Fact Difficulty   76

Addition and Multiplication Basic Facts   77

Basic Fact Fluency   78

About How Much?   79

Do it Mentally   80

Addition with Regrouping   81

Transitional Algorithms   82

Three-Fourths   83

Proportions   85

Percents   86

Thinking About Patterns   87

Equality   89

Algebraic Thinking   90

Find Me   91

Classify Me   93

Compare Shapes   95

Snake and Strip Unit Patterns   96

Measuring   97

Graphing   99

Statistics   100

Probability   101

HELPING CHILDREN LEARN
Helping Children Learn with Games Content   *102*

Advantages of Using Games   102

Games by Topic by Content   103

Buzz-A Counting Game   105

Dots and Numbers   106

Wipe Out   107

Hit the Target   108

Clear the Board!   109

Fill the Frame (or Empty the Frame)   111

The Fact Game   113

Roll A Sum   115

Roll A Product   117

Calculators Versus Mental Computation   119

Capture 5   121

Race-to-a-Flat, Give-Away-a-Flat   124

Sum or Difference Game   126

The Remainder Game   128

Fraction Shape Puzzles   130

Whole Hog   132

Can You Beat the Toss?   135

Make a Match   137

Less is Best   139

Solid Shake   141

Race to a Yard (or Meter)   143

Race to 20   145

Skunk   146

Factor Me Out   147

Helping Children Learn with Technology Content   149

Software Review Form   151

Reviewing Software   152

WWW Lesson Plan   153

Web Sites   154

Integrating Calculators into a Mathematics Lesson   155

Problem Solving on the Web   157

Counting On and On and On   159

Skipping Around   161

Counting Backward   163

Base Blocks on the Internet   165

Chip Trading on the Internet   166

Hitting Hundreds   167

Calculator Fact Practice   169

Guess My Fact   170

21 or Bust!   171

How would you do it? (Whole Numbers)   173

How would you do it? (Fractions)   175

Zeros Count   177

Plug In Puzzles   179

Decimal Maze   181

Completing Patterns   183

Make Me Different   184

Build a Graph   185

Build a Spinner   186

Divisibility Discovery   187

Helping Children Learn: In the Classroom Lessons Content   189

Lesson Plan Cover Sheet   192

Lesson Participant Summary   193

Investigative Lesson Plan Outline   194

Direct Instruction Lesson Plan Outline   195

Exploration Lesson Plan Template   196

After-Teaching Reflection   197

After-Teaching Feedback   198

Different Kinds of Four-sided Figures   199

Patterns with Blocks   201

Composing Fractions   203

Who am I?   205

Alike-and-Difference Trains   207

Hunting for Numbers   209

Skip Counting   211

Decide If It's Up or Down   213

Counting on a Hundred Chart   215

Finding Tens   217

The Power of 10 on the Thousand Chart   219

Thousands Chart   221

Literature Context for Facts   222

Dot Sticks   223

Rectangles and More Rectangles   225

Finding 100   227

How Could It Happen?   229

Sorting Products   231

Number Net   233

Look for Patterns   235

Variation on Look for Patterns (Subtraction)   237

Fraction Strips   238

Comparing Models   241

Know your Coins   243

Balance Me   245

In-Out Machine   247

Solid Activities   249

Gumdrops and Toothpicks   251

Show My Sides   253

Measuring Length with Arbitrary Units   255

Comparing Height and Circumference   257

How Are We Alike? Different?   259

Make Two of Me!   261

What is the Connection Between Volume and Surface Area?   263

What is the Connection between Perimeter and Height?   265

Let's Find Out   267

Peanuts   269

What Are the Chances?   271

Rolling and Recording   273

Can You Make Predictions?   275

What Do You See in Me?   277

Do You Believe That?   279

Appendix A: Blackline Masters Content   *281*

A-1   Base-Ten Blocks   282

A-2   0–9 Numeral Cards   283

A-3   0–9 Dot Cards   284

A-4   Attribute Blocks   285

A-5   Hundreds Charts   286

A-6   Geoboard Recording Paper   287

A-7   Centimeter Grid Paper   288

A-8   Inch Grid Paper   289

Contents by Topic and Experience

	In the School (Observation and Collection of Information)			Helping Children Learn (Activities to do with Children)		
HCLM Chapter Topics	School and Resources	Teacher and Student Observation	Teacher and Student Interviews	Games	Technology Activities	In the Classroom Lessons
1. Issues, Trends, Principles	pp. 3–4		pp. 58–59			
2. Learning	pp. 5–6	pp. 25–30	pp. 60–61			pp. 199–202
3. Teaching, Planning, Adapting	pp. 7–10	pp. 31–40 See also pp. 26–30	pp. 62–64		pp. 151–156	
4. Assessing, Recording, Reporting	p. 11	pp. 41–46	pp. 65–68			See also pp. 67–68
5. Process Standards	p. 12 See also pp. 8–10	pp. 47–48	p. 69 See also p. 70		pp. 157–158 See also pp. 151–154	
6. Problem Solving	p. 13 See also pp. 8–10	See also pp. 33, 42–48	p. 70 See also pp. 62, 69	See also pp. 171–172, 203–204	See also pp. 151–154, 157–158	pp. 203–204
7. Number Sense, Prenumber	p. 14 See also pp. 8–10	p. 49 See also p. 33	pp. 71–73 See also p. 62	pp. 105–106 See also pp. 111–112	pp. 159–164 See also pp. 151–154	pp. 205–212 See also pp. 159–164
8. Place Value	p. 15 See also pp. 8–10	See also p. 33	pp. 74–75 See also p. 62, 67–68	pp. 107–108 See also pp. 124–125	pp. 165–168 See also pp. 107, 151–154	pp. 215–221 Also pp. 165–168
9. Basic Facts	pp. 16–17 See also pp. 8–10	p. 50 See also p. 33	pp. 76–78 See also p. 62	pp. 109–118 Also pp. 145–146	pp. 169–172 See also pp. 159–162, 151–154	pp. 222–226 Also pp. 159–162, 211–212, 273–274
10. Computational Alternatives	See also pp. 8–10, 17	p. 51 See also p. 33	pp. 79–80 See also p. 62	pp. 119–120 See also pp. 121–23, 128–29	pp. 173–176 See also pp. 119–120, 151–156	p. 227–232 Also pp. 173–176, 209, 235
11. Whole Number Operations	p. 18 See also pp. 8–10	See also p. 33	pp. 81–82 See also p. 62	pp. 121–129	pp. 177–178 See also pp. 151–154, 173–174	pp. 233–237 See also pp. 173–174
12. Fractions, Decimals	p. 19 See also pp. 8–10	See also p. 33	pp. 83–84 See also p. 62	pp. 130–136 See also pp. 137–138	pp. 179–182 See also pp. 151–154, 175–176	pp. 238–242 See also pp. 175, 203
13. Ratio, Proportion, Percent	See also pp. 8–10	See also p. 33	pp. 85–86 See also p. 62	pp. 137–138 See also pp. 135–136	See also pp. 151–154	pp. 243–244
14. Patterns, Algebra	p. 20 See also pp. 8–10	See also p. 33	pp. 87–90 See also p. 62	See also pp. 105, 113–114, 145, 147–148	p. 183, See also pp. 187, 151–154, 159–162	pp. 245–248 Also 187, 201, 211, 215, 219, 235, 243
15. Geometry	See also pp. 8–10	p. 52 See also p. 33	pp. 91–95 See also p. 62	pp. 139–142	p. 184, See also pp. 151–154	pp. 249–254, See also pp. 199–200
16. Measurement	p. 21 See also pp. 8–10	p. 53 See also p. 33	pp. 96–98 See also p. 62	pp. 143–144	See also pp. 151–154	pp. 255–256 See also pp. 201, 243
17. Data, Statistics, Probability	p. 22 See also pp. 8–10	p. 54 See also p. 33	pp. 99–101 See also p. 62	pp. 145–146 Also pp. 115–116	pp. 185–186 See also pp. 151–154	pp. 267–276
18. Number Theory	See also pp. 8–10	See also p. 33	See also p. 62	pp. 147–148	pp. 187–188 See also pp. 151–154	pp. 277–280

Preface to Prospective Elementary Teachers

As a prospective elementary teacher, you are being asked to spend a significant amount of time in school classrooms prior to student teaching. What happens in your field experience may vary greatly from day to day, classroom to classroom and teacher to teacher. You observe, put up a bulletin board, help an individual child with a troublesome concept, work with a group of children, grade papers, organize materials for a lesson, teach a lesson to a small group, or teach the whole class. Although this variety provides a wealth of diverse experiences, it also has a downside. You may find that your experiences were very different from those of your peers, giving you little in common to discuss. Furthermore, you may not have observed anything directly relevant to the issues being discussed in your methods class.

As instructors of mathematics methods classes, we have found it useful to provide our students some common in-school experiences to focus discussions and connect their field experience with the mathematics methods class. That is why we have written, *Teaching Elementary Mathematics: A Resource for Field Experiences* (4th edition). The activities in this book are divided into two categories: *In the School* and *Helping Children Learn*.

In the School activities focus on observing and gathering information about the school and its resources, teachers, and children. For example, you might be asked to interview or observe a teacher, check if the school offers a "Math Night for Parents" or has a policy for use of calculators. Guidelines for task-based interviews with children are also provided to help you learn about their attitudes, about mathematics and their confidence, as well as their skills and their thinking.

Helping Children Learn activities focus on learning what children know and what mathematics they are able to do through activities that are somewhat like mini-lessons. All of the activities provide an explicit focus designed to help you learn more about how elementary and middle school children think and what they can do with a range of content typically encountered in school. You present the activity, observe children's responses, and probe when needed to learn what the child is doing and as much about what the child is thinking as you can.

You are not expected to use all of the activities in this book during your methods class or field experience. A range is available to allow you or your instructor to choose activities that are appropriate for your situation. The matrix provides an overview of the activities organized by topic and type of experience. In addition, at the beginning of each section, you will find a table of contents organized by topic.

Many of the activities in this book will also be good resources for you as you student teach and begin your teaching career. Although some activities may be used in grades K–8, other activities are targeted toward narrower grade bands (K–2, 3–5, 6–8) consistent with the NCTM *Principles and Standards for School Mathematics*. With minor variation most of the activities can be adapted and used with a broader range of children. You should summarize and reflect on what happened. As space is limited, you may need to attach your reflection and analysis. We wish you well as you embark on your career, and hope this book helps prepare you in a meaningful way.

Preface to Instructors of Prospective Elementary Teachers

This book is designed to support field experiences of pre-service elementary teachers who are preparing to help children learn mathematics. Although the activities in the book are linked to *Helping Children Learn Mathematics*, 9th edition (HCLM), they can also be used independently with other methods books. The matrix provides a summary of the activities sorted by key topics. Two new activities have been added to each section. Also new to this edition is the category of number theory. In addition, at the beginning of each section, you will find a table of contents of activities related to the topic.

Prospective teachers are often asked to spend a significant amount of time in elementary school classrooms prior to student teaching. *Teaching Elementary Mathematics: A Resource for Field Experiences* (4th edition) is a resource that provides some mathematical focus for field experiences. The activities in this book are divided into two broad categories: *In the School* and *Helping Children Learn*.

In the School activities focus on observing and gathering information about the school and its resources, teachers, parents, and children. They include collecting information about resources, observations, and interviews. Specific questions are included to help students focus on each of these areas.

Helping Children Learn activities focus on helping students find out what children know and what mathematics they are able to do through activities. They include games, technology activities, and In the Classroom (ITC) lessons. The ITC activities are derived from the text, *Helping Children Learn Mathematics* but are designed to stand alone.

You are not expected to use all of the activities in this book. A range is available to allow you (or your students) to choose activities that seem appropriate for their situations. For example, you might assign everyone to conduct an interview while in the schools but the topic and grade level selected will depend on each student's field placement. Or you might have each student develop an Individual Learning Plan (page xv), selecting one or more activities to complete for each content strand. While some activities may be used in grades K–8, other activities are targeted toward narrower grade bands (K–2, 3–5, 6–8). However, we realize that grade bands are artificial, so with minor variation most of the activities can be adapted and used with a broader range of children. Students will also need help determining which grade levels within the band are appropriate for an activity. Once the activity is completed, students should be expected to summarize and reflect on what happened. In many cases, we have provided a structure to focus this reflection, often by including specific prompts. In addition to using the activities in a field experience, many of the activities may also be used during your methods class period. For example, observations could be completed using video clips. Helping Children Learn activities could be completed during the methods class.

We wish to acknowledge the help of the following student reviewers from Emporia State University who provided thoughtful analysis and careful feedback for an early draft. They include John Apel, Emily Devor, Angela Scherer, Sherri Sells, and Kara Warrion. Thanks also to Sue Beck, Morehead State University, Bob Glasgow, Southwest Baptist University, Guy Ragan, Southwest Missouri State University, Barbara Reys, University of Missouri, Edna O. Schack, Morehead State University, and Deanna Wasman, Appalachian State University for reviewing activities and offering suggestions.

This book contains activities we have found most useful in helping elementary teachers learn about mathematics teaching in school-based settings. We have provided a range of activities for you and your students to choose and use during their school-based experiences. We hope these activities will be equally useful to you and your students.

Professionalism and Confidentiality Agreement

I am a guest in the school where I am observing. My task is to objectively collect information so that my classmates and I can learn more about helping children learn mathematics. As my observation time is limited, it is not my job to pass judgments about the teacher, children, or the school.

I agree to protect the confidentiality of the classroom and respect the professionalism of my teacher.

I agree to offer to share my assignments with the teacher before turning them in to my methods instructor. If he/she would like me to make changes, I will respect his/her wishes.

I agree that observation and interview results should be discussed only with the teacher or my methods instructor. There are not "right" answers or behaviors in these exercises.

I have read and agree to follow the Professionalism and Confidentiality Agreement.

_____   _____
Signature   Date

Field Experience Cover Page

Name: _____

Instructions

Attach a copy of this sheet, or a cover page including the following information, for all field experience assignments that are turned in to your instructor.

Date of classroom visit: _____   Duration of classroom visit: _____
(minutes)

_____   _____   _____
School   Grade   Host/Mentor Teacher

Participants: (If children, first names only)

EXPERIENCES (Check all that apply and list the numbers for the experiences attached.)

In the School   Page Numbers for Experiences:

_____ Learning About the School and Resources _____

_____ Observing the Teacher _____

_____ Observing Students _____

_____ Interviewing the Teacher _____

_____ Interviewing a Student _____

Helping Children Learn   Page Numbers for Experiences:

_____ Learning with Games _____

_____ Learning with Technology _____

_____ Learning with In the Classroom Lessons _____

Elementary Mathematics Individual Learning Plan (ILP)

Name _____ Date _____ Grade Level _____

School _____ Cooperating Teacher _____

Approval Signature _____ _____
                         Cooperating Teacher   Instructor

Instructions: From *Teaching Elementary Mathematics: A Resource for Field Experience*, collaborate with your cooperating teacher to select and complete a minimum of one field experience for each of the six categories below.

I. Instruction and Assessment

TEM page #	Title of Experience	Teacher/Grade Level	Participants	Due Date

II. Number and Operations

TEM page #	Title of Experience	Teacher/Grade Level	Participants	Due Date

III. Algebra

TEM page #	Title of Experience	Teacher/Grade Level	Participants	Due Date

IV. Geometry

TEM page #	Title of Experience	Teacher/Grade Level	Participants	Due Date

V. Measurement

TEM page #	Title of Experience	Teacher/Grade Level	Participants	Due Date

VI. Data Analysis and Probability

TEM page #	Title of Experience	Teacher/Grade Level	Participants	Due Date

Field Experience Assessment Form

Name: _____ Section: _____
(Check one and list page number)   Score Rubric Sections
___   School and Resources, p. ___   A   B   C   D
___   Interview, p. ___   A   B   C   D
___   Observation, p. ___   A   B   C   D
___   Game Lesson, p. ___   A   B   C   E
___   Technology Lesson, p. ___   A   B   C   E
___   ITC Lesson, p. ___   A   B   C   E

Rubric

Elements to be Graded (0-5 points)	Weight	Excellent 5 points	4	Needs Improvement 3 points	2	Unsatisfactory 0-1 points	Points Earned
A. Editing (all activities) Self Earned ___ ___	x 1	Editing for spelling/grammar errors is complete and effective		Editing leaves some spelling/ grammar errors		Editing is poor or not evident	_____ out of 5 possible
B. Activity Introduction Self Earned ___ ___	x 1	Intro completely addresses • Who participated • Why chosen • How it went • What you learned		Intro briefly addresses • Who participated • Why chosen • How it went • What you learned		Intro doesn't address • Who participated • Why chosen • How it went • What you learned	_____ out of 5 possible
C. Text Reflections Self Earned ___ ___	x2	Text Reflections • are accurate • are completely filled in • show deep thinking and analysis		Text Reflections • are mostly accurate • mostly filled in • show some thinking and analysis		Text Reflections • are inaccurate • are not completely filled in • show little or no thinking and analysis	_____ out of 10 possible
D. Form/ Product Self Earned ___ ___	x 2	Form/product is • attached to the assignment • accurate • completely filled in • clear, specific		Form/product is • attached to the assignment • mostly accurate • briefly or mostly filled in • somewhat clear, specific		Form/product is • not attached to the assignment • inaccurate • not filled in • not clear, specific	_____ out of 10 possible
E. Teaching Reflection Self Earned ___ ___	x 2	Reflection • is complete • includes all -assessment, -changes, -follow-up • is clear, specific, and accurate • shows deep thinking and self-analysis		Reflection • is partly complete • includes most -assessment, -changes, -follow-up • is somewhat clear, specific, and accurate • shows some thinking and self-analysis		Reflection • is incomplete • does not include -assessment, -changes, -follow-up • is not clear, specific, and accurate • shows little or no thinking and self-analysis	_____ out of 10 possible

Comments:

Self Earned Total

Total Points: ____ ____ / 30

In the School: Learning about the School and its Resources Content

These data collection experiences allow you to learn more about elementary and middle schools and classrooms. This includes collecting information about the school, its policies and procedures, and resources available to teachers. No grade levels are indicated on the activities. All of these activities may be used in K–8 classrooms.

School Resources by Topic

Key Topics	Title	Page
1. Issues, Trends, Principles	Curriculum Guide Mathematics in the School	3 4
2. Learning	Classroom Manipulatives—Finding Them Classroom Manipulatives—Using Them	5 6
3. Teaching, Planning, Adapting	Classroom Sketch Children's Literature in the Mathematics Classroom Mathematics Textbook Lesson Mathematics Textbook Unit	7 8 9 10
4. Assessing, Recording, Reporting	Testing	11
5. Process Standards	Connections in the Textbook and Classroom See also pp. 8-10	12
6. Problem Solving	Problem Solving in the Textbook and Classroom See also pp. 8-10	13
7. Number Sense, Prenumber	Counting in the Textbook and Classroom See also pp. 8-10	14
8. Place Value	Place Value in the Textbook and Classroom See also pp. 8-10	15
9. Basic Facts	Operation Meaning in the Textbook and Classroom Basic Facts in the Textbook and Classroom See also pp. 8-10	16 17
10. Computational Alternatives	See also pp. 8-10, 18	
11. Whole Number Operations	Computation in the Textbook and Classroom See also pp. 8-10	18
12. Fractions, Decimals	Fractions in the Textbook and Curriculum Guide See also pp. 8-10	19
13. Ratio, Proportion, Percent	See also pp. 8-10	

SCHOOL RESOURCES BY TOPIC (continued)

Key Topics	Title	Page
14. Patterns, Algebra	Patterns in the Textbook and Classroom See also pp. 8-10	20
15. Geometry	See also pp. 8-10	
16. Measurement	Measurement Tools See also pp. 8-10	21
17. Data, Statistics, Probability	Probability Models in the Classroom See also pp. 8-10	22
18. Number Theory	See also pp. 8-10	

Curriculum Guide

In this activity you will compare the school's curriculum guide with NCTM's Standards and Expectations *(Principles and Standards for School Mathematics*, NCTM 2000). The NCTM chart can be found in Appendix A of *Helping Children Learn Mathematics, 9e* (Reys et al., 2009) or on the World Wide Web (standards.nctm.org).

1. Obtain the Curriculum Guide for mathematics used by the school for the grade level with which you are working. [This could be a state, district, or school document.] Obtain the NCTM Standards and Expectations for that grade-level band (e.g., Grades 3–5).

   Curriculum Guide examined:

2. Make the following overall comparisons of the two documents:

   (a) Grade-level examined:

   Curriculum Guide   grade(s) _____

   Principles and Standards   grade-band _____

   (b) What major content areas are included in each?

   (c) What process standards are included in each? Are they listed separately or integrated into the expectations? Give an example.

3. Choose one content area of the *Principles and Standards*. Compare the expectations for this area with the relevant statements in the Curriculum Guide. Give an example of how they are the same and one of how they are different. Overall, how do the two documents compare in this content area? (You may want to attach a copy of the relevant pages and make notes on the documents.)

REFLECTION:

1. How do you feel about teaching from this curriculum? Explain why.

Mathematics in the School

These observations and questions are designed to help you learn about the role of mathematics in this school. This initial impression may change during your stay in the school, but think of this as what parents and other visitors may see on a first visit.

OBSERVATIONS:

1. As you enter the school, around the office and halls, is there any indication that children are involved in mathematics? Look for children's work, mathematics artifacts, such as a number line, or problems of the week. Compare/contrast this emphasis on mathematics to that given to language arts, visual arts, science, or other subject areas.

2. Glance in several classrooms. Do you observe mathematics (e.g. posters) on display? Do you observe mathematics materials around the room? Describe what grade levels you observed and what you saw.

QUESTIONS:

3. Ask a teacher, the principal or assistant principal about the role of mathematics in the school. Do they have special activities (fairs, family math nights, teams, or contests) for mathematics? Do they have a set amount of time for mathematics at each level? Do they have any special initiatives focused on mathematics? Are there mathematics resource materials available for teachers to use? Where are they housed? How are they shared?

4. Ask your teacher the same questions, as in #1, about his or her own classroom. How does the amount of time allotted for mathematics compare with other subject areas?

REFLECTION:

1. From what you saw and asked, how would you describe the environment of the school in terms of mathematics?

Classroom Manipulatives—Finding Them

Manipulatives provide valuable support for mathematics teaching and learning. These materials may be on shelves, in cabinets, closets, teacher and children's desks, or in a library or storage area for teachers to check out. The manipulatives needed depend on the grade level, mathematics being learned, and the commitment of the teacher toward using them. This is a fact-finding mission to learn the range of manipulatives available to support the mathematics learning of children.

Once you have done your fact-finding (i.e., talked with teachers, teacher's aid, librarian, etc.) complete the chart below by placing a check by materials available. Then ask a teacher which of the available materials have been used with her/his children, and add any additional materials that are available (used) but not listed below.

Manipulative	Available	Used	Manipulative	Available	Used
Attribute Blocks	[ ]	[ ]	Measurement devices—		
Base ten blocks	[ ]	[ ]	Liter	[ ]	[ ]
Calculators	[ ]	[ ]	Meter sticks	[ ]	[ ]
Cuisenaire rods	[ ]	[ ]	Scales	[ ]	[ ]
Decimal models	[ ]	[ ]	Thermometer	[ ]	[ ]
Fraction models	[ ]	[ ]	Pattern Blocks	[ ]	[ ]
Geoboards	[ ]	[ ]	Play Money	[ ]	[ ]
Geometric models	[ ]	[ ]	Tangrams	[ ]	[ ]
Interlocking Cubes (ex. Unifix etc.)	[ ]	[ ]			

Other Manipulatives:

	Available	Used		Available	Used
_____	[ ]	[ ]	_____	[ ]	[ ]
_____	[ ]	[ ]	_____	[ ]	[ ]
_____	[ ]	[ ]	_____	[ ]	[ ]

REFLECTION:

1. Did you see any of the available manipulatives being used during your classroom visits?
   Yes   No

2. If **Yes,** were the manipulatives used by the teacher? By the children? Explain.

3. If **Yes**, name or describe the manipulative(s) and the mathematical topic being discussed.

Classroom Manipulatives—Using Them

Manipulatives provide valuable support for mathematics teaching and learning. Some popular materials are listed in the previous activity, Classroom Manipulatives-Finding Them. The following questions provide several different perspectives to consider about the use and availability of manipulatives.

OBSERVE A CLASS WHERE MANIPULATIVES ARE BEING USED:

1. Did the teacher use manipulatives for demonstration? **Yes No**
   If yes, name or describe the manipulative(s) and the mathematical topic being discussed.

2. Were the students using manipulatives during the lesson? **Yes No**
   If yes, name or describe the manipulative(s) and the mathematical topic being discussed.

3. Were there other manipulatives visible in the classroom? **Yes No**
   If yes, name or describe them.

ASK THE TEACHER:

4. Do you think manipulatives are useful in helping children learn mathematics? **Yes No**
   Please explain.

   If you answered **Yes** to #1, ask some of these questions.

5. Do you often use manipulatives in your mathematics classes? **Yes No**
   If yes, ask her to name or describe "some favorite manipulative(s)" and to describe what mathematics they help children learn.

6. Are there some manipulatives you would like to have for your classroom? **Yes No**
   If yes, ask her to name or describe them.

7. How do you get new manipulatives? (i.e., Do you recommend their purchase to the principal? Do you pay for them yourself? Is there an annual budget submitted to the district? Is there money from PTA, PTO, etc.?)

REFLECTION:

1. What benefits appear to be gained from the use of manipulatives?

2. What questions or concerns do you have about the use of manipulatives?

Classroom Sketch

The physical arrangement of a classroom can have a large influence on the teaching and learning that goes on within it. Observe the classroom of your field experience.

Draw a sketch of the arrangement of the classroom. Be sure to include teacher and student desks, work areas, location of materials such as overhead projector, computer, etc.

REFLECTION:

1. Describe particular features of the classroom which support a particular philosophy or strategy of teaching mathematics.

Children's Literature in the Mathematics Classroom

Look in the school or public library for five children's books that could be used with mathematics lessons. List the author, title, date, and publisher for each of the books here.

CHECKING THE BOOKS:

Answer the following for each book included above.

1   What grade level(s) would be most appropriate for using this book?

2. What mathematics concept(s) are or could be highlighted?

3. If the main focus of the book is a mathematical idea or concept, describe it. Or, if you would need to extend the story to relate it to math, tell what sort of extension you would suggest. In either case, give one example of how you might use this book as part of a lesson focusing on math (for example, as a lesson launch, as a source of problems, to set the context for a problem-solving activity).

CHECKING THE CLASSROOM:

4. Ask the teacher if he or she uses children's books for teaching mathematics. If so, have the teacher suggest one book and describe how it is used. If not, ask why he or she doesn't.

5. If you observe children's books being used to teach math, what is the reaction of the children?

REFLECTION:

1. What do you think are some of the benefits of using children's books to teach mathematics?

2. Do you think you will use children's books in math? Why or why not?

Mathematics Textbook Lesson

1. Examine the teacher's edition of the mathematics textbook used by the teacher and students in your class. List the grade level and bibliographic information here (author, date, title, publisher).

2. Choose a unit topic: _____

3. Select a lesson from the unit. Identify the:

   Objective:

   Lesson Type: Direct Instruction   or   Investigative
   (circle one)

   Manipulatives/models used to support learning:

   Technology integrated in the lesson:

   Adaptations for diverse learners:

   Amount of time you think it would take you to complete all of the student activities:

4. Use the appropriate lesson plan template (templates are available in the *In the Classroom* lesson section or use the template assigned by your instructor) and write a plan as you would teach it.

REFLECTION:

1. How easy was it to develop a lesson plan from this textbook page? What are the strengths and weaknesses? Explain your thinking.

2. What additional materials or activities would *you* include if you were to actually teach this lesson?

Mathematics Textbook Unit

1. Examine the teacher's edition of the mathematics textbook used by the teacher and students in your class. List the grade level and bibliographic information here (author, date, title, publisher).

2. Choose a unit topic: _____

3. Analyze and describe the following:

   Organization and Structure:

   Worthwhile mathematical tasks, active learning:

   Opportunities for communication both oral and written:

   Manipulatives/models used to support sense making and learning:

   Technology integrated in the unit:

   Multiple means of assessment:

   Adaptations for diverse learners:

   Amount of time you think it would take you to complete all of the unit lessons:

REFLECTION:

1. How easy would it be to develop lesson plans from this textbook unit? What are the strengths and weaknesses? Explain your thinking.

2. What additional materials or activities would you include if *you* were to actually teach this unit?

Testing

In this activity you will document and compare the types of mathematics tests that students experience in your school.

1. Talk with your classroom teacher about the types of assessments he/she uses for classroom grading purposes. These might be teacher-made tests or tests from the textbook. Ask if you can look at some examples. The teacher may also use other sources of information for grading (e.g., written classroom assignments, homework, student interviews, classroom observations), but your focus here is on testing.

2. Talk with the teacher about what other math tests his/her students must take (e.g., school, district, or state-mandated assessments, including standardized tests) and how test results are used. Obtain a copy of each, if possible. Some tests are kept secret, but often test guides are available which provide sample questions and information about the test. Get whatever information you can. A good place to look for information about state or district testing may be on the state or district web site.

3. Make the following comparisons of the various tests you've collected:

    (a) List the grade-level examined for each type of test and give the name of the test.

    (b) How are the formats of the tests alike or different? For each type of test, are there: multiple choice questions? questions where students must work out their own answers and show their work? questions where students must explain their thinking in writing? Are rubrics used for scoring? Is partial credit available? If so, how is it awarded? For each test, are there sections where students may use a calculator, or sections where calculators are not allowed? (Do the sorts of questions where calculators are permitted differ from those where calculators are not permitted? If so, how?) For each answer above, give an example to illustrate.

    (c) What major content areas are included in each test? For example, are there questions on numbers, geometry, measurement, data and probability, and patterns and algebra? How are the questions distributed across these content areas? Are some content areas not included? Are some content areas emphasized more fully? Give examples to illustrate your responses.

    (d) Are there questions where students' mathematical processes (e.g., communication, connections, problem solving, reasoning, representations) are assessed? If so, are mathematical processes tested separately, or do the test questions integrate processes with content? Give examples to illustrate your responses.

4. Choose one content area from the content list in (c) above. Read the description for this content area and this grade-band in *Principles and Standards for School Mathematics* (NCTM, 2000). Compare the expectations revealed by questions on the district or state test with expectations described in the *Standards*. Overall, how do the two documents compare in this content area? Give at least one example of how they are the same and one of how they are different. Would you say the test was "aligned" with the *Standards*?

REFLECTION:

1. What appears to be the role of testing in this classroom or school?

2. Some people believe the United States should require a national test and curriculum. What are your thoughts on this issue?

Connections in the Textbook and Classroom

In this activity you will focus on locating and examining resources, in your school or classroom, that connect mathematics with other school subjects and with real-world applications. Connections is one of NCTM's five "process standards." Begin by reviewing the connections standard in NCTM's *Principles and Standards for School Mathematics* (NCTM, 2000). An overview can be downloaded from www.nctm.org. Next, look for connections in various forms in your school or classroom.

1. Look for math connections that might be displayed on shelves, walls or bulletin boards in the classroom. For example, you might see evidence of children's science or art or cooking projects involving mathematics, or a poster about how math is used in various careers, or children's literature with math-related stories. Describe what you find.

2. Examine the textbook or curriculum materials for this class. List what materials you examined and describe how connections are evident in these materials. For example, you might find suggestions for art projects, or for science fair projects, or for measurement activities, or for poetry that relates to mathematics.

3. Look outside the classroom (in the library or on the web) for at least three supplemental resources about math connections that might be useful for teachers. These might include children's books, teacher resource books, software, videos, lists of websites, posters, suggestions for projects, etc. One good way to find useful resources is to do web searches by linking the words "mathematics," "connections," and some potentially related subject or field of study (for example, look for mathematics and science connections, mathematics and art connections, mathematics and cooking connections, etc.).

4. Observe or ask your teacher about ways that he/she has encouraged students to make mathematical connections. For example, are mathematical concepts or skills sometimes introduced or reinforced through science activities or experiments? Do children sometimes write explanations about mathematical ideas or write their own story problems, and thus practice writing skills in the context of thinking about mathematics? Does the teacher use a "mini-economy"—where children earn rewards for good behavior or good grades while also gaining experience in accounting as they track of their points?

REFLECTION:

1. How does NCTM's vision for emphasizing mathematical connections compare with what you found in this classroom or school?

2. What additional ways of encouraging students to make mathematical connections would you like to consider implementing when you have your own classroom?

Problem Solving in the Textbook and Classroom

In this activity you will focus on locating and examining mathematics problem solving resources in your school or classroom. Begin by reviewing the problem solving standard in NCTM's *Principles and Standards for School Mathematics*, (NCTM, 2000). This may be viewed at http://www. NCTM.org. Next, look for problem solving, in all its various forms, in your school or classroom.

1. What problem solving materials are displayed on walls or bulletin boards? You might see children's problem-solving work; a Problem of the Day, Week, or Month; a problem solving plan or steps; problem solving strategies; etc. Describe.

2. Examine your textbook or curriculum materials for this class. List the material examined and describe how problem solving is evident in these materials. Ex. Problem solving strategies might be taught in specific lessons, or story problems included at the end of each lesson, or problem solving embedded within content lessons, etc.

3. Look for supplemental problem-solving resources available for teachers. These might include children's books, teacher resource books, software, lists of websites, posters, assessment rubrics, etc. Describe what you find.

4. Observe or ask your teacher how problem solving is incorporated in typical mathematics lessons. Describe the role of problem solving in the mathematics lesson. Also describe how students' problem solving work is assessed. Ex. Assessment of daily work, through individual or collaborative problem solving, through student journals, through tests or quizzes, etc.

REFLECTION:

1. How does NCTM's vision for problem solving compare with what you found in this classroom or school?

2. What additional problem-solving resources do you hope to have when you have your own classroom?

Counting in the Textbook and Classroom

Counting is an important process that takes time and practice to develop. It is a major focus during early childhood and primary grades. Find the resource book or teacher's edition being used in mathematics in the K–2 mathematics program and use it to help answer these questions. List the grade level and bibliographic information here (author, date, title, publisher).

CHECKING THE TEXTBOOK:

1. Are specific goals for counting (or writing numbers) stated by grade level?   **Y   N**
   (i.e., Are children expected to be able to count to 100 [or some stated number] by a certain grade?) If **yes**, identify a goal for a particular grade. How do these goals compare to NCTM's *Standards and Expectations*?

2. Are calculator counting activities included? If **yes,** describe an activity.

3. Did you see a hundred-chart in the textbook? If **yes,** Did it start at 0 or 1?

4. Are the titles of specific children's books related to counting mentioned?   **Y   N**
   If **yes,** list one or two titles.

   Are these books available in the classroom or school library?   **Y   N**

CHECKING THE CLASSROOM:

5. Did you see a number line in the classroom?   **Y   N**
   If **yes,** how far did it go?

6. Did you see a hundred-chart in the classroom?   **Y   N**
   If **yes,** did it start with 0 or 1?

7. Did you find other materials (i.e. blocks, calendar, buttons, children's books, teacher resource books, technology) to encourage and support counting?
   Y   N   If yes, list them.

8. Talk to the teacher about how he or she teaches counting. Does the teacher supplement the textbook approach? If so, how? If not, why not?

REFLECTION:

1. Did you feel there were clear goals for counting and sufficient resources available to support the children reaching those expectations? Explain.

2. How would *you* use this text in teaching counting? If you think you would probably choose to supplement the text, explain what supplementary materials you would use and why.

14 • *Teaching Elementary Mathematics: A Resource for Field Experiences* © 2009 John Wiley & Sons   • In the School   • Resources

Place Value in the Textbook and Classroom

Examine a student textbook and teacher's guide for discussion of place value. Checking the table of contents or index will help locate where place value is developed. List the grade level and bibliographic information here (author, date, title, publisher).

CHECKING THE STUDENT BOOK:

1. When was the term 'place value' first introduced? (i.e., working with tens, hundreds, thousands, etc.)

2. What was the first manipulative (physical model) used to help develop place value concepts (i.e., ten frame, base ten blocks, paper strips, etc.)? Identify and briefly describe how the manipulative was used.

3. Were pictures of this model shown in the student book?   **Yes   No**
   If **Yes,** did the pictures clearly show the model in action? Explain.

4. Was more than one manipulative used in the student book?   **Yes   No**
   If **Yes,** identify other models that were used.

CHECKING THE TEACHER'S EDITION:

5. Review a teacher's edition to find models for place value that were not shown in the student book. Identify any models that were not shown in the student book.

6. Did you find other materials (i.e. children's books, teacher resource books, technology) to encourage and support the development of place value ideas?   **Y   N**   List them.

CHECKING THE CLASSROOM:

7. Ask the teacher if he or she uses manipulatives to help develop place value?   **Yes   No**
   Explain why or why not.

8. Are the place value manipulatives shown in the student text available for children to use? Are other place value models discussed in the teacher's edition available?

REFLECTION:

1. Did you feel there were clear goals for place value and sufficient resources available to support the children reaching those expectations? Explain.

2. How would *you* use this text in teaching place value? If you think you would probably choose to supplement the text, explain what supplementary materials you would use and why.

Operation Meaning in the Textbook and Classroom

Examine the mathematics textbook (or any other materials) used by the teacher and students in your class. Analyze how meaning for the four basic operations (addition, subtraction, multiplication, and division with single digits) are presented in the book.

CHECKING THE TEXTBOOK:

1. List the grade level and bibliographic information here (author, date, title, publisher):

2. Depending on grade level, you may find that the text deals with meanings for addition and subtraction, or meanings for multiplication and division, or all four. In which chapters are meanings for operation(s) presented? How much of the text is devoted to helping children make sense of the operation(s)? How is each operation introduced to the students? Is the use of manipulatives an integral part of the work on operation meaning? Are the students asked to engage in problem solving situations? Explain how (or why you say no).

3. Are there activities that engage students in moving from concrete to abstract representations? How is this done? Give some examples.

4. Are there activities presented to allow students to see the relationships between operations? If so, give some examples.

5. What other materials are listed (manipulatives, children's books, teacher resource books, technology) to encourage and support basic operations?

CHECKING THE CLASSROOM:

6. Talk to the teacher about how he or she teaches basic operations. Does the teacher supplement the textbook approach? If so how? If not, why not?

7. What other materials (i.e. manipulatives, children's books, teacher resource books, technology) did you find to encourage and support basic operations?

REFLECTION:

1. Did you feel there were clear goals for basic operations and sufficient resources available to support the children reaching those expectations? Explain.

2. How would *you* use this text in teaching the basic operations? If you think you would probably choose to supplement the text, explain what sorts of supplementary materials you would use and why.

Basic Facts in the Textbook and Classroom

Examine the mathematics textbook (or any other materials) used by the teacher and students in your class. Analyze how the basic facts for the four basic operations are presented in the book. List the grade level and bibliographic information here (author, date, title, publisher):

CHECKING THE TEXTBOOK:

1. Depending on grade level, you may find that the text deals with addition and subtraction facts, or multiplication and division facts, or all four. In which chapters are basic facts presented? How much of the text is devoted to basic fact instruction?

2. Which facts are presented? How are the facts presented and how are they grouped? Are thinking strategies presented? If so, how do they compare with the strategies for basic facts that you know or have learned?

3. Does the text provide for practice of basic facts? If so, how? (Are there timed tests, practice exercises, worksheets, games, problems, etc.)

CHECKING THE CLASSROOM:

4. Talk to the teacher about how he or she teaches basic facts. Does the teacher supplement the textbook approach? If so how? If not, why not?

5. What other materials (i.e. manipulatives, children's books, teacher resource books, technology) did you find to encourage and support basic facts?

REFLECTION:

1. Did you feel there were clear goals for basic facts and sufficient resources available to support the children reaching those expectations? Explain.

2. Do *you* think this text will develop fluency with basic facts as characterized in the *Principles and Standards for School Mathematics*? Explain your thinking.

Computation in the Textbook and Classroom

Examine the mathematics textbook used by the teacher and students in your class and analyze one lesson plan on computation in the teacher's guide. List the grade level and bibliographic information here (author, date, title, publisher):

CHECKING THE TEXTBOOK:

1. What type of computation (addition, subtraction, multiplication, division) was the lesson on?

2. What stages from concrete to abstract are involved in the lesson? How is this done?

3. Does the lesson use the standard algorithm? Are student-invented algorithms encouraged? Are any other algorithms presented? (You might want to look at other computation lessons in the book as well.)

CHECKING THE CLASSROOM:

4. Talk to the teacher about how he or she teaches computation. Does the teacher accept or encourage student-invented algorithms? If so how? If not, why not?

5. What other materials (i.e. manipulatives, children's books, teacher resource books, technology) did you find to encourage and support computation?

REFLECTION:

1. Did you feel there were clear goals for computation and sufficient resources available to support the children in reaching those expectations? Explain.

2. Would you use this lesson for teaching the computation? How? If you think you would probably want to supplement the text, explain what sorts of supplementary materials you would use and why.

Fractions in the Textbook and Curriculum Guide

Examine three successive grade levels of teacher's editions, from the textbooks at your school, for development of fractions. Also, check the curriculum guide for the state, district, or school (if none is used, refer to the *Principles and Standards for School Mathematics*, NCTM 2000).

BIBLIOGRAPHIC INFORMATION:

Textbook (author, date, title, publisher, grade levels examined)

Curriculum Guide (name, date, system)

CHECKING THE TEACHER'S EDITION:

For each of the three grade levels, answer the following questions:

1. What meanings of fractions (part whole, division, ratio, or other) are included? Is it for the first time or a repeat from previous years?

2. What models are used for fractions?

3. Are equivalent fractions used? Are models used or is only a rule given?

4. Are operations with fractions included? Which? Describe how developed.

CHECKING THE CURRICULUM GUIDE:

5. Describe briefly the main emphasis in the curriculum guide for this grade span.

6. How closely does the text follow these guidelines? Explain.

REFLECTION:

1. Do the three years show careful development of fractions? Give examples to justify your answer.

2. How would *you* use this text in teaching fractions? If you think you would probably choose to supplement the text, explain what supplementary materials you would use and why.

Patterns in the Textbook and Classroom

Examine a student textbook and teacher's guide for pattern ideas. List the grade level and bibliographic information here (author, date, title, publisher).

CHECKING THE STUDENT BOOK:

1. What types of patterns are included in the student text? Give sample page numbers for each of the types found.

2. Many patterns can be generalized with a rule (ex. add 2). Do the patterns encourage generalizations? If so, how do the students communicate such generalizations? If not, do you see ways that generalizations could be included?

CHECKING THE TEACHER'S EDITION:

3. Does the teacher's edition give additional suggestions to encourage students to generalize patterns? Give examples.

4. Does the teacher's edition give ways to use patterns in learning mathematics in addition to those in the students' textbook? Give examples.

CHECKING THE CLASSROOM:

5. Do you see any evidence of patterns (on bulletin boards, centers, or elsewhere)? List them.

6. Ask the teacher to identify the new ideas about patterns that are in this grade level.

REFLECTION:

1. Why do you think that patterns are an important part of learning mathematics?

2. Do you enjoy figuring out patterns? Why or why not?

Measurement Tools

Select a grade level: _____

Find out what measurement tools are used by the children in this grade level. You can examine the curriculum materials, talk to teachers, and look in storage areas. List the tools here. For each tool, list the measurement attribute measured (ex. length) and units used (ex. inches, paper clips).

CHECKING THE TOOLS:

Answer the following for the tools included above.

1. What measurement tools included standard units? Nonstandard units?

2. What measurement tools were (or could be) homemade? How could these tools be made with inexpensive materials?

CHECKING IN THE CLASSROOM:

3. Ask the teacher how he/she models correct use of the tools.

4. What sequence of activities does the teacher provide to prepare students to effectively use the tools?

5. If you observe measurement tools being used to teach math, what is the reaction of the children? What seems to give them difficulty using measurement tools?

REFLECTION:

1. What do you think is the benefit of learning to use a variety of tools to measure?

2. What additional measurement tools do you anticipate using? Why?

Probability Models in the Classroom

Examine the resources in your classroom for possible models of probability. Make a list of the resources and briefly describe how ideas of probability might be connected.

FROM YOUR CLASSROOM:

Do you have a panel of light switches? If so, what is the probability that, if you turn on one switch, it will turn on the proper bank of lights?

Do you have chairs/desks in your classroom? If so, is the probability of an odd number of chairs one-half?

Do your classroom windows open? If yes, describe some statements involving probability.

Check how the student chairs are arranged in your classroom.

  a. If your chairs are arranged in rows, describe how you might use probability to locate a certain seat.

  b. If your chairs are arranged in groups or pods, describe how you might use probability to locate a certain seat.

Describe how cubes might be used to develop probability.

FROM A BOOK:

Place a note card between two pages. What is the probability that the left page is an even number?

Is the probability greater than one-half that a picture or drawing will be on the right page?

Is the probability high/low that the word "mathematics" will be found at least once on the page?

REFLECTION:

1. Identify some other things in your classroom that might be used to model concepts related to probability.

2. Do you think ordinary classroom objects would be helpful in developing probability concepts? Why or why not?

In the School: Observing the Teacher and Students Content

These observation experiences allow you to learn more about teaching in elementary and middle schools and the children you will be teaching. The observations include watching the teacher as he/she provides instruction and interacts with the children, watching the whole class of students, or watching individual students during various experiences they participate in during mathematics class. No grade levels are indicated on the observations. All of these observations may be used in K–8 classrooms.

Your teacher is a professional and should be treated as such. Offer to share your results before turning them in. If your teacher would like you to make changes, respect his/her wishes. Your job is to objectively collect information without passing judgments. Remember to protect the confidentiality of the classroom. Observation results should be discussed only with the teacher or your instructor in your methods class.

Observations by Topic

Key Topics	Title	Page
1. Issues, Trends, and Principles		
2. Learning	(Student) Children's Development	25
	(Teacher) Equity for Gender in Whole Class Lessons	26
	(Student) Equity in Single-Gender Group Work	27
	(Student) Equity in Mixed-Gender Group Work	28
	(Student) Equity for Students with Special Needs	29
	(Student) Equity for English Language Learners	30
3. Teaching, Planning, Adapting	(Teacher and Student) The Learning Environment	31–32
	(Teacher) Teaching a Mathematics Lesson	33
	(Teacher and Student) Checking on Technology	34
	(Student) Analyzing Classroom Discourse	35–36
	(Student) Focusing on Individuals	37–38
	(Teacher and Student) Analyzing Textbook Use	39–40
	See also pp. 26–30	
4. Assessing, Recording, Reporting	(Teacher) Proctoring a Test or a Classroom Assignment	41
	(Student) Analytic/Holistic Problem Solving Scoring	42–44
	(Student) Performance Task	45–46
5. Process Standards	(Student) Mathematical Processes	47–48

OBSERVATIONS BY TOPIC (continued)

Key Topics	Title	Page
6. Problem Solving	See also pp. 33, 42–48	
7. Number Sense, Prenumber	Focusing on Counting and Number Recognition See also p. 33	49
8. Place Value	See also p. 33	
9. Basic Facts	(Student) Timed Tests See also p. 33	50
10. Computational Alternatives	(Teacher and Student) Focusing on Computation See also p. 33	51
11. Whole Number Operations	See also p. 33	
12. Fractions, Decimals	See also p. 33	
13. Ratio, Proportion, Percent	See also p. 33	
14. Patterns, Algebra	See also p. 33	
15. Geometry	(Teacher and Student) Focusing on Geometry See also p. 33	52
16. Measurement	Focusing on Measurement See also p. 33	53
17. Data, Statistics, Probability	(Teacher and Student) Focusing on Probability and Data See also p. 33	54
18. Number Theory	See also p. 33	

Watch the children in a mathematics class so you observe their developmental characteristics.

1. What grade level did you observe? _____

2. What is the age span (in months and years) of the children? _____

DEVELOPMENTAL CHARACTERISTICS	
PRIMARY LEARNERS (AGES 4-7)	**INTERMEDIATE LEARNERS(AGES 8-11)**
Cognitive Characteristics (thinking and ways of learning)	
• Piaget's preoperational stage • Centration-able to focus on only one idea or stimulus at a time • Irreversibility-unable to recognize the reversibility of changes to actions or objects • Begins to understand ideas beyond firsthand concrete experiences	• Piaget's concrete operational stage • Able to decenter, can focus on part/whole • Understands reversibility of actions or objects • Able to classify and sequence by attribute • Can use logic and concrete objects to solve problems
Physical Characteristics (muscle and motor skills)	
• Developing control of large and small muscles, fine-motor skills • Short attention span	• Able to complete more complex physical skills
Social Characteristics (self-concept and interpersonal skills)	
• Egocentric-focuses more on self than others, talks at rather than with others • Developing sense of self and abilities • May have a best friend and exclude others • Learning to express oneself and make decisions	• Growing more independent • Small groups of friends have major influence • Hard to accept failure or criticism

3. List the developmental characteristics you observed in this class and any behaviors you noticed to support these observations.

4. For the observed characteristics listed above, what developmentally appropriate practices were used or provided by the teacher?

REFLECTION:

1. Think about the extent to which the children's cognitive, physical, and social developmental needs were being met. What other developmentally appropriate practices would you use to increase the support provided in this mathematics class?

Equity for Gender in Whole Class Lessons

Observing the Teacher

Observe a mathematics class and specifically be sensitive to the verbal and physical clues that suggest boys are treated differently than girls.

Research studies report patterns of behavior* where teachers
When questioning and answering
        Call on boys more than girls
        Wait longer for boys to respond than for girls
        Allow boys to interrupt their speaking more easily than girls
        Accept boys "called out answers" more than girls
When giving feedback and directions
        Give boys more criticism
        Praise girls for the appearance of their work and boys for the content of their work
        Tell boys how to solve problems, but solve the problems for girls
        Allow students to self select groups by sex
        Give girls less time with computers and models than boys
        Assign different tasks on the basis of gender

*A more detailed list of these behaviors is available in the Gender Equity Sources and Resources for Education Students by Jo Sanders, Janice Koch and Josephine Urso published by Erlbaum Publishers, Mahwah, NJ, 1997.

---

1. Did you see evidence of any of the above behaviors suggesting that boys and girls were treated differently? Check all behaviors observed and provide specific examples.

REFLECTION:

1. What do you think causes boys and girls to be treated differently?

2. What will you do to ensure equity in your classroom?

Equity in Single-Gender Group Work

Observe a mathematics class using <u>single-gender</u> cooperative groups.

1. How many groups were involved?_____   How many children were in each group?_____

2. Were there observable differences in these groups <u>attention to the mathematical task</u>? **Yes   No**
   If **Yes**, give an example.

3. Was there an observable difference in the <u>noise level generated</u> from the groups? **Yes   No**
   If **Yes**, give an example.

4. Did you notice any difference in the <u>group dynamics</u> between the boys and girls? **Yes   No**
   If **Yes**, give an example.

REFLECTION:

1. While each <u>single-gender</u> group may have its own unique character, there may be some patterns that you noticed. Based on information from your observation, describe any patterns that you would associate with gender.

Equity in Mixed-Gender Group Work

1. How many groups were involved?_____   How many children were in each group?_____
   Focus your observation on one of the groups. Record the first names of group members:

   _____   _____   _____

   _____   _____   _____

2. Was the group leader a boy or girl?_____ Who decided?_____

3. Did everyone seem to <u>contribute equally</u> to the group's work?   **Yes   No**
   If **no**, who (boy/girl) contributed the most/least?

4. Did everyone <u>speak equally</u> in the group?   **Yes   No**
   If **no**, who (boy/girl) spoke the most/least often?

5. If manipulative materials are being used, did everyone have <u>equal use</u>?   **Yes   No**
   If **no**, who (boy/girl) has the most/least use?

6. Did you observe any examples of "learned helplessness"?   **Yes   No**
   If **yes**, who (boy/girl) exhibited this trait?

7. Did you find evidence that boys are greater risk takers than girls?   **Yes   No**
   If **yes**, describe a situation you observed.

8. Did you notice any difference in the group dynamics between the boys and girls?   **Yes   No**
   If **yes**, give an example.

REFLECTION:

1. Based on your observation of the <u>mixed-gender</u> groups describe any patterns or trends that suggest either gender equity or inequity within the groups?

Equity for Students with Special Needs

Observe in a mathematics class where students identified for special education services are included in the room.

1. About how many children appeared to be in need of special help? _____

2. How many children did the teacher report had been identified to receive special education services? _____ What types of special needs have been identified in the class? How many of each?

3. Focus your observation on one or two of the children with special needs.

   First name: _____ Special Needs: _____

4. What type of adaptations were made for the child? Was the child successful? Explain.

5. Who provided special help to the child? (circle all that apply)
   (Classroom teacher, special education teacher, assigned aide, another child, volunteer, you)

6. About how much time (approximate minutes) was spent helping the child? _____

7. Describe the nature of the special help provided.

8. Was there sufficient time and staff to provide help to each special needs child? **Yes No**
   If **no**, how many were unattended? _____ What seems to determine who gets help?

REFLECTION:

1. Think about the extent to which the children with special needs were being served. What would you do to increase the support provided in this mathematics class?

Equity for English Language Learners

Observing Students

Observe in a mathematics class where students identified for English Language Learner services are included in the room.

1. How many children did the teacher report were English Language Learners? ____

2. Briefly describe the range of English proficiency of these students.

Basic Principles of Instruction to meet the needs of English Language Learners*

1. **Give students comprehensible input.**
    Use clear, concise, understandable language
    Avoid slang
    Emphasize key vocabulary and concepts
    Use visuals, models, or physical actions to illustrate key vocabulary and concepts
2. **Give students opportunities to increase verbal interaction.**
    Allow students to respond using their level of proficiency (ex. action, single word, select response from provided choices)
    Provide ample wait time
3. **Teach in a way that contextualizes language.**
    Use a manipulative or graphic organizer to connect old and new knowledge
    Connect to students' lives
    Use both English and words from students' native languages
4. **Use teaching strategies and groupings that reduce the anxiety of the students.**
    Involve as many senses as possible
    Provide ways to respond besides writing or speaking English
    Encourage interaction with a partner or small group
5. **Assign activities that offer students opportunities for active involvement.**
    Have students use manipulatives or every day objects

*Specific instructional strategies for each of these principles may be found in: Herrell, A. L. *Fifty Strategies for Teaching English Language Learners*. Upper Saddle River, NJ: Merrill, 2000.

---

3. List the principle numbers above that you saw the teacher implementing and for each, briefly describe what was specifically done to support the English Language Learners.

REFLECTION:

1. Think about the extent to which the English Language Learners were being served. What would you do to increase the support provided in this mathematics lesson?

Time	Physical Space and Materials

Context	Respect and Value Students' Ideas

The Learning Environment

Observing the Teacher and the Students

Observe in an elementary or middle school classroom during at least one entire mathematics lesson. Use the observation sheet on the previous page so you can make special notes about the four items in the learning environment underlined and described below.

In 1991, the National Council of Teachers of Mathematics (NCTM) published *Professional Standards for Teaching Mathematics*, a book that promotes a vision of mathematics teaching in which *developing mathematical power in all students* is central.

> Mathematical power includes the ability to explore, conjecture, and reason logically; to solve non-routine problems; to communicate about and through mathematics; and to connect ideas within mathematics and between mathematics and other intellectual activity. Mathematical power also involves the development of personal self confidence and a disposition to seek, evaluate, and use quantitative and spatial information in solving problems and in making decisions. Students' flexibility, perseverance, interest, curiosity, and inventiveness also affect the realization of mathematical power. (NCTM, 1991).

This vision of mathematics teaching was reaffirmed in 2000 with the publication of *Principles and Standards for School Mathematics* (NCTM, 2000).

What does the classroom environment look like when a teacher is committed to pursuing this vision? According to *Professional Standards for Teaching Mathematics*, the teacher of mathematics should create a learning environment that fosters the development of each student's mathematical power by—
- providing and structuring the <u>time</u> necessary to explore sound mathematics and grapple with significant ideas and problems;
- using the <u>physical space and materials</u> in ways that facilitate students' learning of mathematics
- providing a <u>context</u> that encourages the development of mathematical skill and proficiency;
- <u>respecting and valuing students' ideas</u>, ways of thinking, and mathematical dispositions . . . . (NCTM 1991, p. 57, emphases added)

Read pp. 57–61 in *Professional Standards for Teaching Mathematics* for a more complete description of the Learning Environment Standard. These pages also include three vignettes (elaborated examples) of classroom environments that exemplify the standard. (Available on the World Wide Web at www.standards.nctm.org.)

REFLECTION:

1. Summarize your observation and discuss each of the four items, comparing and contrasting what you observed in the classroom with the vision provided in NCTM's "Learning Environment Standard."

2. What will *you* do to support the learning environment in your own classroom?

Teaching a Mathematics Lesson

Observing the Teacher

Watch the teacher teach a mathematics lesson. Grade: _____ Topic: _____

Lesson Type: Direct Instruction   or   Investigative
(circle one)

1. Use the appropriate lesson plan template and fill in the components of the lesson you observed.

2. Would you characterize it as attending to <u>procedural</u> or <u>conceptual</u> knowledge? Tell why.

3. Describe how students were actively involved in the mathematics lesson.

4. Describe how communication was integrated in the mathematics lesson.

5. Describe how the teacher utilized questioning during the mathematics lesson.

REFLECTION:

1. What was effective about the lesson?

2. If *you* were teaching this lesson, what might you do differently?

Checking on Technology

Technology assumes many different roles in the classroom. For example, it may be used by the teacher to demonstrate or by students to carry out an assignment. As you observe in the classroom be alert for technology that is being used or is available for use.

1. Were these technologies

	Available?	Used?
Overhead projector	Yes No	Yes No
VCR and Video Monitor	Yes No	Yes No
Calculators	Yes No	Yes No
Computers	Yes No	Yes No
Other _____		

2. How many calculators were available? _____
    (a) Was a calculator used by the teacher?   **Yes   No**
        If **yes**, how was it used? If **no**, how could it have been used?

    (b) Did students use a calculator?   **Yes   No**
        If **yes**, how was it used? If **no**, how could it have been used?

3. How many computers were available? _____
    (a) Were computers connected to the Internet?   **Yes   No   Not sure**

    (b) Was a computer used by the teacher?   **Yes   No**
        If **yes**, how was it used? If **no**, how could it have been used?

    (c) Did students use a computer?   **Yes   No**
        If **yes**, how was it used? If **no**, how could it have been used?

4. Did you notice any math computer software packages present in the classroom or loaded on a computer? **Yes No**   If yes, list a title and publisher for one of them and briefly describe its purpose.

REFLECTION:

1. In your opinion, would you characterize this classroom as being rich in technology to support mathematics teaching and learning? **Yes   No**   Explain.

2. How would *you* use technology in this classroom to support mathematics teaching and learning?

Analyzing Classroom Discourse Observation Sheet

Time	Lesson Segment	Talk: Who and What

Analyzing Classroom Discourse

Observing Students

For this observation you should focus your attention on the *talk* in the classroom—both of the teacher and of the students. Your goal is to document and analyze classroom discourse—conversations that the teacher has with students and that the students have with each other.

1. Plan to sit where you can hear as much of the classroom conversation as possible.

2. Use the observation sheet on the previous page to keep running notes throughout the lesson.

3. In the Time column, make note of the time whenever you enter an observation in one of the other columns (e.g., 9:00, 9:05, 9:07 and so on).

4. In the Lesson Segment column, make notes about the major segments of the lesson. If the teacher is talking to the whole class, note this. If the teacher stops lecturing and tells the students to work individually, note this. If the teacher tells the children to share their work in small groups, note this. In other words, the first two columns together give a time specific outline of the various segments of the lesson.

5. In the Talk: Who & What column, make notes about what you hear. When the teacher asks a question, note it (and try to capture how it is phrased). If students respond, note as much of what they say as you can. Note who is talking to whom. (You don't need to know the children's names. You can refer to them as A, B, C, or Boy 1, Girl 2, etc.) If the class is working in small groups, listen in on one group, while also keeping an ear out for what the teacher is saying as he or she interacts with that group and others.

REFLECTION:

1. Analyze the discourse (talk) during the lesson. What proportion of the time was the teacher talking? How carefully did he/she listen to and respond to what students said? How many different students had a chance to talk? Did anyone dominate the conversation?

2. What types of questions were asked (by teacher or by students)? (Yes/no? Probing? Routine? Challenging?) Give some examples of good questions that were not asked, but could have been. Were students challenged to clarify and justify their ideas? If so, how? Did students react to and challenge each others' ideas, or was talk mostly teacher to student and student to teacher? Back up your analysis by using specific examples.

3. How did the discourse in this classroom enhance (or impede) student learning?

Focusing on Individuals Observation Sheet

Time	Lesson Segment	Child 1	Child 2

Focusing on Individuals

Observe a mathematics lesson. For this observation you should focus your attention on just one or two students. Your goal is to document what they are doing at all times during the lesson, in an attempt to see how the lesson impacts them individually.

1. Choose one or two students to observe. (Ask the classroom teacher for advice.)

2. Use the observation sheet on the previous page to keep running notes throughout the lesson.

3. In the <u>Time</u> column, make note of the time whenever you enter an observation in one of the other columns (e.g., 9:00, 9:05, 9:07 and so on).

4. In the <u>Lesson Segment</u> column, make notes about what is supposed to be going on. If the teacher is talking to the whole class, note this. If the teacher stops lecturing and tells the students to work individually using manipulative materials, note this. If the teacher tells the children to share their work in small groups, note this. In other words, the first two columns together give a time specific outline of the various segments of the lesson.

5. In <u>the Child 1 and Child 2</u> columns, make notes about what children are doing throughout the lesson. Note if they are listening, or talking, or staring out the window, or using materials or a calculator, or writing, etc. Make notes about the looks on their faces (eager, excited, bored, frustrated, etc.) Try to position yourself so you can make notes about everything they say and do. If possible, get a copy of the work your focus students did during the class.

REFLECTION:

1. Write two brief narratives about the lesson, each from the point of view of one of your focus students. How would <u>they</u> report what happened during math class that day?

2. Did your focus students engage in the lesson in different ways? How? What were they doing whenever they were off task? What do you think caused their inattention? What could the teacher have done to bring them into the lesson?

3. Speculate about what the focus students learned about mathematics during this lesson. Back up your speculations by pointing to specific things that they did or said or wrote.

Analyzing Textbook Use

Research documents that the district adopted mathematics textbook determines what mathematics is presented and often how it is taught. For this observation you should focus your attention on how the textbook is used by the teacher and the students. Get a copy of the textbook and sit where you can see the teacher and observe the students.

During and/or after the observation, answer the following questions:

1. What textbook series was used? (include title, publisher, and copyright date)

2. Did the teacher use the textbook?   **Yes   No**

   If **yes**, what is the name of the lesson?

      What pages were covered during the lesson?

      What is the major mathematical content for this lesson?

      What is the title of the chapter or unit for this lesson?

      What is the major mathematical content for the chapter?

      Was the textbook used
            to guide the lesson?   **Yes   No**
            for selecting problems to demonstrate?   **Yes   No**
            for practice in class exercises?   **Yes   No**
            for assigning homework?   **Yes   No**

      Additional notes about the teacher's use of the textbook:

3. Were any other print materials used by the teacher?   **Yes   No**
   If **yes**, what was the source? How were they used?

(continued on next page)

ANALYZING TEXTBOOK USE (continued)

4. Did the students use the textbook?   **Yes**   **No**

   If **yes**, was the textbook used
         to demonstrate how to do the math?   **Yes**   **No**
         for the in class practice?   **Yes**   **No**
         for homework?   **Yes**   **No**

   Additional notes about the students' use of the textbook:

REFLECTION:

1. In your opinion, to what extent did the textbook influence the content and presentation of this mathematics lesson?

2. How would *you* use the textbook in this classroom to support mathematics teaching and learning?

Proctoring a Test or a Classroom Assignment

Observing the Teacher

Watch the teacher while the students are taking a test or working on a written classroom assignment. Obtain a copy of the test or assignment beforehand. Try to sit where you can survey the whole class unobtrusively.

Grade: _____   Topic: _____

1. THE TASK: Describe the test or assignment. Does it include questions that involve facts? skills? concepts? problem solving? investigations? explanations? What types of questions are included (multiple choice, short answer, open response, etc.). Are students instructed to show their work? Are they supposed to write explanations? If this is an individual test or assignment, are students supposed to work entirely on their own or may they talk with others about their work? If this is a collaborative assignment, how are the students arranged? What ground rules for collaboration, if any, are laid before the students start on the assignment?

2. BEFORE: Watch and listen as the teacher distributes the test or assignment. What does he/she say before distributing the papers? How are papers distributed (by teacher to each student? by teacher to each row or group? by students themselves—how?). Are directions given before or after papers are distributed? What sorts of directions are given? How does the teacher ensure that students are listening to the directions?

3. DURING:
   (a) How does the teacher respond to students who raise their hands with questions? What sorts of questions or comments does he/she make? Are directions reiterated? Are students directed to reread or to think about the meaning of the problems? Are the students told how to proceed? What sorts of hints are given, if any? Give examples.

   (b) If there are no students with hands raised, what does the teacher do? Does the teacher sit at his/her desk? Circulate around the room? Does he/she look over the students' shoulders? (If so, you may want to ask afterwards what he/she was looking at or listening for.)

   (c) Are there occasions when the teacher addresses the whole group? What precipitates these announcements and what are their topics? How much of the class time is allocated to talking to the whole class (versus having the students work independently)?

   (d) How does the teacher deal with students who finish early?

4. AFTER: How does the teacher end the class session? Does he/she make announcements about time remaining even before time is up? How are papers collected? What happens with students who are not yet finished?

REFLECTION:

1. What was effective about the ways that the teacher handled the classroom? How did his/her actions and responses fit with the type of assignment that the students were working on?

2. If *you* were proctoring this test or assignment, what might you do differently?

Analytic Scoring Scale

Understanding the Problem

0:   Complete misunderstanding of the problem

1:   Part of the problem misunderstood or misinterpreted

2:   Complete understanding of the problem

Planning a Solution

0:   No attempt or totally inappropriate plan

1:   Partially correct plan based on part of the problem being interpreted correctly

2:   Plan could have led to a correct solution if implemented properly

Getting an Answer

0:   No answer, or wrong answer based on an inappropriate plan

1:   Copying error, computational error, partial answer for a problem with multiple answers

2:   Correct answer and correct label for answer

A scale for scoring problem solving (Reprinted with permission from Charles, Lester, and O'Daffer, *How to Evaluate Progress in Problem Solving,* © 1987 by the National Council of Teachers of Mathematics

Holistic Scoring Rubric

1	**Needs more instruction**—Student work may include evidence that the problem was not understood completely; may use inappropriate methods or faulty reasoning; may make significant errors.
2	**Good work**—Task is completed with some minor errors. Work shows basic understanding of the problem and uses anticipated approaches.
3	**Very good work**—Task as stated is completed with no errors, work is clear and complete.
4	**Exemplary work**—Goes well beyond expectations of the task (e.g., problem solving in more than one way or student has extended the problem and completed a more difficult version).

Analytic/Holistic Problem Solving Scoring

Get permission from the classroom teacher to administer a problem to approximately 10 or more students in the class. (Maybe the teacher will be willing to have the entire class do the problem, or a subgroup of the class can work on the problem while other groups are doing something else.) If possible, have the children work in pairs on the problem, you will be able to learn a lot about their thinking by circulating around the room and listening as they talk with one another. If this is not feasible, you should still circulate to watch individuals. Perhaps you can find a time to talk with them about their work afterwards. Use the analytic scoring scale or holistic scoring rubric on the next page to score the students' work.

Finding a good problem: Consult your instructor, your mathematics methods textbook, a student textbook for the grade level you are working in, the classroom teacher, or a supplementary problem-solving book to identify one or more word problems that should be challenging, yet doable, for students you are observing. By definition, a *problem* is a situation in which a person does not know immediately what to do to get it. If a problem is so easy that children know the answer, or how to obtain the answer immediately, there is no problem at all. Such a task is simply an exercise. Your problem should require some analysis and thought. Strategies such as act it out, think of a simpler problem, make an organized list, look for a pattern, or make a drawing may be useful in attacking the problem you pose. Here are some example problems:

Grades 1–2

A bus has 10 rows of seats. There are 4 seats in each row. How many seats are there on the bus? There are 18 cookies in a package. If 4 children are sharing the cookies, how many can each child have?

Grades 3–4 (may also be good for Grades 5–6)

A snail is at the bottom of a jar that is 15 cm high. Each day the snail can crawl up 5 cm, but each night he slides back down 3 cm. How many days will it take the snail to reach the top of the jar?

I counted 76 cycle riders and 19 cycle wheels go past my house. How many bicycles and how many tricycles passes?

Grades 5–6

A patch of lily pads doubles its size each day after it starts growing in a pond. If a pond was completely covered just today, what part of it was covered in lily pads five days ago?

In how many ways can you add 8 odd numbers to get a sum of 20? (You may use a number more than once.)

I bought some items at the store. All were the same price. I bought as many items as the number of cents in the cost of each item. My bill was $2.25. How many items did I buy?

When introducing the problem, explain to the students that you have a challenging problem for them to solve. Encourage them to be creative and thoughtful while solving the problem. Have them report their solution and thinking on paper to be handed in. Remind them they may use pictures, symbols, and/or words in their report.

ANALYTIC/HOLISTIC PROBLEM SOLVING SCORING (continued)

Use the analytic scoring scale (previous pages) to assign each student three scores for his/her work on the problem. The scale provides scores for three aspects of the problem-solving process: understanding the problem, planning a solution, and getting an answer.

Or

Use the holistic scoring rubric (previous pages) to assess students' work on the problem. Each student will receive a single score. It may help to sort the students' work into three piles: (1) students who do not understand, (2) students who are developing, but not quite there, (3) students who have solved the problem well.

REFLECTION:

Include a copy of the problem you used and of the students' work, along with answers to the following questions.

1. What grade level did you use? Why did you chose this problem for your problem-solving assessment? What mathematical concepts and skills does it involve? What problem-solving strategies do you consider most useful in solving it? Explain.

2. How appropriate was the problem for these students? Was it too easy or too hard? By doing this problem were the children able to demonstrate what they know and understand about mathematics, as well as what they still need help with?

3. Describe what you learned about the student's problem-solving abilities and understandings of the mathematics involved in the problem by using the analytic scoring scale to evaluate their work. If you have previously used an analytic or holistic scoring rubric, how did using this scoring system compare?

4. What, if anything, might you do differently if you were planning another problem-solving assessment for students such as these?

Performance Task Template

Grade: _____

Objective(s):

Task Description:

Directions to Students:

Benchmark Performance Levels: (rubric optional)

Performance Task

Use the performance task template on the previous page to create a performance task that is at a reasonable level for the students in your class. Get permission from your teacher to administer the task to at least three target students. (It may be helpful to get advice from the teacher about an appropriate task and expectations.)

A performance task can be defined as any assessment of student learning that requires evaluation of student writing, student work, or student behavior. Performance tasks often mirror the real world, are open-ended, and require time for grappling with a problem. A problem with a single correct answer, unaccompanied by explanation, is not a performance task. Examples of performance tasks might include measuring objects with a ruler or meter stick, estimating the number of candies in a jar; deciding what size and shape garden is best for planting 24 plants 1 foot apart with a minimum of fencing; explaining which of several recipes for powdered lemonade makes the most lemony drink; or determining how to scale up a recipe for 4 people to feed 8 (or 10 or 100).

1. Administer the task and observe while the children work. (It often is helpful to pair children when observing their work on a performance task so that you can hear their talk as they work.) Make notes about how the students approach the task and what they do and say. You might plan a checklist ahead of time to help you keep notes about student performance in certain areas of particular interest (for example: strategies used—trial and error, organized list, look for a pattern; skill in measuring—decides appropriately what units to use, lines ruler up with edge of object correctly, reads measurement accurately to nearest quarter inch; or attitudes—confidence, curiosity, enthusiasm, perseverance).

2. Analyze the students' written work. You should judge students' work on a performance task by comparing it with benchmark performance levels that you establish beforehand. One way to do this efficiently (especially when you have many students) is to begin by sorting responses into three piles: (1) needs more instruction, (2) on the right track but needs some improvement, (3) proficient. Put papers in the first pile, if you think you'd need to talk to the child in order to help him or her. Put papers in the second pile if the work is not totally correct, but you think the student could correct the work if you returned the paper with a small sticky note attached. Put papers in the third pile if they are entirely (or almost entirely) correct. Note that you are not comparing the students with one another; instead, you are comparing their work against your predetermined standards of achievement. You may create a rubric to describe your expectations. If possible, talk directly with the students about their work. How is what you learned from the written assignment different from what you learned from talking together?

REFLECTION:

1. Write a written summary about the performance of your target students. Describe what they did, how it was correct or not, and what steps you would take next if you were their teacher.

2. How appropriate was your assessment for students of this age? Explain.

3. What have you learned about the strengths and weaknesses of students of this age?

4. How would you design or score this assessment differently if you were using it again?

Mathematical Processes Observation Sheet

Time	Lesson Segment	Process Examples

Mathematical Processes

Observing Students

Sit in the back of the classroom and scan the room throughout an entire math lesson, looking for instances of children using one or more of the 5 mathematical processes.

Mathematics is much more than computing or learning about shapes. According to *Principles and Standards for School Mathematics* (NCTM 2000), "doing mathematics" means being actively involved in a wide variety of physical and mental actions—actions that can be described by verbs such as exploring, investigating, patterning, experimenting, modeling, conjecturing, and verifying. *Principles and Standards* highlights this active vision of learning and doing by identifying five "process" standards: *problem solving, reasoning and proof, communication, connections,* and *representations.* (If you are not familiar with these standards, consult your mathematics methods text, *Principles and Standards,* or on the World Wide Web (www.standards.nctm.org) for more information before beginning this observation.)

1. Use the observation sheet on the previous page to keep running notes throughout the lesson.

2. In the <u>Time</u> column, you should make note of the time whenever you enter an observation in one of the other columns (e.g., 9:00, 9:05, 9:07 and so on).

3. In the <u>Lesson Segment</u> column, you should make notes about what is supposed to be going on at various times during the lesson. If the teacher is talking to the whole class, you simply note this. If the teacher stops lecturing and tells the students to work individually using manipulative materials, you note this. If the teacher later tells the children to share their work in small groups, you note this. In other words, the first two columns together give a time specific outline of the various segments of the lesson.

4. In the <u>Examples</u> column, you enter abbreviations for the process standards (PS, R&P, Comm, Conn, Rep), along with a brief description of what you observed and who was involved. Be as complete as possible in capturing what students say or do.

REFLECTION:

1. Which mathematical processes were evident in the lesson?

2. What role did the teacher play in getting students involved in these mathematical processes?

3. Which mathematical processes were absent? If you were planning another lesson for this same class, what would you do to bring these processes into the lesson?

Focusing on Counting and Number Recognition

Observing Students

Observe a young child (pre-K–1st grade) playing a board game.

Setting up for the observation:

- For each child, provide a counter and a game board or chart (See below. Chart may be made on one-inch grid paper from Appendix A.). If only one child, you may serve as his/her opponent.
- Have ten cards with a 0–9 on each card. (See Appendix A.) Mix and place face down. Or use a six-sided die with dots instead of numeral cards.

START	1	2	3	4	5	6	7	8	9
10	11	12	13	14	15	16	17	18	19
20	21	22	23	24	25	26	27	28	END

Observation:

Ask each child to place his/her counter on START. Players take turns drawing a card and moving the number of spaces that correspond to the number on the card. Once one player reaches or passes the cell marked END the game is over. You may play several times.

1. Do children recognize the names of the numbers shown on the cards? Describe. Or do the children display group recognition for the numbers on the die, or do they need to count the dots on each face? Describe.
2. Are the children counting out loud and using a 1-1 correspondence between the number name being counted orally and the cells being counted? Is the counting accurate? Describe.
3. Observe and describe any shortcut counting procedures the children use.
4. Did each of the cards pose the same difficulty for the children? If not, describe.

Variations

- Increase the numbers on the counting board, cards or die. Or show 5 columns, not 10.

START	1	2	3	4
5	6	7	8	9
10	11	12	13	14
15	16	17	18	19
20	21	22	23	24
25	26	27	28	END

- Shade one or more columns on the counting board to facilitate their counting.

START	1	2	3	4	5	6	7	8	9
10	11	12	13	14	15	16	17	18	19
20	21	22	23	24	25	26	27	28	END

REFLECTION:

1. For each child, briefly describe what adaptations you would provide the next time they play the game and what skills you hope to develop or reinforce.

Timed Tests

Observe children as they take a timed test on basic facts.

1. What facts were students being tested on? How many items were on the test? How much time was provided? What sorts of time constraints were there (per item, for the entire test)?

2. How were the facts presented (orally, in a list, in a table, flash cards, other)?

3. Observe the students as they are taking the test. What behaviors and emotions could you document? (For example, did you notice children using their fingers to count?)

4. How did the children get feedback on their own progress? Did they grade their own papers and chart their own results, or did the teacher (or someone else) do this?

5. Ask the teacher how he or she uses the results from these tests.

6. Talk to at least five children or adults about their feelings about or memories of timed tests on basic facts. What do they say about their experiences?

REFLECTION:

Think about the experiences of the students you observed and the people you talked to.

1. What benefits of timed tests can you identify? What problems or concerns can you identify?

2. What do you think about the value or purpose of giving students timed tests on basic facts? Will you give timed tests when you are a teacher (and if so, how and why)? If you will not give timed tests, explain why not.

3. What methods will *you* use to help children learn their basic facts and to find out whether they know them?

Focusing on Computation

Observe a computation lesson in a classroom. What grade level(s) did you observe?

OBSERVATION:

1. What was the purpose of the lesson? Briefly describe the lesson.

2. What materials were used? What manipulatives were used? If used, by whom and how?

3. Did the students use

Mental computation?	**Yes**	**No**
Estimation?	**Yes**	**No**
Calculator computation?	**Yes**	**No**
Written computation?	**Yes**	**No**

4. Were students encouraged to discuss their solutions and strategies? **Yes**   **No**
   Were they encouraged to solve problems in a variety of ways that made sense to them?
   Yes   No   Explain.

5. Did you see examples of children displaying number sense or lack of number sense? Provide examples.

REFLECTION:

1. Do you think that the objectives of the lesson were met? Justify your answer.

2. How would you change the lesson? (If you respond that you would make few changes, then describe what you would do for the next computation lesson.)

3. Why is it beneficial to have children compute in a variety of ways that make sense to them?

Observing Teacher and Students

Observe a geometry lesson in a classroom. What grade level(s) did you observe?

OBSERVATION:

1. What was the purpose of the lesson?

2. What materials were used? Were there sufficient materials for all students? If so, how were the materials distributed? If not, how did the teacher manage without materials for each student?

3. Briefly describe the lesson.

4. Did all students participate? How would you describe their participation?

REFLECTION:

1. Do you think that the objectives of the lesson were met? Justify your answer.

2. How would you change the lesson? (If you respond that you would make few changes, then describe what you would do for the next geometry lesson.)

3. Often teachers skip geometry. Why do you think this happens?

Observing Students

Observe students measuring with a ruler. Plan an activity for a small group of students in which they have to measure objects in the room, including one that is shorter than the ruler, one that is longer than the ruler, one that is around a cylinder, and one that is around a rectangular object. What grade level (s) did you observe?

OBSERVATION:

1. *Object shorter than the ruler.* How did the students line up the ruler with the object? Did they begin at 0 or 1? Did they use inches or centimeters? Did they measure to the nearest inch (or centimeter)? Did they report the measurement correctly (number and unit)? What else did you notice?

2. *Object longer than the ruler.* How did the students move the ruler? How did they calculate the length? Could some children do task 1, but not this one?

3. *Cylindrical object.* What suggestions did the students have for measuring around with the ruler? What else did you notice?

4. *Perimeter of a rectangular object.* Did the students measure all four sides? How did they handle the four lengths to find the distance around? Were they concerned that the measurements did not turn out exactly?

REFLECTION:

1. How did the four tasks differ as far as students' ability to complete the task? Did they learn from each other?

2. Did you encounter students who had more difficulty in measuring with a ruler than you expected? What were these difficulties? What experiences would you next provide for them?

Focusing on Probability and Data

Observe a probability or data lesson in a classroom. What grade level(s) did you observe?

OBSERVATION:

1. What was the purpose of this lesson?

2. Briefly describe the lesson.

3. Did the students use:

textbook or worksheet	**Yes** **No**	
hands-on materials	**Yes** **No**	(describe below)
graphs	**Yes** **No**	(describe below)
calculator	**Yes** **No**	

   For each "yes" answer, briefly describe how that item was used and whether you believe using it was appropriate and effective or not.

4. Was this part of a series of lessons involving question-posing, data collection, data analysis, and/or question-answering from data? If so, who posed the question(s) and/or decided how the data would be collected, displayed, and analyzed? Individual students? Groups of students? Teacher?

5. What did students need to know already about probability or data in order to be successful in this lesson?

6. Did all students participate? How would you describe their participation?

REFLECTION:

1. Do you think that the objectives of the lesson were met? Justify your answer.

2. How would you change the lesson? (If you would make few changes, then describe what you would do for the next probability/data lesson.)

In the School:
Interviewing the Teacher
and Students Content

The **teacher interview** experiences allow you to learn more about the beliefs of teachers in elementary and middle schools. This includes talking with the teacher to learn more about their classroom and their teaching. No grade levels are indicated on the activities. These activities may all be used in K-8 classrooms. You do not have to use all of the teacher interview questions found in this resource book. If the interview seems too long, select questions you and your instructor feel are appropriate for your setting.

Schedule a convenient time to meet with your teacher. You may also provide your teacher with the questions ahead of time so he/she has time to think about them before the interview. If you are worried about taking notes during the interview, you might ask your teacher if he/she is comfortable with you making an audiotape. Or you may wish to make brief notes during the interview and then fill in more detailed comments and observations later. If you think of related questions during the interview, ask them but be sure to note any adaptations you make. This is your opportunity to learn more about a teacher and your role in his/her classroom.

Remember your teacher is a professional and should be treated as such. Offer to share your results before turning them in. If your teacher would like you to make changes, respect his/her wishes. Your job is to objectively collect information without passing judgments. Remember to protect the confidentiality of the classroom. Interview results should be discussed only with the teacher or your instructor in your methods class.

The **student interview** experiences give you practice conducting an assessment interview and give you insight into how children develop, what they know, and what they are able to do at various levels. Each interview should take approximately 30 minutes or less and are classified into three grade level bands. Specific grade level suggestions may be found on each interview. Select questions appropriate to your setting. Schedule a convenient time and location and have all materials ready to go. Find a quiet place for you and the child. Make them feel at ease by telling them that you are trying to learn how they think so you will know more when you are teaching.

Have the child record all written work on paper, later label each sheet with the child's first name and the task, and attach it to the interview. Using a clean sheet for each new task will make interpretation of results easier for you and those with whom you share results. You may wish to only make brief notes during the interview, recording student responses and your observations. Then fill in more detailed comments and observations later. You may also get permission to audio tape the interview so you may listen again and not be bothered taking notes.

Remember the purpose of this interview is to assess what the child knows and can do rather than report what he/she can't do. So you will need to probe, ask why, or how they would explain their answers to other students (or to younger children). *Your job is to assess and accurately record the child's responses, not to teach the child or correct his/her responses.* Be flexible. If the question asked is too difficult for the child, make it easier. Also, if the child is not challenged by a question, pose a more difficult one. Be sure to note any adaptations you make. The interview does not have to be conducted all at one time. If you are losing the child's interest or attention, or if the class schedule is limited, break the interview into smaller parts.

Offer to copy your results and share with the child's teacher if he/she is interested. Remember to respect the dignity of the child and protect the confidentiality of the classroom. Results should be discussed only with the teacher or your instructor in your methods class.

Interviews by Topic

Key Topics	Interview	K–2	3–5	6–8	Page
1. Issues, Trends, and Principles	(Teacher) Resources for Teaching Mathematics	X	X	X	58
	(Teacher) Equity	X	X	X	59
2. Learning	(Teacher) Teaching, Learning	X	X	X	60
	(Student) Attitudes about Mathematics	X	X	X	61
3. Teaching, Planning, Adapting	(Teacher) Teaching a Topic	X	X	X	62
	(Teacher) Grouping in the Classroom	X	X	X	63
	(Teacher) Teaching with Technology	X	X	X	64
4. Assessing, Recording, Reporting	(Teacher) Assessment	X	X	X	65–66
	(Student) Primary Interview on Place Value	X			67–68
5. Process Standards	(Teacher) Doing Math	X	X	X	69
6. Problem Solving	(Student) Problem Solving Strategies	X	X	X	70
	(Teacher) See also p. 62, 69				
7. Number Sense, Prenumber	(Student) Conservation and Counting	X			71
	(Student) Counting	X			72
	(Student) Early Number Sense	X			73
	(Teacher) See also p. 62				
8. Place Value	(Student) Place Value		X		74
	(Student) See also pp. 67–68				
	(Teacher) Developing Place Value Concepts				75
	(Teacher) See also p. 62				
9. Basic Facts	(Teacher) Basic Fact Difficulty		X	X	76
	(Student) Basic Fact Fluency	X	X	X	77–78
	(Teacher) See also p. 62				
10. Computational Alternatives	(Student) About How Much?		X	X	79
	(Student) Do It Mentally		X		80
	(Teacher) See also p. 62				
11. Whole Number Operations	(Student) Addition with Regrouping		X		81
	(Student) Transitional Algorithms	X	X	X	82
	(Teacher) See also p. 62				
12. Fractions, Decimals	(Student) Three-Fourths		X	X	83–84
	(Teacher) See also p. 62				
13. Ratio, Proportion, Percent	(Student) Proportions			X	85
	(Student) Percents			X	86
	(Teacher) See also p. 62				
14. Patterns, Algebra	(Student) Thinking About Patterns	X			87–88
	(Student) Equality		X		89
	(Student) Algebraic Thinking		X	X	90
	(Teacher) See also p. 62				

INTERVIEWS BY TOPIC (continued)

Key Topics	Interview	K–2	3–5	6–8	Page
15. Geometry	(Student) Find Me (Student) Classify Me (Student) Compare Shapes (Teacher) See also p. 62	X X	X X X	 X X	91–92 93–94 95
16. Measurement	(Student) Measuring (Teacher) See also p. 62	X			96–98
17. Data, Statistics, Probability	(Student) Graphing (Student) Statistics (Student) Probability (Teacher) See also p. 62	X	X X	X X X	99 100 101
18. Number Theory	(Teacher) See also p. 62				

Interviewing the Teacher

The following questions will help you think about the views of teachers as to where they turn when they need new ideas or help in reaching students. You may wish to ask several teachers including one that is in the first few years of teaching and one that has taught for a good length of time.

1. What is the best source you have found when planning for teaching mathematics?

2. How do you use guidelines such as the state, local, or national standards?

3. What textbooks and other materials have you found useful?

4. Do you have a favorite web site or other electronic material?

5. What professional development opportunities are available for mathematics teaching?

6. Are there local, regional, or state groups that focus on teaching mathematics? Who are they and how often do they meet?

7. Do the teachers in this school share ideas about teaching mathematics? Is there a math resource teacher or someone who is available to help with teaching mathematics?

REFLECTION:

1. What is your assessment of the help you would receive in beginning to teach mathematics in this school?

2. What opportunities or resources do you think would be helpful to have available?

Equity

The following questions will help you learn about all children learning mathematics as well as obtaining the views of the teacher with whom you will be working. The Equity Principle in *Principles and Standards for School Mathematics* (NCTM 2000, pp. 14–16) states: "Excellence in mathematics education requires equity—high expectations and strong support for all students." The full text of this principle also can be found on the World Wide Web (www.standards.nctm.org). Before asking your teacher the following questions, answer them for yourself as if you were the teacher.

QUESTIONS:

1. What does the statement that "all students can learn mathematics" mean to you?

2. Do you hold the same high expectations for all your students? How do you communicate those expectations?

3. Children often need further assistance to meet high expectations. What is one thing you do in the classroom to ensure that all children learn? Is there school-wide assistant (special teachers, technology, or programs) available?

REFLECTION:

1. How did your answers to these questions match the teacher's responses?

2. What happens when you do <u>not</u> believe that children can learn mathematics?

Interviewing the Teacher

The following questions will help you think about how children learn as well as obtaining the views of your cooperating teacher. Here are some questions to ask your cooperating teacher. Before asking the teacher, answer them for yourself as if you were the teacher.

1. How do you believe children learn mathematics?

2. What are the characteristics of learners at this age?

3. What types of instructional activities best help children learn mathematics at this age?

4. What percent of class time is devoted to conceptual development? Practice?

5. How do you feel about mathematics and teaching mathematics?

6. How do your attitudes and actions influence your students' attitudes toward mathematics?

7. How do you support students who display mathematics anxiety?

REFLECTION:

1. How did your answers to these questions match the teacher's responses?

2. How did this interview give you better insight into what happens in this classroom?

Attitudes about Mathematics

Materials Needed: none

The following questions will help you think about students' attitudes toward mathematics. Ask these questions so you can learn about their attitudes and perceptions about mathematics.

1. What school subject do you like most? _____ Are you good at it? **Y** **N**
   (If they say recess, ask what they like most after recess!)

2. What school subject do you like least? _____ Are you good at it? **Y** **N**

3. If I say, "Let's do some mathematics"—what would you do?
   (i.e., What comes to mind when you think of doing mathematics?)

4. Do you think knowing mathematics will help you when you grow up? **Y** **N** Tell why.

5. Who do you think is better at mathematics? ____Boys ____Girls ____Both the same
   Tell why.

6. Do you think your teacher likes to teach mathematics? _____ Tell why.

7. What helps you learn math?

REFLECTION:

1. Did you ask additional questions to learn a bit more? If so, what questions did you ask?

2. Based on the information you collected, how would you describe this child's feelings about mathematics? What do you think are some of the factors that contributed to their feelings?

Teaching a Topic

Interviewing the Teacher

The following questions will help you learn about teaching a specific mathematics topic (i.e. place value or fractions). Here are some questions to ask your cooperating teacher.

1. I would like to find out more about _____.

   Topic

2. What do children already know about this topic when they come to this grade level?

3. What are the key outcomes children in this grade level learn for this topic?

4. What will children learn about this topic next year?

5. Are there particular materials you use to teach this topic at this grade level?

6. What gives children at this grade level difficulty with this topic? What helps them overcome these difficulties?

REFLECTION:

1. How did answers to these questions improve your insight about teaching this topic?

Grouping in the Classroom

Interviewing the Teacher

The following questions will help you learn about how teachers group students for learning activities. In a typical elementary school classroom, the children are similar in age, but may differ considerably in their achievement in mathematics, their mathematical ability, and their attitudes toward mathematics. As a result teachers often find it useful to group children purposefully for instruction (either in mixed-ability or like-ability groups). Talk to a teacher about what sorts of grouping patterns he or she uses in classroom instruction, and why.

1. Which of the following grouping patterns do you use often in your classroom? (Circle all that apply) Individual seatwork, pairs of students working together, small groups of students working together, work centers around the room for individual or small group work, whole class lecture, whole class discussion. Which ones do you use most often? Why? Which ones do you use infrequently? Why?

2. Do all students in your class do the same assignments, or is work differentiated by ability grouping? If grouping is by ability, how frequently are the groups changed? How do tasks assigned to lower groups differ from those assigned to other groups?

3. Are there different sorts of tasks that you use with different sorts of groupings? For example, what tasks do you assign for pairs of students that you don't assign for individuals or small groups? When do you lecture? When do you hold whole class discussions? For what sorts of work do students work individually?

4. For each of the grouping patterns that you use, how do you organize the class?
For example, when students work in small groups, do the groups do the same tasks or different tasks? How do you manage the task of planning for a variety of different groups or a variety of different grouping patterns? When you are working with one group, what are other groups doing? How do you manage to keep students on task?

5. What sorts of management strategies do you recommend for teaching with various grouping patterns? For example, do you use students as group leaders? Do you have folders or boxes where group materials are kept? Do you communicate with groups by written instructions in a logbook or on the blackboard? Do your students or groups use special signals to indicate when they need your help?

6. How do you manage grading when students work in groups? Do you grade group assessments (quizzes, projects, reports, etc.)? How do you ensure that the individuals have been fairly assessed on what they, individually, have done, know, and can do?

For background information before conducting your interview, read Larson, Carol Novillis. "Organizing for Mathematics Instruction." *Arithmetic Teacher*, 31 (September 1983), pp. 16–20.

REFLECTION:

1. Based on this interview, how do you plan to use grouping in your mathematics classroom?

Using Technology in the Mathematics Classroom

The following questions will help you think about the role of technology in the teaching of mathematics. You may wish to ask more than one teacher, including one that is in the first few years of teaching and one that has taught for a good length of time.

CALCULATORS

1. Do students use calculators in your mathematics class? Why or why not?

2. If yes, how frequently are students allowed to use calculators? How are the calculators used by students? Is calculator use unrestricted?

3. Do you provide instruction in the use of calculators?

COMPUTERS

4. Do students use computers in your mathematics class? Why or why not?

5. If yes, how frequently are students allowed to use computers? How are the computers used by students in mathematics class?

6. Do you have favorite web sites or software for students to use in mathematics?

OTHER TECHNOLOGY

7. What other technology do you use in mathematics class? How is it used?

8. Where do you find ideas for technology activities?

9. What other technology resources do you wish you had for teaching mathematics?

REFLECTION:

1. What is your assessment of the technology resources available in this school? Does it appear that the teacher you interviewed is making good use of the technology resources? Why or why not?

2. What technology do you hope to have available and use when teaching mathematics?

Assessment

Interviewing the teacher

To learn about the sorts of assessment a teacher uses in mathematics classroom instruction and why, interview the teacher using the questions below. Your goal for this interview is to learn about the teacher's views and beliefs on assessment, how he/she uses assessment in teaching, and how his/her practices fit with those recommended by the Assessment principle from *Principles for School Mathematics* (NCTM 2000, pp. 22-24): "Assessment should support the learning of important mathematics and furnish useful information to both teachers and students."

1. What purposes do you have for using assessments in your mathematics teaching?

2. Each month, how often do you use each of the following types of assessment:
   (i)   Teacher made tests or quizzes
   (ii)   Tests supplied by textbook publishers such as end of unit or chapter tests
   (iii)   Individual homework
   (iv)   Group projects or group problem solving
   (v)   Oral responses of students during classwork or class discussions
   (vi)   Standardized state or district assessments
   (vii)   Other, specify_____

3. If you give tests, which types of test items do you typically use to assess your students' learning, and why:
   (i)   Multiple choice
   (ii)   Short constructed response (short answer or fill-in-blank)
   (iii)   Constructed response (answer with work shown and explanation of reasoning)
   (iv)   Essay

(Continued on next page.)

4. How do you combine the results of various assessments to assign math grades?

5. How are your assessments alike or different from the tasks your students do during everyday classroom activities? Why?

6. In your opinion, how can technology be used to support and enhance assessment?

REFLECTION:

1. To what extent do the teacher's assessment practices align with the Assessment Principle? Give supporting examples to support your assertions.

2. To what extent does the teacher you interviewed view assessment as an integral part of the learning and teaching process? Explain.

Primary Interview on Place Value

Materials: Unifix cubes, paper and pencil, base-ten blocks.

Tasks:

1. Can you show me twenty-four Unifix cubes? Observe if child counts accurately (says numbers in proper order, uses one-to-one correspondence, has a method for keeping track of which cubes have been counted).

2. Now let's suppose we want thirty-four cubes. Can you show me that? Does child count out ten more or count over from beginning?

3. Can you write the number thirty-four here?

4. Let's put the thirty-four cubes into groups of ten. How many tens do you think we can make? Do you think you'll have any cubes left over? Shall we count out the thirty-four cubes into piles to make sure?

5. Let's look at thirty-four, the number you wrote. Can you show me with the cubes what the 3 means? Can you show me what the 4 means?

6. Now let's make four piles of ten cubes each. And let's have five leftover. Do you know how many cubes we have here altogether? How can you tell? (Does student know to count the piles by ten and add the leftovers? Or does he or she count all?)

7. a. If the child has trouble with the questions above, check further by asking again to count out several different numbers of cubes—for example, 17, 26, or 30—and to predict how many tens and how many left over. Ask the reverse question. For example, if we have 2 tens and 7 left over, how many cubes would that be?

   b. If the child has no trouble with the questions above, probe for understanding of place value of larger numbers such as 123 or 347 using base-ten blocks and asking how many piles of one hundred could be made and how many piles of ten and how many ones. Also ask the reverse question: if we have three flats and six sticks and two units, how many cubes would that be altogether? Extension: Check to see how many different ways the child can show 136.

Interview Reminders:

Listen and watch carefully! Let them do it! Don't teach!

Be flexible. Ask for more examples, if needed.

Ask: How would you show a friend? How would you explain it to a little kid?

Primary Interview on Place Value

Interviewing a Student   Grades 1–3

Materials Needed: *Primary Interview on Place Value*, counters (around 50 connecting cubes), base-ten blocks (flats, longs, and units may be constructed from grid paper).

The following questions will help you learn about children's beginning understanding of place value. Place value concepts are foundational to student number sense. Many young children can count to one hundred or beyond, but actually have little or no sense of what numbers like twenty-four or fifty-three or seventy-nine actually mean. Before students can make sense of addition or subtraction of multi-digit numbers, it is essential that they develop a good understanding of place value.

Conduct an interview on place value, like the one on the reverse of this page (*Primary Interview on Place Value*), with at least four different primary aged children. If possible, take them out of the classroom individually to conduct the interview. Tape record it so you can review your questions and their answers. Each interview should take approximately 15–30 minutes.

Make notes about what the students do during the interview. You may also want to comment aloud on things they are doing so the tape recorder can pick up your comments and remind you later of student actions (for example, you might say, "OK, Jeremy, you've counted out three piles of ten and put out four other cubes too," or, "I see you are touching each of the cubes and pushing them aside while you count them silently.")

REFLECTION:

1. What sorts of strengths with counting, place value, or number sense did some of the students evidence during your interviews? What do they already understand well?

2. What sorts of difficulties or misconceptions with counting, place value, or number sense did some of the students evidence during your interviews? What do they still need more experience with?

3. Give some examples of the types of tasks, questions, or probes that you found useful (or problematic) in getting students to explain their thinking about place value. Discuss why you think these task or questions worked well (or not so well).

4. What surprised you most about the students' responses to your interview questions?

5. If you were these students' teacher, what sorts of activities would you plan next, to help them in further developing their number sense?

Interviewing the Teacher

The following questions will help you learn about a teacher's view of mathematics. Talk to one or more elementary teachers about their vision of what it means to "do mathematics." Your goal is to understand how these teachers' views of mathematics fit (or do not fit) with a view that includes the five mathematical processes identified by *Principles and Standards for School Mathematics* (NCTM 2000)—*problem solving, reasoning and proof, communication, connections,* and *representation.* (If you are not familiar with these standards, consult your math methods text or *Principles and Standards* on the World Wide Web (www.standards.nctm.org) before beginning to plan this interview.)

GETTING READY:

You might begin with an open-ended question such as: "What does it mean, to you, to 'do mathematics'?"

Follow-questions might include:
Everyone is concerned about students learning "the basics" these days. To you, what are the basics in mathematics?

What are your major goals for the mathematics learning of your students? How do your goals fit into the big picture of what you believe mathematics really is?

An interesting way to probe deeper may be to ask the teacher to react to a list of statements such as the following:
> Mathematics helps us understand the world around us.
> Mathematics is hierarchical.
> Technology has radically changed what it means to do mathematics.
> Accuracy and efficiency are key words in mathematics.
> Many situations in the real world can be modeled mathematically.
> Skills first; understanding follows.
> Mathematics is an important tool for learning other subjects.
> The mind is a muscle and learning mathematics makes it stronger.

(You may extend this list by writing other probing or controversial statements.)

REFLECTION:

1. Describe briefly what each teacher believes it means to "do mathematics." Give specific examples to support your assertions about what the teachers believe. (For example, which of the following were mentioned as part of their visions? Learning basic facts. Performing computations. Solving problems. Learning about geometric figures and their properties. Making and testing conjectures. Searching for patterns. Communicating about mathematical ideas. Using tables, graphs, figures, and symbols. Solving equations. Using mathematics as a tool in other subjects.)

2. Compare and contrast the teachers' visions of doing mathematics. Discuss how their visions fit (or do not fit) with NCTM's vision of the five process standards.

Problem Solving Strategies

Materials Needed: counters, paper and pencil, problems.

The following questions will help you learn about children's use of problem solving strategies. Ask the teacher to identify at least two children to work on a problem while you watch. Your task is to identify the strategies each child uses and to write an evaluation of their efforts. If you can get more than two children, you may choose to have them work in pairs so that you can listen while each pair talks about the problem together.

Problem solving is one of the five process standards described by *Principles and Standards for School Mathematics* (NCTM, 2000). By definition, a *problem* is a situation in which a person wants something and does not know immediately what to do to get it. Identify problem(s) appropriate for use with children in the classes you visit by consulting *Principles and Standards*, your mathematics methods textbook or instructor, the textbook being used in those classes, or the classroom teacher. (For some problems, see Analytic/Holistic Problem Solving Scoring Observation.)

If a student doesn't know how to solve a problem, how can he or she ever hope to get started? Strategies such as act it out, make a drawing or diagram, look for a pattern, construct a table, identify all possibilities, guess and check, work backward, write an equation, or think of a simpler problem are useful in attacking problem-solving situations. Make a list of the problem-solving strategies that may be useful for each of the problems you plan to use for this assessment.

1. Examine the students' work while you talk with them about how they approached the problem. Ask questions such as: "What would be a reasonable answer?", "How did you know what to do at first?", "How did you decide to do that?", "What did you do next?", "How did that help you?", "What made you think of doing ___?", and "What else could you have done?"

2. Talk more generally about problem-solving strategies. Ask questions like: "What do you do if you're not sure how to get started on a problem?" and "If a friend of yours was stuck on a problem, what strategies might you suggest that he or she use?"

REFLECTION:

Include a copy of the problem and grade level, a copy of the children's work, and answers to the following questions. (You might also evaluate the students' work using an analytic or holistic scoring system (see Analytic/Holistic Problem Solving Scoring Observation).)

1. Why did you chose this problem for your problem-solving assessment? What mathematical concepts and skills does it involve? What problem-solving strategies did you consider most useful in solving it? Explain.

2. How appropriate was the problem for these students? About how long did the student spend on the problem? Was it too easy or too hard? What strategies did they use? How? Were the strategies appropriate? Helpful?

3. Describe what you learned about each student's problem-solving abilities and understandings of the mathematics involved in the problem.

4. What might you do differently if you were designing another assessment for these students?

Conservation and Counting

Materials Needed: 10 each of two colors of counters or cubes.

The following questions will help you learn about a child's conservation of number. Use the following questions to conduct an interview with a young child to determine if he/she is a conserver.

Conservation of Number

Piaget described a child as a conserver if he/she recognizes that two equal quantities are the same amount even though one appears to be more. A nonconserver will be "fooled" by the visual arrangement or appearance of the objects.

---

1. Use cubes to build two trains. Use two colors of cubes but the same number of each color.

   Ask: Which is more? Once it is established that the trains are equal in length, point to one train (black) and ask "How long is this train?" Observe how the child counts. Then point to the other train (white) and ask "How long is this train?" Does the child count again?

2. Break up one train (i.e., separate the cubes). Again ask: Which is more?

   If the child says one row is more, ask "How many black cubes? How many white?" Does the child count again after the cubes have been rearranged?

3. Provide some counters (about 20) for the child to estimate. Ask "About how many counters are here?" After an estimate is made, ask them to count them and observe how they count. Once a number of counters is established, mix the counters again (be sure to NOT add or remove any counters) and ask "How many counters are here?"

Gearing Up:
Determine how the child answers questions, such as:
If the black train has 8 cubes, and the white train has 1 less, how many cubes are in the white train?
If the black train has 8 cubes, and the white train has 2 more, how many cubes in the white train?

REFLECTION:

1. If you noticed any counting errors, describe them and tell what counting principles (described on the following page) were not applied?

2. Tell how their responses provide you insight into whether or not they are conservers.

Counting

Interviewing a Student   Grades K–1

Materials Needed: 20 counters.

The following questions will help you learn about a child's counting skills. Counting is an important process that takes time and practice to develop. There are identifiable counting stages and counting principles that research has identified. This activity provides some structure to focus on different aspects of counting, namely rote counting, counting objects, and writing numbers in order.

Ask a child to count or observe a young child counting. You might begin by asking them to:

1. Rote count aloud:
   Can you count? How far can you count?
   Please count for me to _____ (you decide a goal).
   Record how far they counted before the first error.

Did the child use number names in the proper order? If not, how far did the child count before errors occurred? Ask them to count again and see if the errors occur with the same names.

2. Count objects:
   Place some counters for the child to count.
   Ask them to count and tell you how many.

Did you notice the child using 1–1 correspondence in applying a number name to an object? If not, describe their error patterns.

3. Recording:
   Ask if they can "write" their numbers. If so ask them to count and write the numbers as they count. Review their written numbers and describe their progress.

REFLECTION:

Keep the following counting principles in mind as you reflect on what you observed.

Principles Children Apply when Counting
1. One to One—Each object is assigned only one number name.
2. Stable Order—The number names must be used in the same order every time one counts.
3. Order Irrelevance—The order in which the objects are counted doesn't matter.
4. Cardinality—The last number name used gives the number of objects.

---

1. Did you witness all four of the counting principles?   **Y**   **N**
   If **no**, which one(s) did not appear?

2. Illustrate what the child did or said to convince you that a particular counting principle was or was not being followed.

72 • *Teaching Elementary Mathematics: A Resource for Field Experiences* © 2009 John Wiley & Sons • **In the School** • **Interviewing**

Early Number Sense

Materials Needed: none

The following questions will help you learn about a child's number sense. Use whatever questions seem appropriate and probe for explanations from the child. Try to capture the "words students use" to describe how they did it. This will provide you additional clues about their thinking, and their level of number sense. Record their responses in the space provided.

Counting forward:

Ask a child to count by 2 to 30. (Record how far they got without an error and note how long it takes them. Allow child to try again if they want to do so.)
Count to 60 by other numbers, such as 3, 5, and 10
Begin at 2 and count by tens until you get over 100.
Begin at 23 and count by hundreds.

Counting backward:

Ask a child to begin at 30 and count back by 1.
Begin at 97 and count back by tens.

Next and before:

What number comes before seventeen? thirty? two hundred?
What number comes after thirty-nine? two-hundred nine? Three-hundred-fifty?

How many?

How many tens are in forty? forty-seven?
How many tens are in ninety? one-hundred fifty?
How many hundreds are in one-hundred? one-hundred seventy? three-hundred? one-thousand?

Gearing Down: Develop and ask easier questions which provide the child with success.

Gearing Up: Develop and ask more challenging questions if these are too easy.

REFLECTION:

1. What questions/answers informed you most about this child's number sense? Explain how their answers helped your understanding.

2. Identify additional questions that you asked to help you better understand their level of number sense.

Place Value

Materials Needed: paper and pencil or marker.

The following questions will help you learn about a student's understanding of place value. It provides a series of questions about numbers with increasing magnitude. Stop the tasks when the child is unable to accurately respond. Try to capture the "words students use" to describe how they did it. This will provide you additional clues about their thinking and their level of number sense. Say:

I am going to say a number and I want you to write it:
- fifty six
- three hundred forty eight
- four hundred five
- one thousand
- two thousand thirty seven
- twelve thousand four hundred eight

Now I am going to write some numbers and I want you to say them:
- 82
- 457
- 305
- 3000
- 4036
- 12078

Gearing Down: Select smaller numbers until you find their level of success.

Gearing Up: Consider any of the following questions to gain additional insight about their number sense.

1. Write a large number. Name the number you wrote.

2. Can you write a larger number?   **Yes   No**   If **Yes,** ask them to write and then name it.

3. Keyon wrote 12345. Julia said that is not right, and you should write it as 12,345.
   Does it matter whether you use a comma to write the number? Explain.

4. How many tens are in 40?   500?   6000?

5. Consider the number 6789.
   How many hundreds does it have?
   How many tens does it have?
   How many thousands does it have?

REFLECTION:

1. Do you think this child has a good grasp of basic place value concepts? Use information you have collected to support your answer.

Developing Place Value Concepts

Interviewing the Teacher Grades 1–3

The following questions will help you learn about a primary teacher's approach to helping children learn about place value. Talk to a teacher in grade 3 or below.

QUESTIONS:

1. About how many students in your class have not yet developed a secure understanding of the concept of place value in our base-ten number system? How do you know?

2. Give several examples of tasks or questions you might use to gauge a student's level of place value understanding.

3. Give several examples of the sorts of tasks, problems, games, or questions you use to help children learn about place value.

4. Which of the following hands-on materials do you use in lessons about place value?
   a. Counting chips
   b. Bean sticks
   c. Calculators
   d. Coins
   e. Linking cubes
   f. Abacus
   g. Base-ten blocks
   h. Two-color Counters

   How do you use these materials?

   Are there other materials that you use? What and how?

   Which materials do you prefer to use? Why?

REFLECTION:

1. After talking with the teacher, think about his or her students. Is this a class that is strong in its understanding of place value? (What makes you think this?) What else might this teacher consider doing to help his or her students with place value understanding?

2. Think about yourself as a future primary teacher. What will you do to help your students develop sound place value understanding?

In the School • Interviewing • *Teaching Elementary Mathematics: A Resource for Field Experiences* © 2009 John Wiley & Sons • **75**

Basic Fact Difficulty

The following questions will help you learn about an upper grade teacher's approach to teaching basic facts. Talk to a teacher in grade five or above about what he or she does with students who are not fluent in basic facts. Here are some questions you might want to ask:

1. How many students in your class have difficulty with basic facts? How do you know what facts are difficult? What facts are the most difficult? Do you have specific suggestions for how students can be helped to learn these "tough" facts?

2. Do any of your students receive special instruction in fact strategies? If so, what does this instruction entail? How do you help the students keep track of their progress in learning basic facts?

3. Do your students use calculators routinely for classwork and homework? If so, how do you think this calculator use helps or hinders those who have trouble with basic facts? If your students do not use calculators, why not? How do you think their not using calculators helps or hinders those who have trouble with basic facts?

REFLECTION:

1. After talking with the teacher, think about his or her students. Is this a class that is strong in its knowledge of the basic facts? What else might the teacher consider doing to help his or her students with basic facts?

2. Think about yourself as a future intermediate grade teacher. What might you want to do to help your students with their basic facts? What fact strategies might you encourage your students to use?

Addition Basic Facts

+	0	1	2	3	4	5	6	7	8	9
0	0	1	2	3	4	5	6	7	8	9
1	1	2	3	4	5	6	7	8	9	10
2	2	3	4	5	6	7	8	9	10	11
3	3	4	5	6	7	8	9	10	11	12
4	4	5	6	7	8	9	10	11	12	13
5	5	6	7	8	9	10	11	12	13	14
6	6	7	8	9	10	11	12	13	14	15
7	7	8	9	10	11	12	13	14	15	16
8	8	9	10	11	12	13	14	15	16	17
9	9	10	11	12	13	14	15	16	17	18

Multiplication Basic Facts

x	0	1	2	3	4	5	6	7	8	9
0	0	0	0	0	0	0	0	0	0	0
1	0	1	2	3	4	5	6	7	8	9
2	0	2	4	6	8	10	12	14	16	18
3	0	3	6	9	12	15	18	21	24	27
4	0	4	8	12	16	20	24	28	32	36
5	0	5	10	15	20	25	30	35	40	45
6	0	6	12	18	24	30	36	42	48	54
7	0	7	14	21	28	35	42	49	56	63
8	0	8	16	24	32	40	48	56	64	72
9	0	9	18	27	36	45	54	63	72	81

Basic Fact Fluency

Materials Needed: A 10 x 10 chart showing addition (or multiplication) fact combinations from 0+0 through 9 + 9 (or 0 x 0 through 9 x 9) may be found on the previous page.

Your goal in this interview is to document a student's mastery of basic facts (addition or multiplication), to look for patterns in the facts he/she has trouble with, and to formulate a plan for future instruction. You are looking for fluency: ability to compute accurately and relatively quickly. Whenever you, as a teacher, have time to meet with individual students, an individual interview provides a very useful and informative alternative to a timed fact test.

1. Explain to the student that this interview will be entirely oral—no paper or pencil allowed. You will read one fact at a time aloud and the student will respond with an answer. Explain that you may occasionally stop to ask "how did you get that?" Explain that you will not talk about whether the answers are right or wrong until the end of the interview. Assure the child that the purpose of the interview is to help him/her by finding out what facts are already known and which ones still need work. The interview is not designed for assigning a grade.

2. Read facts aloud randomly from the chart (e.g., 2 + 5? 4 + 9? 0 + 2? 3 + 0?). The child should reply out loud. If a student response is correct, circle it. If the student response is incorrect, write the student's answer in the chart next to the correct response. (Be sure to read addends or factors consistently in the proper order: that is, say "3 + 4" when 3 is in the left column and 4 is on the top row, but say "4 + 3" when 4 is in the left column and 3 is in the top row. Students may know one of these facts but not know the other, and you want to be sure to capture this.) Keep your paper shielded so the student cannot see what you are writing. When you write something for each response, the student will not be able to tell if answers were correct or incorrect. If a student answer seems strange, ask "how did you get that?" You may ask this even if the answer is correct. Make notes about strategies.

3. When you have read all 100 fact combinations, examine the table. Look for patterns in the student's correct and incorrect responses, and in his/her strategies. You may want to do this with the student, talking aloud as you think about the error patterns. For example, a student may have trouble with multiplying by 7 (most of the answers in the 7 row going across and the 7 column going down are wrong). Or a student may have trouble only with larger sums (most wrong answers are in the bottom right corner of the chart—involving addends 8 or 9. Be sure to praise the student for patterns of correct answers, "I see you know your fives."

Gearing Down: You may assess in several small sessions rather than all 100 facts at once.

REFLECTION:

Attach a copy of the fact chart from your interview. After the interview is over, think about what next steps you would recommend for this student.

1. Write a brief summary detailing your findings and your recommendations for this student.

2. What error patterns or erroneous strategies were observed?

3. Which facts or fact families should he/she concentrate on next?

4. What fact strategies might be helpful? Offer examples to illustrate your recommendations.

About How Much?

Materials Needed: none

The following questions will help you learn about computational estimation strategies students use. Think about how you would estimate 29 x 24. When asked to estimate, some children equate estimation with guessing. Make it clear that whether they estimate or guess—you want to know how they did it. During the interview, try to capture the "words students use" to describe how they estimated. This will provide you additional clues about their thinking. Children may want to write something. Don't encourage them to write, but if they need to do so, observe what they write.

Present this computation orally or visually: 29 x 24
Ask the child to estimate. Ask them to think out loud so you can know how they did it. Record your observations here.

If for whatever reason, you don't understand what they said or did, consider follow-up probes, such as:
Tell me your thinking.   Can you explain it another way?
Think out loud for me as you do it.   How did you do that?
Repeat this interview with at least one more child.

WHAT WE FOUND:

Several different strategies were used, including:
Rounding 24 to 20 and 29 to 30 and making an estimate of 600
Rounding 24 to 25 and 29 to 30 and making an estimate of 750
Rounding 24 to 25 and 29 to 28 and estimating 700—this person thought of 25 as quarters and said 28 quarters is $7 and made 700 as their estimate.

REFLECTION:

1. Did you find any of the strategies similar to "What we found?" If so, which ones?

2. Describe other estimation strategies that were used.

3. What evidence did you find that the students wanted to compute an exact answer and then round to make their estimate?

Do it Mentally

Materials Needed: none

The following questions will help you learn about mental computational strategies students use. Think about how you would compute 99 + 165. Would you use written computation or do it mentally? Some children may ask you if they can write the computation down. Encourage them to do it mentally. If they can't, then allow them to do the computation with paper and pencil, and observe how they record their solution. Try to capture the "words students use" to describe how they did it.

Present this computation orally: 99 + 165
Ask the child to compute it mentally (i.e., in their head).
Ask them to think out loud so you can understand how they did it.

If for whatever reason, you don't understand what they said or did, use follow-up probes:

Tell me your thinking.   Can you explain it another way.
Think out loud for me as you do it.   How did you do that?
Repeat this interview with at least one more child.

WHAT WE FOUND:

From a second grader:
"I added 100 to 165 and got 265. This was 1 too much so I subtracted 1."
From a fourth grader:

"I added 9 plus 5 and got 14. I then added 6 plus 6 and got 12 then added one more to get 13. Then I added 1 plus 2 and got 3. So my answer is 3 something, but I forgot the rest."
This fourth grader's comment may reflect an emphasis on written computation that encourages students to apply written computation methods mentally.

Gearing Down: Try using: 49 + 51

Gearing Up: Change the order and say "What is the sum of 165 + 99?"
Change the computation to "99 + 99" or "165 + 101."
How much does it cost? $3.99 + $5.99

REFLECTION:

1. Write up the results of the interview that reflects the question and the response of the child, describing exactly how they did the mental computation.

2. Describe the strategies that were used to solve these computations.

3. Did you find evidence that "written algorithms" were applied mentally? Explain.

Addition with Regrouping

Materials Needed: three problems (see below), base-ten manipulatives, paper and pencil.

The following questions will help you learn about children's skill with whole number addition involving regrouping. Develop three items that would assess students' understanding of adding two three-digit numbers with regrouping. Attach a copy of the items you developed. Why did you choose these?

Try your items with several children and analyze their responses.

1. How did each child solve the problems? Did he or she use any manipulatives or pictures? What algorithms, if any, did he or she use?

2. What errors, if any, did each child make? What might this tell you about his or her understanding of addition with two-digit numbers?

REFLECTION:

1. How well did these items work for assessing the students' understanding of three-digit addition with regrouping? Would you use them again? What changes, if any, might you want to make in the items or in how they were administered?

2. If these were your students, based on what you learned about each student's understanding of three-digit addition, what are some things you might do next with them?

Transitional Algorithms

Materials Needed: base-ten manipulatives, paper and pencil.

The following questions will help you learn about the use of transitional algorithms to assist a student who is having difficulty with computation. Ask your cooperating teacher if you can spend some time working with a student who is having trouble with paper-and-pencil computation (addition, subtraction, multiplication, or division, depending on age and grade level). See if you can figure out what the child's problem is. You might try helping him or her by suggesting the use of a transitional algorithm.

A transitional algorithm is an alternative to the algorithm traditionally taught in school; although it may not be as efficient, it is generally easier to understand and to model. Consult a mathematics methods textbook or *The Teaching and Learning of Algorithms in School Mathematics* (1998 NCTM Yearbook, Lorna J. Morrow and Margaret J. Kenney, eds.) for examples of transitional algorithms. A student who understands and can use a transitional algorithm accurately often can later be prompted to move toward using the more efficient traditional algorithm.

1. What is the age and grade level of the child? What type of computation is he or she having trouble with?

2. What did you do with the child? If you used manipulatives to model the computation, explain how.

3. What does this child understand about this type of computation? What problem is he or she having?

4. Did you work with the child on using a transitional algorithm? Which one?

5. How did you introduce the algorithm to the child? Was this helpful to the child? How do you know?

REFLECTION:

1. What went well as you worked with this child? What, if anything, would you have done differently?

2. Did you get a good feel for what this child understood and what problem he or she was having with the computation? As a teacher, what might you want to do next with this child?

Three-Fourths

▼ In which of the following models does the shading show three-fourths of the whole? Why or why not?

A Whole: large rectangle

F Whole: large rectangle

B Whole: box of marbles

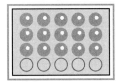

G Whole: box of candy

C Whole: large rectangle

H Whole: large rectangle

D Whole: large rectangle

I Whole: large triangle

E Whole: box of shapes

J Whole: large rectangle

Three-Fourths

Materials Needed: *Three-Fourths*, 20 objects, paper and pencil.

The following questions will help you learn about a child's understanding of fractions. This sheet (*Three-Fourths*) presents many examples and non-examples of three-fourths. Your task is to ascertain which model the child understands (see notes below on models).

Sit with an individual child, show them *Three-Fourths*, and ask them three questions:
1. What is the whole? (Have young children show you the whole.)
2. Does the shaded part show three-fourths of the whole?
3. Why or why not?

Gearing Up:
1. Ask the child to draw another model of three-fourths, a model of two-fifths, and a model of three-sevenths.
2. Ask the child to show you three-fourths of 20 objects.
3. Show the child 12 objects. Tell them this is two-thirds of a box of candy. Ask them how many candies were in a whole box, and to justify the answer. (18 candies)

Descriptions of Models:
A.   Region model showing three-fourths.
B.   Set model showing three-fourths. More difficult for many children than the model in A because the whole consists of a number of elements.
C.   Region model showing three-sevenths. Many children confuse this since there are three shaded parts and four non-shaded parts. The ratio of the shaded to the non-shaded is 3 to 4 often represented by 3/4; but the shaded part does not show 3/4 of the whole rectangle.
D.   Region model, but more complicated than the simple one in A. Be certain that a child can identify the fourths (the vertical strips).
E.   Set model showing three-fourths. Watch to see if the different size objects present any problem.
F.   Region model showing three-fourths.
G.   Set model showing three-fourths. Contrast this one with B in which the four parts (the rows) are easily identified.
H.   Region model that does not show three-fourths.
I.   Area model showing three fourths. See if any children realize the areas of the small triangles (assuming bases are the same).
J.   Region model showing three-fourths.

REFLECTION:

Record the child's answers and explanations.

1. Which models did the child understand? What evidence do you have?

2. Is there a difference between the set and region model?

Proportions

Materials Needed: none

The following questions will help you learn about the understanding and strategies used to solve problems involving proportions. Developing facility with proportional reasoning requires complex thinking. Ask several different students the following question. If there is any doubt about what the child said, try follow-up probes, such as: Tell me how you did that. Can you explain it differently? Think out loud for me so I can better understand what you are doing.

Rustin and Whitney were buying snacks. They could spend $2.00 for 16 ounces of Superade or $1.60 for 12 ounces of cran-apple juice. They bought the juice. Did they make the most economical choice?

What research* has found:
One correct solution: $2.00 ÷ 16 = 12.5¢ per ounce for Superade. $1.60 ÷ 12 = 13.3¢ per ounce for cran-apple. No, they did not make the best economical choice.

Another correct solution: No, they didn't make the best choice because 48 ounces of Superade cost $6.00 and 48 ounces of juice cost $6.40.

Other answers: Yes, because each drink you buy is 40¢ cheaper, so you are saving lots of money.
No, because Superade is cheaper, because it has more ounces to it.
Yes, because it really didn't cost that much money.
No, because what if some of the kids don't like cran-apple juice?
What does "economical choice" mean? We never learned that.

*Miller, J. L. & Fey, J. T. "Proportional Reasoning," *Mathematics Teaching in the Middle School*, 5 (5), 310–313, January 2000.

Gearing Down: Try using: A punch recipe uses 2 cups of juice and 3 cups of ginger ale. If we use 4 cups of juice, how many cups of ginger ale will be needed? (6 cups)

Gearing Up: Here is another question requiring students to use proportional reasoning.
A picture is 5 cm x 7 cm. If it is to be enlarged to be 8 cm wide, how long will it be?

REFLECTION:

1. Did your students give one of the responses above? If so, which one? If not, summarize their strategy.

2. Do you think the cost per ounce problem is more difficult that the enlargement problem? Tell why.

 *Percents*

Materials Needed: none

The following questions will help you learn about a student's understanding of percents. Percents are often used, but sometimes some basic fundamental ideas are not well understood. For example, one national survey showed that about one-third of 17 year olds and adults did not know that 100 is the comparison base for percent.

Ask students some of the following questions. In each case, if there is any doubt about what the child said, try follow-up probes, such as: "Tell me how you did that," "Can you explain it differently?" or "Think out loud for me so I can better understand what you are doing."

- What is 50% of $80?
- What is 100% of 50?
- What does 1/2% on a milk carton mean?
- 25 is what percent of 75?

Gearing Down:
Can you eat 50% of a cake? Can you eat 100% of a cake? Can you eat 150% of a cake? Tell how.
Can a price increase 50%? Can a price increase 100%? Can a price increase 150%? Tell how.

Gearing Up:
Is it possible to get a 100% raise? If so, can you give an example?
If the cost of a CD is $6, and it is increased 200% how much does it cost?
Suppose an item was originally priced at $5 and is decreased by 50%. When it didn't sell, it was later decreased by 50% again. Does that mean it is now free? Explain.

REFLECTION:

1. Which of the bulleted questions were the easiest?

2. Which of the bulleted questions was most difficult?
   Tell why.

3. Select a question that produced different responses from different children. Summarize their responses and how their answer helped you better understand their knowledge of percent.

4. Do you think the **Gearing Up** questions help assess student's understanding of percent?
   Tell why.

Name: _____

Class: _____

Thinking About Patterns

▼ Provide children with a variety of patterns like these, asking them questions like:

• How do you describe this pattern?

• What shape (or object) goes in the empty space? Why?

• Are some of these patterns alike? How?

1. What pattern block shape should come next?

2. One of the shapes is missing in this string of shapes. What shape and what color would you insert? Why?

3. What animal should be in the next place? Why?

Thinking about Patterns

Materials Needed: *Thinking about Patterns*, pattern blocks or other materials that vary by color or shape. Have some additional patterns in mind such as ones that repeat every four elements (for example, a red square, a blue square, a green square, and a yellow square or a red triangle, a blue square, a green triangle, and a yellow square).

Here are some additional questions to ask about each pattern:

Pattern 1. If the child places a green triangle, ask why. Then, see if they can continue the pattern. Ask the child can they make another pattern like this one with the yellow and red pattern blocks.

   If the child places a blue rhombus, ask why. He or she may be seeing another pattern such as the blue blocks increasing by one each time (1 triangle, 1 rhombus, 1 triangle, 2 rhombuses, 1 triangle). If they indicate that it is a blue rhombus, ask them to continue the pattern until you can tell what they are doing.

Pattern 2. If a child puts a red circle, ask why. If a child puts a green square, ask why. If a child has difficulty placing any shape, then you put the shape and ask what would come next after the green square and red circle. (Note; if you do not have red circles and green triangles, substitute yellow hexagons for the circles and orange squares for the green squares from the pattern blocks). See if you can ascertain whether it is the missing element (not at the end of the string) that is bothering the child, by giving similar pattern (2 of a shape, 1 of another shape, 2 of the first shape, etc.).

Pattern 3. This is a more difficult pattern. Do not be surprised if it causes difficulty for younger children. The squirrel is a 1, 2, 1 pattern with a rabbit in between. See if the pattern is easier with the pattern blocks. If a child is still trying to figure out the pattern, have them tell you how many squirrels they see between the rabbits. Carry the pattern out with some more elements. Does either of these actions help the child? Also, be on the look for a child who has a different answer; let them give their rule and continue the pattern.

REFLECTION:

(To answer these questions, you may have to do more variations of the three patterns; chose one reflection question to investigate further with children.)

1. Which patterns were easy for children---alternating, repeating with a core of 2 elements, repeating with a core of 3 elements, ones that seem to be made from two patterns (such as rabbit and squirrel)?

2. Is it easier for children to continue a pattern or to find a missing element?

3. Did it help to have the pattern blocks for the children to handle?

Materials Needed: Interview questions and recording paper.

The following questions will help you learn about students' understanding of equality. Interview at least four students individually who have been identified by the teacher as having different levels of mathematics proficiency. Have the students solve each problem separately, ask them to tell why they answered the way that they did, and record their responses.

INTERVIEW QUESTIONS:

What number(s) will make the sentence true?

1. $4 + 7 = \square$

2. $6 + 5 = \square + 2$

3. $9 + \square = 15$

4. $\square = 8 + 6$

5. $3 + 7 = 7 + \square$

6. $23 + 41 = 22 + \square$

7. $8 + \square = 5 + \bigcirc$

8. $5 + \square = \bigcirc + 5$

ANSWERS YOU MAY EXPECT:

In addition to the correct answer, look for the following that may indicate misconceptions about equality. Some errors may be due to fact errors.

1. A student who gets this one and misses many of the others may only understand equality as meaning, "get an answer."
2. If answered 11, adds the first two numbers. Also, probe the student who answers 9 of how he or she arrived at this correct answer.
3. An answer of 24 may indicate just adding the two numbers, not balancing the equation.
4. See if the box being on the left gives any trouble.
5. This is an example of the commutative property. Does the student see immediately the answer is 7 or does he or she have to add 3 and 7 and then subtract 7 from the 10?
6. Watch to see how the student approaches this. Some children will say that because 22 is 1 less than 23, you must add 42 (one more than 41). Others will find the sum and subtract 21.
7. This has many answers. Each number in the box must be 3 less than the one in the circle. Does the student notice that there is more than one answer?
8. The numbers in the box and circle must be the same, but can be any number. Again, look to see if the student finds one answer, several answers, or generalizes.

REFLECTION:

1. Does the student look at equality as meaning you should complete an operation or do they understand the balancing idea? How do you know?

2. Do you think the curriculum that the students are using encourages an understanding of equality? Why or why not?

3. What would *you* do next to further develop these students' understanding of equality?

Algebraic Thinking

Materials Needed: 30 light cubes and 6 dark cubes or tiles.

Students may 'see' the same information very differently depending on how the information is represented or how they perceive the representation. This interview is designed to help you capture different ways that students think algebraically. Show this series of figures built from dark and light cubes to several students:

Figure 1   Figure 2   Figure 3

Ask each student questions such as:
How would Figure 4 look? Sketch or describe.
How would Figure 5 look? Sketch or describe.
How many dark cubes would you need to build Figure 10? How many light cubes?
How many dark cubes would you need to build Figure 100 (or N)? How many light cubes?

Provide students with paper or actual cubes to build the figures. Observe how the students proceed. Observe how students decide the number of cubes needed for Figure 10, 100 or N:
Do they sketch the dark cells first and then fill in the frame?
Do they sketch the top row first and work down?

WHAT WE FOUND:

Deciding the number of white cubes is the most interesting question, because multiple solutions exist. Here are some strategies we found in talking with students about Figure 10:
"There are 10 white cubes in the top and bottom row and there are two in the middle row."
"There are 3 white cubes on each end, and there are two rows of 8 white cubes."
"There are the 4 corners, a white cube on each end of the dark cubes and two rows of 8 white cubes."

Most students will describe these relationships in words. Once they are described, ask them how they might be represented with symbols. For example, the above descriptions could be expressed symbolically for Figure 10 as: symbolically for Figure N as:

$2(10) + 2$ $2(N) + 2$
$2(3) + 2(8)$ $2(3) + 2(N-2)$
$4 + 2 + 2(8)$ $4 + 2 + 2(N-2)$

REFLECTION:

1. What different strategies did you find? Did students describe their strategies orally or symbolically?

2. Generalization is central to algebraic thinking. We found it is much easier for students to describe a solution for a specific number than for N. Is this consistent with your experience? Why do you think this is more difficult? What would you do to encourage this type of thinking?

Find Me

▼ These are triangles:

▼ These are not triangles:

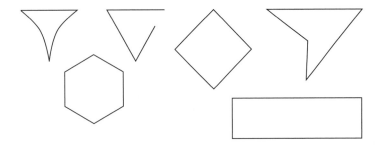

▼ Which are triangles? Tell why the others are not triangles.

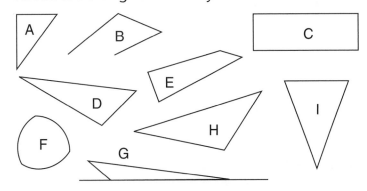

Find Me

Materials Needed: *Find Me*

The following questions will help you learn about children's understanding of triangles. By listening to the responses of individual children, you will be able to have a deeper understanding of the knowledge of children. You are asked to interview children in two different ways. First, by discussing examples and non-examples of triangles together and then asking children to identify triangles. Second, by asking children without the discussion.

Version One

Choose three students of different abilities. Show each student *Find Me*, have them tell why the examples of the triangles are triangles, and why the ones that are nonexamples are not triangles. Then, have them tell whether A-I are or are not triangles and why. At the end, ask the student to draw a triangle.

Version Two

Choose three students of different abilities. Show each student *Find Me*, and have them tell whether A–I are or are not triangles and why. At the end, ask the student to draw a triangle.

REFLECTION:

1. Did the two versions make a difference? How? For which students?

2. What type of triangle did each child draw? What does this experience tell you about the model of a triangle that a child holds in his or her mind?

Classify Me

▼ Mark each of the figures with a

1. if it is a quadrilateral.

2. if it has two pairs of parallel sides.

3. if it has all right angles.

4. if it has all congruent sides.

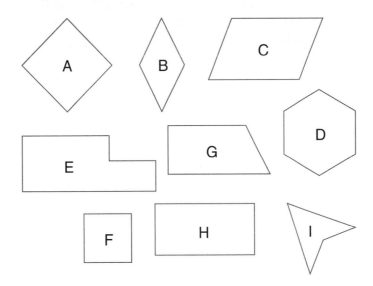

• Any figure marked 1 and 2 is a _____.

• Any figure marked 1, 2, and 3
is a rectangle as well as a _____.

• Any figure marked 1, 2, and 4 is a _____
as well as a _____.

• Any figure marked 1, 2, 3, and 4 is a _____
and a _____ as well as a square.

Classify Me

Materials Needed: *Classify Me*

The following questions will help you learn about a student's understanding of quadrilaterals. By listening to the responses of individual children, you will be able to have a deeper understanding of the knowledge of children about quadrilaterals.

Give the student a copy of *Classify Me.* If he or she needs assistance in reading or following directions, help the student noting how you helped. When he or she has completed numbering the quadrilaterals, ask the questions at the bottom of the sheet. See if the child can tell the defining characteristics (from the four listed at the top) of each type of quadrilateral: parallelogram, rectangle, rhombus, and square.

REFLECTION:

1. Did the child understand that a figure could be a rectangle as well as a parallelogram?
   Did the child understand the classification scheme of all rectangles being parallelograms? For which classifications did they have difficulty?

2. How else could you assess students' understanding of the classification of quadrilaterals?

3. Can the child turn the classification around to give the characteristics of a square? Of a rhombus? Of a rectangle? Of a parallelogram?

Compare Shapes

Materials Needed: A copy of the shapes at the bottom of the page.

The following questions will help you learn about the growth in students' ability to describe how two shapes are the same and different. This is an interview that you should do with your classmates across as many grades as you can. Show at least three children the two shapes at the bottom of this page. Ask them to describe how these shapes are the same and how they are different. Record all the responses.

Work with your classmates to see how the responses they received were the same and how they were different. Your instructor may want to organize how you work together. See how your responses compared to those (see description below) expected at the grade levels below for students who have been given opportunities to study geometry as recommended by the *Principles and Standards for School Mathematics* (NCTM 2000).

Typical Responses

Grades K–2 Each has four sides. A is a rectangle. B is not. A can be folded to match. They each have corners, four corners. B looks lopsided.

Grades 3–5 Each has 4 sides and 4 corners. A is a rectangle, B is a parallelogram. A has perpendicular sides. B has 2 pairs of parallel sides. So does A. The angles of A are equal, they are right angles. The length of opposite sides are equal. They aren't congruent.

Grades 6–8 All of the above. Both are parallelograms and quadrilaterals. They have the same height. They have the same area, but they aren't congruent. They are convex. Opposite angles are equal. The perimeter of B is longer. They are not similar.

REFLECTION:

1. Do children use their own vocabulary and descriptions or geometric descriptions? Does this change across the grades?

2. Did you see growth across the grades? What type?

3. What attributes did all students mention? Did older students drop some of the earlier descriptions?

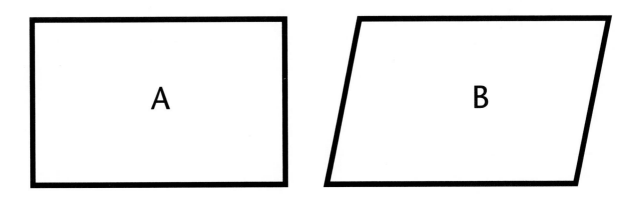

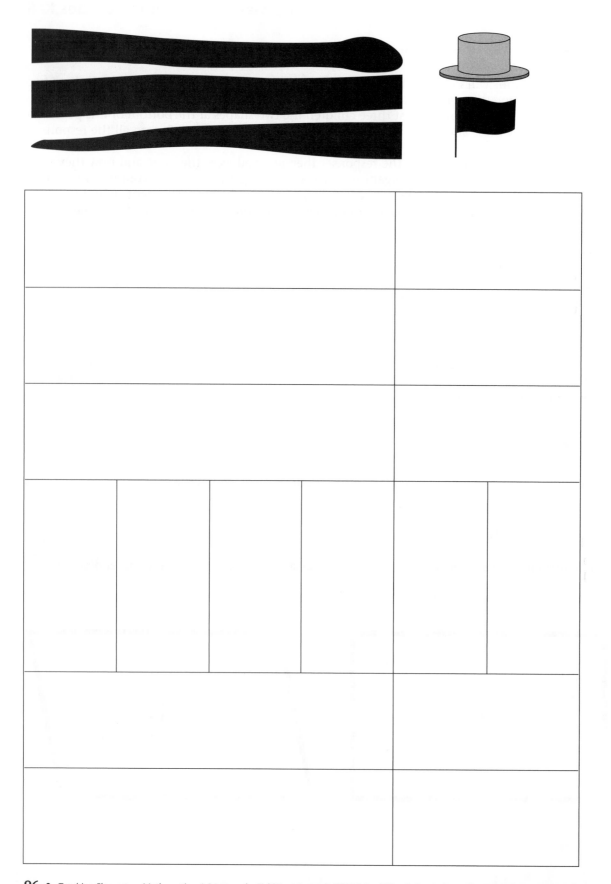

Materials Needed: Use the pattern on the previous page and cut an 8 inch (2 piece) and 12 inch (3 piece) paper snake and identify them either by color or by hat and flag as shown. Also cut paper strip units: five 4-inch strips (color blue) and ten 2-inch strips (color red).

The following questions will help you learn about a child's concept of measurement. Young children often do not coordinate the number in a measurement with the unit. In this series of comparison tasks, you ask each child about the length of two snakes. First find out if he or she knows which snake is longer and how they know. Then, you will measure each snake with different units and ask again which is longer. Finally, you will use the same units to measure the lengths to make the comparison.

Research shows that young children, who can often compare directly or visually, will change their minds about the comparison when numbers become involved.

1. Ask the following questions: "Which is longer, the snake with the hat or the snake or with the flag?" (Let the child hold the snakes to make the comparison.) If you cannot tell how he or she is comparing, ask him or her how she knows which is longer. (See if the child makes a visual comparison or lines the snakes up in any way. If the child says, "I just know," then ask them how they would show someone how much longer one snake is than the other.)

2. Measure the flag snake with the 2-inch strips and the hat snake with the 4-inch strips. Ask the child how long is the flag snake with the flag in blue strips. Write down the answer (4 blue strips). Then ask how long the hat snake is in red strips (3 red strips). Leave placed as shown here. Then ask the child which snake is longer

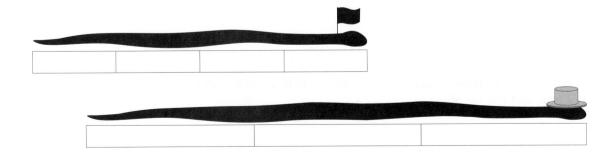

3. Repeat task by interchanging the strips as shown. Repeat questions from number 1.

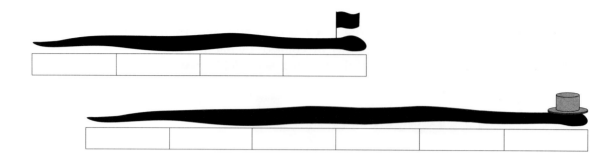

4. Use the 2-inch strips for both snakes. Repeat questions from number 1.

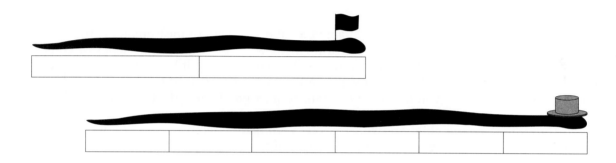

REFLECTION:

1. How did the children handle the change of units? If they changed their answer about which snake was longer, did it bother them?

2. Was there evidence that they realized that it would take more of the shorter strip to measure the length? Do you see why when children only measure in one unit that they may not understand the significance of the unit?

3. What type of activities would you provide to help children understand the importance of both the unit and the number of units?

Graphing

Materials Needed: one sheet of cm grid paper, pencil, crayons, or markers.

The following questions will help you learn about children's ability to interpret graphs.

Cougar Wins over 5 Seasons

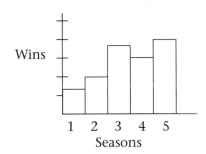

Eagle Wins over 5 Seasons

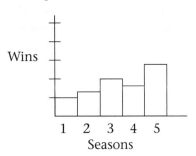

1. Display only the two graphs at the top of the page and share the following scenario.
   The coach of a traveling softball team, the Cougars, was trying to recruit Linda to play for them during the summer season. The Cougar coach showed her some graphs that compared five seasons of wins for the Cougars with the other team Linda was considering, the Eagles. Should Linda play for the Cougars? What's wrong with these graphs?

2. If the student doesn't notice that there is no scale indicated on the vertical axis, point it out. The two graphs are misleading because the scales are not the same. Now write in the following scales: Cougars: 5, 10, 15, 20, 25   Eagles: 10, 20, 30, 40, 50

3. Show the student a data table with the actual number of wins for each team.

Season	1	2	3	4	5
Cougars	7	10	18	15	20
Eagles	10	13	20	18	25

Have the student use the data table and grid paper to make bar graphs for the two teams. Each team should use the following scale: 5, 10, 15, 20, 25. Ask the student to identify which team has the best record (Eagles). Discuss why it is important to read graphs carefully.

For additional interview and analysis examples, see Reys et al., *Helping Children Learn Mathematics*, (Eighth edition) Chapter 16. See also Sakshaug, L. Which Graph is Which? *Teaching Children Mathematics*. March 2000, Volume (6) pp. 454–455 NCTM.

REFLECTION:

1. What did the student identify as misleading about the two graphs?

2. Describe how the student used the data to construct bar graphs on the grid paper.

3. What experiences would you provide next to continue the development of graphing?

4. Did anyone ask about the number of losses for each team? Would this be useful to know?

Statistics

Interviewing a Student   Grades 6–8

The following questions will help you learn about a student's understanding of statistics.

Materials Needed: *Peanuts* (may be found with In the Classroom Lessons), beans or other counters, calculator.

1. Ask the student if they have heard of the statistics mean, median, mode, and range. If so, have them tell you what they know about each one. Record their responses below. If the student is not familiar with any of these statistics, they will not be able to complete the rest of this interview. An alternative learning activity you could complete with them is *Peanuts*.

Mean-

Median-

Mode-

Range-

2. Have the student use the *Peanut* data to show how to find the mean, median, mode, and range. (Item 2) They may use numbers or counters. Record their responses.

Mean-

Median-

Mode-

Range-

3. Have the student examine their results from item 2 and ask: If you were the president of the candy company, which statistic would you want to use to promote your candy? Why?

For additional interview and analysis examples, see Zawojewski, J. and Shaughnessy, "M. Mean and Median: Are they really so easy?" *Mathematics Teaching in the Middle School,* March 2000, pp. 436–440. See also Friel, S. "Teaching Statistics, What's average?" *The Teaching and Learning of Algorithms in School Mathematics, 1998 NCTM Yearbook* (eds. Lorna J. Morrow and Margaret J. Kenney). Reston: Virginia, 1998, pp. 208–217.

REFLECTION:

1. Did the student's explanations seem primarily conceptual or procedural? Explain.

2. Did any misconceptions emerge during the student's explanation and demonstration? Explain.

3. What experiences would you provide next to continue the development of statistics?

Probability

Materials Needed: optional—a paper bag with three red counters, one yellow counter, and one blue counter or a picture of the bag and its contents. Display or sketch the bag and its contents.

The following questions will help you learn about student's understanding of probability.

1. What can you tell me about probability?

2. How many balls are in the bag?

3. If I were going to conduct an experiment by drawing counters from the bag and recording my results, what color counters could be drawn?

4. What is the probability of drawing a red counter? What is the probability of drawing a counter that is not red?

5. What is the probability of drawing a green counter?

6. What is the probability of drawing a red, yellow, or blue counter?

7. Should the bag be shaken before each draw? Why or why not?

8. Should people be allowed to choose their favorite color?

9. Should the person choosing be blindfolded?

10. Should a transparent bag be used?

11. If a yellow counter has just been drawn and returned to the bag, what is the probability the next ball will be yellow?

12. If four consecutive red counters have been drawn and returned each time to the bag, what is the probability the next counter will be red?

For additional interview and analysis examples, see Jones, G., Thornton, C., Langrall, C. and Tarr, J. "Understanding Students' Probabilistic Reasoning." In *Developing Mathematical Reasoning in Grades K–12, 1999 NCTM Yearbook* (ed. Lee V. Stiff). Reston: Virginia, 1999, pp. 146–155.

REFLECTION:

1. Discuss the student's understanding of key probability concepts.
   Sample Space—questions 2 and 3
   Probability of an Event—questions 4–6
   Randomness—questions 7–10
   Independence of Events—questions 11 and 12

Helping Children Learn with Games Content

These game experiences allow you to learn more about using educational mathematics games with children and to observe what children know and can do. What makes a game different from other activities is in a game, the participants try to be the first to reach a particular goal. Most of these games may be played with a small group or whole class of children. The games are classified into three grade level bands with specific grade level suggestions on each game lesson plan. Keep in mind that the games included here may be easily geared up or down by changing the rules or mathematics content. We have included some suggestions for gearing down or up.

Advantages of Using Games

For students, games:

1. provide hands-on activities, require active participation,

2. are very motivational,

3. can provide individual reinforcement or enrichment,

4. can help develop positive self-concepts,

5. and can lead them to use new problem-solving strategies.

For teachers, games:

1. can be made inexpensively, used, reused and adapted,

2. allow time for observation and informal assessment,

3. make math easier to teach as motivation increases,

4. provide another way to develop concepts, and encourage practice.

Games by Topic by Content

Key Topics	Game	K–2	3–5	6–8	Page
1. Issues, Trends, and Principles					
2. Learning					
3. Teaching, Planning, Adapting					
4. Assessing, Recording, Reporting					
5. Process Standards					
6. Problem Solving	See also pp. 171–172, 203–204				
7. Number Sense, Prenumber	Buzz-A Counting Game Dots and Numbers See also pp. 111–112	X X	X		105 106
8. Place Value	Wipe Out Hit the Target See also pp. 124–125	 X	X X	 X	107 108
9. Basic Facts	Clear the Board! Fill the Frame (or Empty the Frame) The Fact Game Roll a Sum Roll a Product See also pp. 145–146	X X X	X X X X	 X X	109–110 111–112 113–114 115–116 117–118
10. Computational Alternatives	Calculators Versus Mental Computation See also 121–123, 128–129		X	X	119–120
11. Whole Number Operations	Capture 5 Race-to-a-Flat Sum or Difference Game The Remainder Game	X X X	X X X X	 X	121–123 124–125 126–127 128–129
12. Fractions, Decimals	Fraction Shape Puzzles Whole Hog Can You Beat the Toss? See also pp. 137–138	X	 X X	 X X	130–131 132–134 135–136
13. Ratio, Proportion, Percent	Make a Match See also pp. 135–136			X	137–138
14. Patterns, Algebra	See also pp. 105, 113–114, 145, 147–148				
15. Geometry	Less is Best Solid Shake	X	X X	 X	139–140 141–142

GAMES CONTENT (continued)

Key Topics	Game	K–2	3–5	6–8	Page
16. Measurement	Race to a Yard (or Meter)	X	X		143–144
17. Data, Statistics, Probability	Race to 20 Skunk See also pp. 115–116	X	X X	X X	145 146
18. Number Theory	Factor Me Out		X	X	147–148

Buzz-A Counting Game

Objective: To provide practice in counting and in recognizing numbers with certain characteristics.

Getting Ready: Buzz is a counting game that can be played by a group or whole class. Players may form a circle or remain seated. You need to make clear the order of their participation (i.e., who goes first, next and so on).

RULES OR PROCEDURES:

Children count aloud (one person at a time and taking turns) until a given number or multiple of that number appears. When this number appears, the person whose turn it is says "Buzz".

For example, you might say: "We are going to play the 'Three Buzz Game' and count to thirty."

Then the children begin to count as follows: 'One' 'Two' 'Buzz' 'Four' 'Five' 'Buzz' 'Seven' 'Eight' 'Buzz' 'Ten' 'Eleven' 'Buzz' . . .

The counting continues until the goal (thirty) is reached. If anyone forgets to say Buzz or says Buzz at the wrong time, the round is over and the game starts all over again. Beginning a new round with a different person starting encourages everyone to think and be alert.

Gearing Down: Limit the range of the count to 10 or 20. To provide additional support, have children work with a partner.

Gearing Up: First and second graders might count by taking turns as described above, whereas at the third grade, 'Buzz' may be substituted for all even numbers or multiples.

At the fourth and fifth grades you might have them "Buzz" on multiples of four and "Bang" on multiples of three. Thus certain numbers (12, 24, 36) will produce a "Buzz Bang" when they are counted.

A further variation is to "Buzz" for all multiples of 4 and "Wizz" for any number with 4 as a digit. Thus the 10—16 sequence would be 'ten' 'eleven' 'Buzz' 'thirteen' 'Wizz' 'Fifteen' 'Buzz' and if you counted as high as forty-four it would be a 'Buzz Wizz Wizz'.

REFLECTION:

1. Watch the students as they play the game. Pay attention to who is able to 'buzz' at the right time and who needs more help. See if you can determine what strategies, if any, that students are using. What were you able to learn about the students' knowledge of counting and numbers?

2. How appropriate was this game for the students? Is this something you might like to do some day with your own students? What changes might you make?

Dots and Numbers

Objective: To provide practice in recognizing numerals and connecting them to quantities.

Getting Ready: Prepare two sets of cards—on one set write numerals for which children need practice and on the other card show the number of dots. Patterns for 0–9 may be found in Appendix A.

RULES OR PROCEDURES:

Dots and Numbers can be played by a group or whole class. Place the numeral cards face down in a box and place the corresponding dot cards (happy faces, or whatever) face up on a table or on a felt board. Ask a child to get a card from the box and match it with the correct quantity card. If correct, the child may choose the next player. If incorrect, the child gets another chance or can choose another player to help. At the end of the game, the one with the most matches is the winner.

Gearing Up: The size of the quantities can be increased to challenge students and extend this idea to place value. For example, cards may be constructed to show 15 dots and 51 dots, or 25 dots and 52 dots (show groups of ten to facilitate counting). Then children will need to choose two of the number cards and place them in the proper order to name the quantity.

REFLECTION:

1. Watch the students as they play the game. What were you able to learn about the students' knowledge of numerals and number quantities? Did they use group recognition or counting to determine the number of dots?

2. How appropriate was this game for the students? Is this something you might like to do some day with your own students? What changes might you make?

Wipe Out

Objective: Identifying the actual place value of digits in a multi-digit number.

Getting Ready: Each player or team will need a calculator. You'll also need paper and pencil to record each player's score.

RULES OR PROCEDURES:

Each player enters a number into the calculator with a predetermined number of digits. Then he or she identifies one of the digits in the number to be wiped out (changed to zero) by the opponent. A digit may be wiped out by adding or subtracting a number. A point is scored each time a digit is successfully changed to zero.

Sample round:
Joe enters 635 and names the 3 to be wiped out and hands the calculator to Louis. Louis wipes out the 3 by subtracting 30 and scores one point. Louis enters 241 on his calculator. He names the 4 to be wiped out and hands the calculator to Joe. Joe tries to wipe out the 4 by subtracting 4. Since the 4 is not "wiped out" no point is scored. Play continues until all digits are changed to zero.

Gearing Down: Use 2- or 3-digit numbers to begin and model each number with base-ten blocks.

Gearing Up: Select larger numbers to wipe out. Play without a calculator. Require the operation to be addition only. Play Go Fish: Players take turns asking for specific digits. "Do you have any three's?" If the opponent's number has a three in the hundreds place, he or she must subtract 300 while the person asking gets to add 300 to his or her number. Play for a predetermined number of turns. The player with the largest total score wins.

A more challenging version of this game is available in NCTM's 1992 Yearbook, *Calculators in Mathematics Education*, "Wipe Out-Refined," by Martha Hopkins, pages 239–240.

REFLECTION:

1. After playing this game, what have you learned about the children's understanding of place value? What place value experiences would you provide next?

2. How appropriate was this game for the students? Is this something you might like to do some day with your own students? What changes might you make?

Hit the Target

Objective: To develop place value and reasoning skills.

Getting Ready: This place value game involves both logic and chance. It can be played by two players, in a small group or with the whole class. You will need paper, or a chalkboard or overhead projector for recording guesses in a table.

RULES OR PROCEDURES:

The leader should make sure students know what is meant by a 'two-digit number'. Once everyone is clear on what a digit means, here is how a game might go in a small group or whole class that is lead by one person. The leader chooses a 'two-digit' number, say 57 but does not tell the students the mystery number. The challenge for the students is to guess the mystery number. Ask one student to guess the number, and make a table to record the guesses.

Tell students that each of their guesses will reveal some clues. In the table below, the Hit means a correct digit has been guessed. A Miss represents an incorrect digit. Bull's-eye means both a correct digit and its place have been guessed. Here is a table that records four guesses for the number 57.

Guess	Miss	Hit	Bull's-eye
23	2	0	0
45	1	1	0
56	1	0	1
75	0	2	0

After each guess, encourage students to examine the table and tell what they know for sure. This encourages students to reflect on the table before making another guess. For example, the first row reports that neither digits 2 or 3 are in the mystery number. From the last row, it can be reasoned that the digits are correct but just reversed. At this stage someone should be ready to identify the mystery number correctly.

There are various strategies for the game. For example, students can move systematically through numbers trying digits in pairs, such as 01, 23, until 89 is reached. It often surprises students to learn that the most information results from two misses, because two misses means both digits can be eliminated. The references below detail additional strategies.

Gearing Down: Limit the range of possible numbers to 20, 30, or 50. Have the students use a hundreds chart to cross out or cover numbers that have been eliminated. Have students provide the number so the teacher can model thinking strategies.

Gearing Up: This game can be expanded to three or more digits as students learn the rules and develop their reasoning skills, but the strategy remains the same.

REFLECTION:

1. Play the game a few times and describe strategies that students use.

2. How appropriate was this game for students? What changes might you make the next time this game is used?

For more information or game options see Aichele, D. B. "Pico-Centro—A game of logic," *Arithmetic Teacher*, 19 (May 1972), 359–61 or Stewart, W. R. "Recreation: Hit, Miss, Bull's-Eye," *Mathematics Teacher*, 67 (December 1974), 693–694.

Clear the Board!

| 1 | 2 | 3 | 4 | 5 | 6 | 7 | 8 | 9 | 10 |

Clear the Board!

| 1 | 2 | 3 | 4 | 5 | 6 | 7 | 8 | 9 | 10 |

Clear the Board!

| 1 | 2 | 3 | 4 | 5 | 6 | 7 | 8 | 9 | 10 |

Objective: To use logical reasoning to practice basic addition facts and to practice adding two-digit numbers.

Getting Ready: For each student you will need a game board (3 copies on previous page), several counters, and two dice. (Each group will need a pair of dice if they play in small groups.)

Clear the Board!

1	2	3	4	5	6	7	8	9	10

RULES OR PROCEDURES:

Ask a student to roll the dice and call out the sum. Players then use the counters to cover either the space with that sum or any two spaces whose numbers add up to that sum.

When a player is unable to cover up any numbers, he or she adds the numbers on his or her board that are still not covered to determine his or her score for the round. Play continues for as many rounds as desired. Students keep a running total of their scores on each round and this determines their final scores. The person with the lowest total wins the round.

Gearing Down: Play the game using a game board with fewer numbers. For younger children, using only one die might also be appropriate.

Gearing Up: Play the game using a longer game board with more sums. Challenge the students to come up with their own games for practicing addition.

REFLECTION:

1. Watch the students as they play the game. Pay attention to who has facts memorized and who needs more help learning thinking strategies. See if you can determine what strategies, if any, that students are using to derive the sums. What were you able to learn about the students' knowledge of basic addition facts? About their use of strategies?

2. How appropriate was this game for these students? Is this something you might like to do some day with your own students? What changes might you make?

Fill the Frame (or Empty the Frame)

Grades K–2

Objective: To practice basic addition and/or subtraction facts.

Getting Ready: Students can play individually, in pairs, or in small groups. Each student will need one ten-frame or five-frame (frames may be made from one-inch grid paper) and several counters, and each group of students will need a set of numeral cards (four each of numerals 1–5). A pattern for five- and ten-frames may be found on the following page. A pattern for numeral cards may be found in Appendix A.

Ten Frame

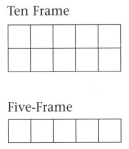

Five-Frame

RULES OR PROCEDURES:

Version 1 (Make Ten):
The players take turns drawing a card and placing that number of counters on their ten-frame, filling the top row first. Players should be encouraged to verbalize how many spaces are filled and how many more are needed. The winner is the first to completely fill their ten-frame.

Version 2 (Take Ten):
Start with all the spaces on the ten-frame filled with counters. Players then subtract the number of counters drawn on their turns.

(adapted from Kaye, P., *Games for Math*. New York: Pantheon Books, 1987.

Gearing Down: Play the game using a five-frame rather than a ten-frame. Use dot cards instead of numeral cards.

Gearing Up: Players can use several ten-frames at one time. They could also play by either two cards or with cards that have more than numerals 1–5. Challenge the students to come up with their own games for practicing the basic addition and subtraction facts.

REFLECTION:

1. Watch the students as they play the game. Pay attention to who has facts memorized and who needs more help learning thinking strategies. See if you can determine what strategies, if any, that students are using to derive the sums or differences. What were you able to learn about the students' knowledge of basic addition and/or subtraction facts?

2. How appropriate was this game for the students? Is this something you might like to do some day with your own students? What changes might you make?

Five and Ten Frames

✕	9	12	15	✕
16	18	20	21	24
25	27	28	30	32
35	36	40	42	45
48	49	54	56	63
✕	64	72	81	✕

Factor List

3	4	5	6	7	8	9

The Fact Game

Objective: Using logical reasoning to practice basic multiplication facts and to learn about factors and multiples.

Getting Ready: For each pair of students you will need one *Fact Game* board and game markers (two colors).

RULES OR PROCEDURES:

The first player places a marker on a number in the factor list. The second player places another marker on any number in the factor list (this may include the factor already marked) and then covers the product of those two factors on the fact game board with a marker.

Now the second player moves *either one* of the factor markers to another factor and then covers the new product with a different marker. Play continues with each player moving one paper clip and covering a new product. If the product has already been covered, the player does not get to place a marker for that turn.

The winner is the first player to cover three squares in a row—horizontally, vertically, or diagonally.

Adapted from: Lappan, Fey, Fitzgerald, Friel, and Phillips, *Prime Time: Factors and Multiples*, Connected Mathematics, Dale Seymour Publications, 1996.

Gearing Down: Play the game with a smaller game board, using a smaller number of factors. Add 1 and 2 to the factor list and 1, 2, 3, 4, 5, 6, 7, 8, 10, and 14 to make a top and bottom row on the game board.

Gearing Up: Challenge the students to come up with their own games for practicing the basic multiplication facts.

REFLECTION:

1. Watch the students as they play the game. Pay attention to who has facts memorized and who is struggling with their facts. See if you can determine what strategies, if any, that students are using to derive the products. What were you able to learn about the students' knowledge of basic multiplication facts? About their use of strategies?

2. How appropriate was this game for the students? Is this something you might like to do some day with your own students? What changes might you make?

1	2	3	4	5
6	7	8	9	10
11	12	13	14	15
16	17	18	19	20

Roll A Sum

Grades 2–5

Objective: Developing and practicing addition facts.

Getting Ready: This is a game for two players. You'll need two red cubes with 0, 10, 9, 8, 7, and 6 on their faces and two green cubes with 0, 1, 2, 3, 4, and 5 on their faces, two *Roll A Sum* game boards (one for each player), and counters or markers.

Roll A Sum

1	2	3	4	5
6	7	8	9	10
11	12	13	14	15
16	17	18	19	20

RULES OR PROCEDURES:

Each player rolls one of the red cubes. The player with the largest number plays first.

A player selects any two of the four cubes and rolls them. The sum of the two numbers is covered on the player's game board. If the sum is already covered, the player loses their turn.

Players take turns rolling the dice. Play continues until one player has either four markers in a vertical row or five markers in a horizontal row.

Allowing the players to choose their cubes allows both probability and strategy to be used. Thus players with some knowledge of which cubes will produce which sums will have an advantage to winning the game. Have students discuss strategies they used.

Gearing Down: The game can be varied by covering the four corners with markers, or having three horizontal or vertical markers in a row.

Gearing Up: The game can be varied by covering the entire board (blackout) with markers. You can also increase the number of dice used.

REFLECTION:

1. What strategies did students use as they played the game?

2. What were you able to learn about the students' skill with addition facts?

3. How appropriate was this game for the students? Is this something you might like to do some day with your own students? What changes might you make?

Roll A Product

0	1	2	3	4	5
6	7	8	9	10	12
14	15	16	18	20	21
24	27	28	30	32	35
36	40	42	45	48	50
56	60	63	64	70	72
FREE	81	90	FREE	100	FREE

Roll A Product

Objective: Developing and practicing multiplication facts.

Getting Ready: This is a game for two players. You need two red cubes with 0, 10, 9, 8, 7, and 6 on their faces and two green cubes with 0, 1, 2, 3, 4, and 5 on their faces, two *Roll A Product* game boards, one for each player, counters or markers.

Roll A Product

0	1	2	3	4	5
6	7	8	9	10	12
14	15	16	18	20	21
24	27	28	30	32	35
36	40	42	45	48	50
56	60	63	64	70	72
FREE	81	90	FREE	100	FREE

RULES OR PROCEDURES:

Each player rolls one of the red cubes. The player with the largest number plays first.

A player selects any two of the four cubes and rolls them. The product of the two numbers is covered on the player's game board. If the product is already covered, the player loses their turn.

Players take turns rolling the dice. Play continues until one player has either four markers in a vertical or horizontal row. The cell marked FREE can be used to make their vertical or horizontal row.

Allowing the players to choose their cubes allows both probability and strategy to be used. Thus players with some knowledge of which cubes will yield certain products will have an advantage to winning the game. Have students discuss their strategies.

Gearing Down: The game can be varied by covering only three cells (vertical, horizontal, or diagonal) with markers.

Gearing Up: The game can be varied by covering an entire row or column with markers. The game can also be varied by allowing children to roll 3 or 4 cubes. Then have them choose to use 2 or 3 of the cubes to form a product.

REFLECTION:

1. What strategies did students use as they played the game?

2. What were you able to learn about the students' skill with multiplication facts?

3. How appropriate was this game for the students? Is this something you might like to do some day with your own students? What changes might you make?

Name: _____

Class: _____

Calculators Versus Mental Computation

▼ Divide the class into pairs of students. In each pair, one student has a calculator and must use it to do computations. The other student doesn't have a calculator and must do computations mentally.

▼ Write computation problems on the board, one at a time.

▼ In each pair, the student who first has an answer raises his or her hand. The other student finishes the computation but doesn't raise his or her hand.

▼ After everyone has finished the computation, ask the students with their hand raised for their answer and whether they used a calculator. If their answer is correct, mark it in the appropriate column of the chart below.

Computation	First and Correct Using a Calculator	First and Correct Using Mental Computation
1. 4×1000	☐	☐
2. $400 + 50 + 8$	☐	☐
3. $99 + 99 + 99 + 99$	☐	☐
4. $1000 - 200$	☐	☐
5. $50 + 50 + 50 + 50 + 50 + 50$	☐	☐
6. $1/2 + 3/4$	☐	☐
7. $6300 \div 7$	☐	☐
8. $10 \times 10 \times 10 \times 10$	☐	☐
9. $0.75 + 0.25 + .050$	☐	☐
10. $\$1.00 - \$0.25$	☐	☐

▼ Write two lists on the board—one list showing the computations that more students did correctly and faster using a calculator, the other list showing the computations that more students did correctly and faster using mental computation.

▼ Discuss the differences in the two lists.

Calculators Versus Mental Computation

Grades 3–6

Objective: Encourage recognition of the power of mental computation and wise use of calculators.

Getting Ready: *Calculators Versus Mental Computation* can be adapted as a game which uses calculators and paper and pencil. Children can play in pairs or small groups. It can also be done as a whole class activity by dividing the class into two groups. One half of the class MUST use a calculator and the other half of the students MUST do these computations in their head. Examine all of the computations and think about which ones you think students with a calculator would be favored to do the fastest. Initially most students think the calculator will be an advantage and want to use them. Toss a coin or whatever to determine who gets to use the calculator.

RULES OR PROCEDURES:

This is a race, and the objective is to get the correct answer the fastest. Also make sure the children realize that one group cannot use a calculator, and the other group MUST use the calculator to get their answer.

Ask students to put their thumb up when they have a answer. Whoever puts their thumb up first with the correct answer is the fastest for that round and scores a point.

Present the computations one at a time, either orally "four times seventy" or visually. If the computations are being presented visually, make sure the children do not see the computations early. After each computation, decide who was the fastest and note it on the record sheet. Then give the next computation.

REFLECTION:

1. When you explained the rules for the game, did children seem to prefer to use the calculator?

2. Did the computations you thought would favor students with calculators do so? If there were any surprises, can you explain them?

3. If you were going to create some computations to give the NON-calculator group an advantage, what would be some computations you would give them?

4. If you were going to create some computations to give the calculator group an advantage, what would be some computations you would give them?

5. How appropriate was this game for the students? Is this something you might like to do some day with your own students? What changes might you make?

Name: _____

Class: _____

Capture 5

Materials

1. A chart divided into 100 squares numbered from 1 to 100.
2. A deck of 52 change cards numbered + 1, – 1, + 2, – 2, + 3, – 3, + 5, + 10, – 10, + 20, – 20, + 30, – 30, (each one of these numbers appears 4 times).
3. Student sheets for recording moves.
4. 12 markers of the same color.
5. 1 game piece per person or group.

How to Play

1. Place each marker on any number on the chart.
2. Place your game piece on any number without a marker. That is where you will begin playing.
3. Place the change cards face down.
4. Take 5 cards from the deck of change cards.
5. Spread them on your table in the order in which you want to use them.
6. A number with a minus (–) sign tells you to take steps backward. A number with a plus (+) sign tells you to go forward.
7. You can use one or more than one card at a time.
8. If your last count in on a marker, capture that marker.
9. You can only use your card or cards once. After you have used them place them face down on a discard pile, and replace them from the change card pile.
10. If your card or cards are not good, replace them with new ones from the deck and reshuffle the deck.
11. If you replace a card or cards you lose your chance to play.
12. Begin the game by placing markers on the squares shown in the chart below.

Activity

1. Jane's game piece was on 9 and she captured a marker on 25. She wrote her equation as :
   9 + 3 + 10 + 2 + 1 = 25. How many spaces did Jane move? Explain how you found this out.

   Rewrite Jane's equation to show how far she moved:
   9 + _____ = 25.

2. Lee's game piece was on 52 and he captured a marker on 85. He wrote his equation as:

52 + 3 + 20 + 10 = 85. How many spaces did Lee move? Explain how you found this out.

Rewrite Lee's equation to show how far he moved:
52 + _____ = 85.

3. Kanye's game piece was on 10 and he captured a marker on 33. He wrote his equation as:
   10 + 20 + 2 + 1 = 33. How many spaces did Kanye move? Explain how you found this out.

   Rewrite Kanye's equation to show how far he moved:
   10 + _____ = 33.

4. Alona's game piece was on 72 and she captured a marker on 59. She wrote her equation as:
   72 – 10 – 1 – 2 = 59. How many spaces did Alona move? Explain how you found this out. Rewrite Alona's equation to show how she moved.

   Rewrite Alona's equation to show how far she moved:
   72 – _____ = 59.

5. Ramona's game piece was on 97 and she captured a marker on 56. She wrote her equation as:
   97 – 30 – 10 – 3 + 2 = 56. How many spaces did Ramona move? Explain how you found this out.

   Rewrite Ramona's equation to show how far she moved:
   97 – _____ = 56.

6. Partner with one of your classmates. Now place the 12 markers wherever you want and start a new game of your own.

1	2	3	4	5	6	7	8	9	10
11	12	13	14	15	16	17	18	19	20
21	22	23	24	25	26	27	28	29	30
31	32	33	34	35	36	37	38	39	40
41	42	43	44	45	46	47	48	49	50
51	52	53	54	55	56	57	58	59	60
61	62	63	64	65	66	67	68	69	70
71	72	73	74	75	76	77	78	79	80
81	82	83	84	85	86	87	88	89	90
91	92	93	94	95	96	97	98	99	100

(Source: Adapted from Economopoulos, K., and Russell, S.J. Putting Together and Taking Apart: Addition and Subtraction. A Unit in the *Investigations in Number, Data, and Space Curriculum.* White Plains, NY: Dale Seymour, 1998, pp. 112-117 and pp. 180-184.)

Capture 5

Objective: Use a hundreds chart to add and subtract multiples of 10's and 1's.

Getting ready: Children can play in pairs or in small teams. For each group of players you need a hundreds chart (Appendix A); a deck of 52 change cards (on the following page); paper for recording moves; 12 markers of the same color; 1 game piece per person or team.

Rules or Procedures:

Go over the following rules with the players.

The goal is to capture the most markers. The game officially ends when the remaining cards on the change card pile cannot capture any more markers.

Players place the 12 markers on any numbers on the chart. (Teams could take turns.) Then each team places their game piece on any number without a marker. That is where they start. Place the deck of change cards face down. (You will also soon create a discard pile.)

Each team takes 5 cards from the deck and spreads them on the table. They take turns playing. A number with a minus (-) sign tells you to move backwards. A number with a plus (+) sign tells you to move forward. You can use one or more than one card at a time. If your last count is on a marker, you capture that marker.

You can only use your card(s) once. After you have used them, place them face down on the discard pile and on your next turn, replace them from the change card pile. If your card(s) are not good, you may use your turn to place them in the discard pile and replace them with new ones from the deck. If you replace a card(s), you lose your chance to play on that turn.

After going over the rules, together work through the activity examples on the Capture Card. When students seem to understand the procedures, let them play the game.

Gearing Down: Let students play in teams rather than pairs, and encourage discussion about how to play the cards. Also, change cards could be placed individually face up on the table, instead of face-down in a pile, so that the team can pick their cards logically.

Gearing Up: Adjust some of the change cards to include a multiple of the number on the card (ex: -2 x 5 would move -10 spaces). A die could be rolled to generate the multiple.

REFLECTION:

1. What was the most common method of computation used by students (counting on or back by tens or ones, mental computation, paper and pencil)?

2. Did the students' calculation strategies change with time? If so, how?

3. How appropriate was this game for these students? What changes might you make?

Change Cards for the Capture Game

+1	+1	+1	+1	-1	-1
-1	-1	+2	+2	+2	+2
-2	-2	-2	-2	+3	+3
+3	+3	-3	-3	-3	-3
+ 5	+ 5	- 5	- 5	+10	+10
+10	+10	-10	-10	-10	-10
+20	+20	+20	+20	-20	-20
-20	-20	+30	+30	+30	+30
-30	-30	-30	-30		

Race-to-a-Flat, Give-Away-a-Flat

Objective: Developing students' understanding of regrouping for addition or subtraction.

Getting Ready: Each student will need a place-value mat (see next page for a sample), and each group of 3–5 students will need connecting cubes or base-ten blocks (can be made from cm grid paper) and a pair of dice. A pattern for base-ten blocks is available in Appendix A.

RULES OR PROCEDURES:

Version 1 (Race-to-a-Flat)

Each group will need to choose one person to be the base-10 "banker." Players take turns rolling the dice, adding the numbers on the tops of the two dice, and then asking the banker for that number of units. For example, if a player rolls a 4 and a 5, he or she would ask for 9 units. The player then puts the blocks on his or her place-value mat in the units column.

There can never be ten or more blocks in any column on the place-value mat. Whenever he or she can, a player must trade 10 units for a long, or 10 longs for a flat. When all the trading is complete it is the next player's turn to roll the dice, collect units, and trade blocks. The first player to trade up to a flat is the winner.

Questions to discuss in small groups and as a class:

1. Is it possible to get one long with one roll of the dice?
2. Is it possible to get two longs with one roll of the dice?
3. Can you win the game with one roll of the dice?
4. What is the fewest number of rolls required to get to a flat?
5. What is the most number of rolls required to get to a flat?

Version 2 (Give-Away-a-Flat)

Each group will need to choose one person to be the base-10 "banker." The banker distributes one flat to each player who places it in the flats column on her or his place-value mat. Players take turns rolling the dice, adding the numbers on the tops of the two dice, and then giving away that number of units to the banker. Clearly, trades will have to be made during each player's first turn and possibly again during subsequent turns. The first player to return all of his or her base-10 blocks to the banker is the winner.

Questions to discuss in small groups and as a class:

1. Is it possible to give away one long with one roll of the dice?
2. Is it possible to give away two longs with one roll of the dice?
3. Can you win the game with one roll of the dice?
4. What is the fewest number of rolls required to give away all of the pieces?
5. What is the most number of rolls required to give away all of the pieces?

Gearing Down: Play *Race-to-a-Long* or *Give-Away-a-Long*.

Gearing Up: Have students come up with variations of the game that would be more challenging to them. For example, they might use three or four dice. Encourage students to mentally calculate how many blocks they think they will have before they actually add or subtract the blocks from their mats.

At intervals during either *Race-to-a-Flat* or *Give-Away-a-Flat*, call out "Audit Time!" Each player must report how many units are on his or her mat altogether before play can be resumed. Players should double check each others' reports. (Some penalty could be imposed for incorrect reporting.)

At intervals during *Race-to-a-Flat*, call out "Tax Time!" On each players' next turn, he or she must subtract the number of units rolled (instead of adding).

At intervals during *Give-Away-a-Flat*, call out "Pay Day!" On each player's next turn, he or she must add the number of units rolled (instead of subtracting).

REFLECTION:

1. What were you able to learn about the students' knowledge of regrouping for addition and/or subtraction?

2. How appropriate was this game for the students? Is this something you might like to do some day with your own students? Would you make any changes?

Place Value Mat

Flats ☐	**Longs** ▯	**Units** ▫

Sum or Difference Game

Grades 2–5

Objective: Use logical reasoning and mental math to calculate sums and differences.

Getting Ready: For each team or pairs of opponents, you'll need a game board (on the following page), a calculator, and markers (different colored chips, paper, or use a pencil to mark A's and B's).

RULES OR PROCEDURES:

Two teams (or two individual people) play this game. The teams take turns. Choose two numbers from the box. Choose addition or subtraction. In your head, add or subtract the numbers and announce the sum or difference.

The other team uses the calculator to find the sum or difference. If you were correct, place a marker on the answer on the game board. A team may put markers on the board in any order, starting anywhere, however the winning team or player is the first to create an unbroken path from one side of the board to the other. You may also try to block your opponent's path.

REFLECTION:

1. What strategies did students use as they played? How were their mental computation skills?

2. How appropriate was this game for the students? Is this something you might like to do some day with your own students? What changes might you make?

*Adapted from *Ideas from the Arithmetic Teacher: Grades 1–4, Primary* (p. 49), compiled by George Immerzeel and Melvin Thomas, National Council of Teachers of Mathematics, 1982.

126 • *Teaching Elementary Mathematics: A Resource for Field Experiences* © 2009 John Wiley & Sons • **Helping Children Learn** • **Games**

Sum or Difference Game

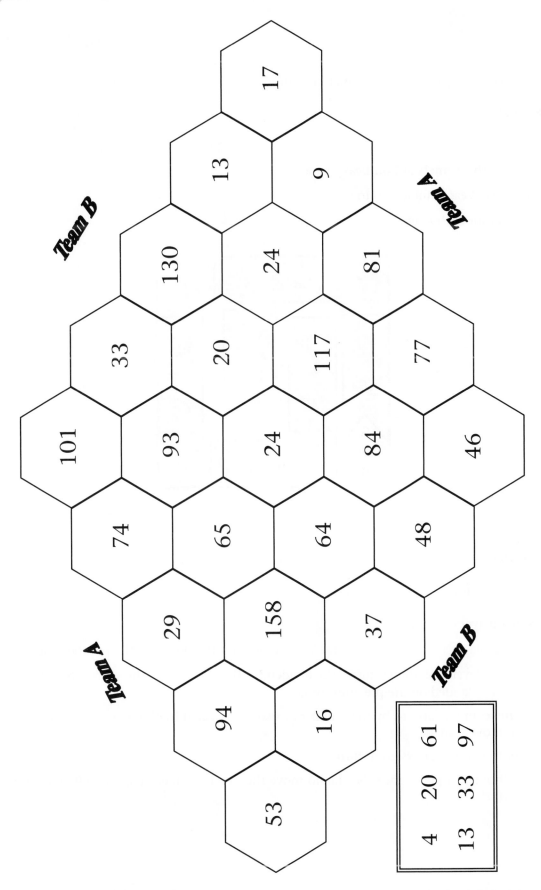

The Remainder Game

Objective: Using a game to practice mental computation involving division.

Grade level: 3–5

Materials:

- A copy of this gameboard on heavy paper
- Four cards of each numeral 0 to 9
- A counter for each player

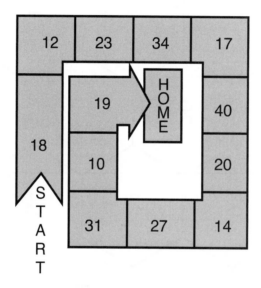

Game Rules:

1. Place the cards face down in a pile.

2. The first player draws a card.

   - For a player's first turn, divide the first number on the board by the number drawn.

   - For a player's additional turns, the dividend is the number on the space where his or her counter landed on the previous turn.

3. Move the counter forward by the number of spaces indicated by the remainder. If the remainder is 0, no move is made.

4. Each of the other players go in turn.

5. To get "home," a player must be able to move the exact number of spaces left. The first person home wins!

The Remainder Game

Grades 3–6

Objective: To practice mental computation involving division.

Getting Ready: Have a copy of *The Remainder Game* for each group of 2–4 students and a different colored game piece for each player. Prepare 4 sets of 1–9 cards (Appendix A). Optional: 40 counters, fact chart, scrap paper and pencil.

Launch: Begin by telling a brief division story using the problem 47 divided by 9. Act it out with counters or draw pictures on the board to explain. Also, think aloud how to solve mentally. Remind the children that when we divide, we use the word "remainder" to refer to the left-overs, or the parts that are "remaining." So, in the story, we see that 47 divided by 9 is 5 with remainder of 2. Emphasize that today's game will focus on the remainder.

Investigate: Have children play the game in groups of 2–4, following the directions on the sheet. Encourage students to calculate mentally if possible. Have them think about which remainders come up most often, which remainders are rare, and to think about why.

Summarize:
Ask the children questions such as the following about what happened when they played.

- What was the lowest remainder (smallest jump) you got? (They should say 0.)

- Give some examples of division problems that would give a remainder of 0 (ex. 12 ÷ 3)? What is special about division problems with remainder 0? (The divisor is a factor of the dividend—in other words, it forms equal groups with no leftovers.)

- What is special about division problems with remainder 8? (The divisor must be 9 or more.) (Use blocks to show why, in division, the remainder is smaller than the divisor. If the remainder is bigger than the divisor, then you haven't shared as much as you could.)

Gearing Down: Provide a multiplication chart (p. 77) for those who don't know their facts. (For example, for 47 ÷ 9, they should put their finger on the 9 row, and run the finger across until they find the highest number smaller than 47. That number will be 45. The remainder is the difference between 47 and 45 (2). (The quotient of 5 is found by running your finger up from 45, to discover that you are in the 5 column.)

Gearing Up: You can adjust the difficulty of this game in several ways: use cards 1–12 (or 1 to any larger number), and/or replace the numbers on the game board with higher numbers. Ask the children to share a few division stories of their own where sharing results in a remainder. Encourage classmates to do the division mentally, and to explain their thinking to the class.

REFLECTION:

1. How many of the children seemed to have firm knowledge of their multiplication facts?

2. Were there students who knew their facts, but still had difficulty figuring out the remainders in their heads? How did you help them? What else could a teacher do to help them?

PUZZLE 1

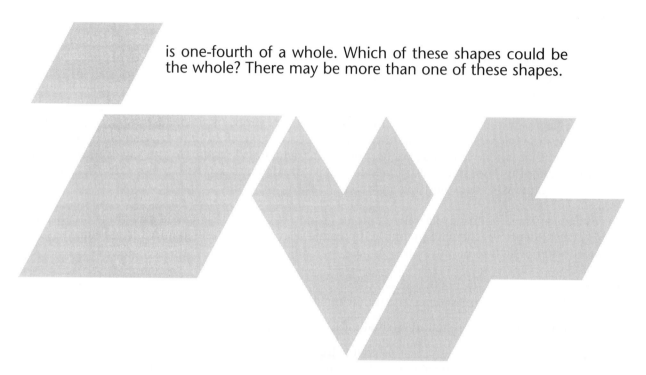

is one-fourth of a whole. Which of these shapes could be the whole? There may be more than one of these shapes.

PUZZLE 2

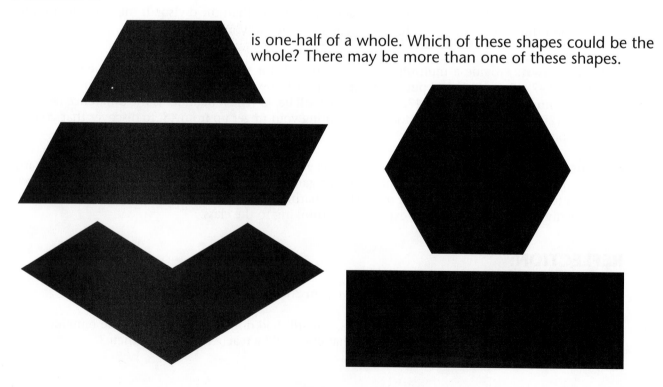

is one-half of a whole. Which of these shapes could be the whole? There may be more than one of these shapes.

Fraction Shape Puzzles

Grades 1–2

Objective: To make wholes, given a fractional part of the whole.

Getting Ready: Students can make these puzzles individually or in pairs. Each student or pair will need four of each pattern block (pattern below), shown here as white, gray, and black, and the puzzle sheet on the previous page. Do puzzle A with the students before they do their own. Have the children justify their answers.

PUZZLE A

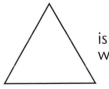 is one-fourth of a whole. Which of these shapes could be the whole? There may be more than one of these shapes that fits.

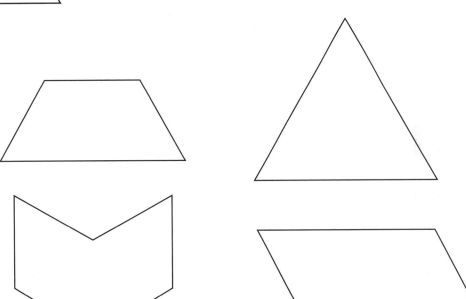

REFLECTION:

1. Did any of the wholes give students difficulty? For example, they can make the first shape above with triangles, but it only takes 3. Did they realize that the triangle would be a third, not a fourth? What else did you notice?

2. The last shape (rectangle) in Puzzle 2 is the whole. Do not expect all students at this age to see this, but look for the ones that say "If you could cut the pieces, I could make it like this." (Be sure that they show you what they mean.) Do you see how?

$\dfrac{1}{2}$	$\dfrac{1}{3}$	$\dfrac{1}{6}$	$\dfrac{2}{6}$	$\dfrac{1}{9}$	$\dfrac{2}{9}$
$\dfrac{3}{9}$	$\dfrac{1}{18}$	$\dfrac{2}{18}$	$\dfrac{3}{18}$		

Whole Hog

Materials

- A copy of the H grid.
- Squares of paper
- Markers

▼ Cut 10 squares of paper. Write one of these fractions on each square:

$$\frac{1}{2} \quad \frac{1}{3} \quad \frac{1}{6} \quad \frac{2}{6} \quad \frac{1}{9} \quad \frac{2}{9} \quad \frac{3}{9} \quad \frac{1}{18} \quad \frac{2}{18} \quad \frac{3}{18}$$

Game Rules:

1. Shuffle the fraction cards and put them in a pile face down.

2. Each player picks a card from the top of the pile and turns it face up.

3. The player with the smaller fraction colors in that fractional part of her or his H.

4. Put both cards at the bottom of the pile.

5. If the player with the smaller fraction cannot color the fractional part shown on the card (because not enough of the H is left uncolored), both players put their cards at the bottom of the pile and pick again.

6. Continue playing until one player colors the whole H. That person is first to go Whole Hog and loses the game.

▼ Make a new H and play again.

Whole Hog

Objective: Practice in comparing fractions.

Getting Ready: Make two gameboards (the H) and the 10 squares with fractions as shown on *Whole Hog.* You will each need color counters or a crayon. A pattern for the game board and fraction squares is available on previous pages.

RULES OR PROCEDURES:

Explain the rules and play the game with the student. Help if you need to help the student, but watch carefully to see if they can identify the smaller fraction and the fractional part of 18. Remember that you are coloring in the fractional part of the whole H. For example, if 1/3 is the smaller fraction drawn on the first round, then 6 squares (1/3 of 18) would be colored or covered. This would leave 12 squares on that person's H. If that person draws 1/2 the next time (the smallest fraction) then he or she would color or cover 1/2 of 18 (not 1/2 of the remaining 12). The loser is the first one to completely color or cover the H.

Gearing Down: Have 18 chips available so that the student can model the fractional part of the set. For example, suppose 2/9 is drawn. The student could make "ninths" or nine equal sets. There would be two chips in each equal set, so 1/ 9 of 18 is 2 and 2/9 of 18 is 4.

Gearing Up: Have students make their own gameboards and fractions that are appropriate for that gameboard. See if they can find what size gameboards work well and why.

REFLECTION:

1. Which fractions were easy for the student to compare? Which gave them difficulty?

2. Did they understand how to find a fractional part of 18? What did they do?

3. What was the reaction to the game? Did the student enjoy it? If so, why do you think he or she did? If not, why do think he or she did not?

4. How appropriate was this game for the students? Is this something you might like to do some day with your own students? What changes might you make?

Can You Beat the Toss?

Materials: Paper and pencil for children, a penny for the teacher

Directions:

▼ The teacher reads a number.

▼ Each child writes the number in either decimal or fraction notation.

▼ Each child receives 1 point if he or she writes the number correctly.

▼ The teacher tosses a coin.

- If it's *heads*, then those who wrote a *decimal* receive one more point.

- If it's *tails*, then those who wrote a *fraction* receive one more point.

Suggested Numbers:

two-tenths   one and three-tenths

seven-tenths   twenty-two and five-tenths

five and seven-tenths   thirty-four and no-tenths

eleven and four-tenths

Challenge Numbers:

sixteen-tenths   five and eleven-tenths

Can You Beat the Toss?

Grades 3–6

Objective: Write numbers as fractions or decimals.

Getting Ready: You'll need a copy of *Can You Beat the Toss?* Read the directions and list a set of numbers and challenge numbers. Decide how many numbers you will use, and how you will have the children check what they wrote. For example, you may want to read all the numbers, letting each child write either the decimal or fractional notation, have the children check the correctness of what they wrote, and then toss the coin for each number to see whether a decimal or a fraction notation won for that number. Alternatively, you may want to check and toss the coin after each number is read.

RULES OR PROCEDURES:

This is a game of skill (writing the correct decimal or fraction notation given the words) and of luck (choosing the type of notation).

Explain the rules (on *Can You Beat the Toss?*) and play the game with a small group of students, or a whole class.

Gearing Down: This is a practice game for connecting the words with symbols. If students are not ready to play this game, then they need more introduction to the concepts of fractions or decimals and how we represent fractions and decimals with words and symbols.

Gearing Up: Use the challenge numbers or use a mixture of hundredths (or thousandths) and tenths.

REFLECTION:

1. What is the advantage of playing games with some luck involved?

2. What was the reaction of the children to this game?

3. How long did it take to play the game, once the children understood the rules? Is this a game that you could use on the spur of the moment when you have just a few minutes before going to lunch or to music?

4. How appropriate was this game for the students? Is this something you might like to do some day with your own students? What changes might you make?

Make a Match

Objective: Comparing fractions, decimals, and percents and their equivalents.

Getting Ready: You'll need to make a deck of 24 cards with one benchmark fraction, their decimal, or percent equivalent written in symbolic form on each card. Include the fractions 1/2, 1/4, 2/4, 3/4, 1/10, 1/5, 1/3, 2/3, the decimals 0.5, 0.25, 0.75, 0.1, 0.2, 0.33, 0.66, and the percents 50%, 25%, 75%, 10%, 20%, 33%, and 66%. You can add 8 more cards by including a picture of each amount. (Shade a 10 x 10 grid.) A pattern for the cards is available on the following page.

RULES OR PROCEDURES:

Once the deck of cards is completed, various games may be played.

Concentration—Place all cards face down in a rectangular array. Players take turns turning over two cards. If the two cards are equivalent, they keep the match and take another turn. If they are not, the cards are turned face down again and the other player takes a turn. The winner is the person with the most matches.

Rummy—Make two of each card so you have 48 cards in the deck. Deal 7 cards to each player. Play by standard Rummy rules with the following modifications. Players try to collect: 1) Three or more cards that are equivalent, 2) Three or more cards ordered from smallest to largest, 3) Cards which add to one whole. Lay-downs may be played on by any player. Play continues until one player has laid down all his cards. The winner of the round scores 5 points, and each player, including the winner, scores 1 point for each card laid down. When one player has accumulated 100 points, he wins the game.

Battle—Two players divide the deck in half. At the same time each player turns over one card from his/her stack. The player with the highest card takes both cards. Play continues until one player has all the cards.

Gearing Down: Include both symbols and pictures on each card. Start with just two representations such as fractions and decimals. Provide 10 x 10 grids so students can illustrate the symbols.

Gearing Up: Expand the deck of cards beyond the benchmark fractions, decimals, and percents.

REFLECTION:

1. After playing this game, what have you learned about the children's understanding of fractions, decimals, percents and their equivalents? What experiences would you provide next?

2. How appropriate was this game for the students? Is this something you might like to do some day with your own students? What changes might you make?

$\dfrac{1}{2}$	$\dfrac{1}{4}$	$\dfrac{2}{4}$	$\dfrac{3}{4}$	$\dfrac{1}{10}$	$\dfrac{1}{5}$
$\dfrac{1}{3}$	$\dfrac{2}{3}$	0.5	0.25	0.5	0.75
0.1	0.2	0.33	0.66	50%	25%
50%	75%	10%	20%	33%	66%

Less Is Best
(A game for two or more)

▼ Choose a partner to play this game:

- Put an assortment of pattern blocks in a box.

- Without looking, each player chooses 3 blocks and puts them together to make a new shape.

- Count the number of sides on each of the new shapes.
  Whoever has the shape with the fewest sides wins—less is best!

▼ Make a table to record your scores, and play several rounds to determine the winner.

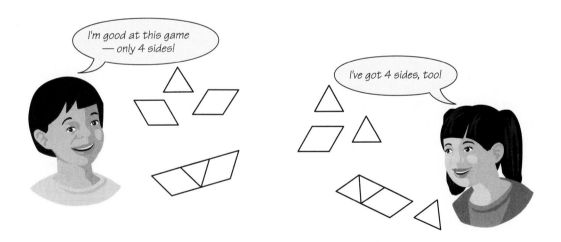

Cos	4			
Marrietta	4			

Less is Best

Objective: Making shapes with fewest sides.

Getting Ready: Review a copy of *Less is Best*. Put a small assortment (about 30) pattern blocks in a container for each pair of children.

RULES OR PROCEDURES:

Tell the children that they are going to play a game in which less is best.

Have pairs of children make a chart to record the scores and pick up one container. Play the game (with transparent pattern blocks if available) with the class.

Discuss strategies the children used.

Gearing Down: Use only two shapes instead of three. Or have children just count the number of sides of shapes they make and see if they can make another with a different number of sides.

Gearing Up: Have children use four triangles and see if they can make shapes with 3, 4, and 5 sides. Have them make up other puzzles for their friends to solve.

REFLECTION:

1. What strategies did you notice children using?

2. Did you notice children counting the number of sides of the individual pieces rather than the sides of the shape they made? What did you do (or what would you do if you notice this happening)?

3. How appropriate was this game for the students? Is this something you might like to do some day with your own students? What changes might you make?

Solid Shake

Grades 3–6

Objective: Identify properties of solid geometric shapes.

Getting Ready: Play with a student. Each of you needs 6 chips or markers you can identify as yours. Use two dice of different colors and the *Attribute Grid* and *Game Board* provided on the next page.

RULES OR PROCEDURES:

Decide who goes first and which die represents across (the other will be the down on the attribute grid).

Toss the dice. Find the space indicated by the dice on the attribute grid. Place a chip on a solid with that attribute. (There may be more than one, but you must chose only one.)

Take turns tossing the dice and placing your chips on the game board. If all the solids that fit the description are covered, you lose your turn. The first person to get three chips in a row wins.

Gearing Down: Play the same game, but have the solids available.

Gearing Up: Make a playing board using only the names of the solids.

REFLECTION:

1. Did the student need the solids? Do you think he or she could have played with just the names of the solids on the game board?

2. Was the vocabulary familiar to the student? If not, how did you help?

3. Was this a game that the student enjoyed playing? Why or why not?

4. How appropriate was this game for students? Is this something you might like to do some day with your own students? What changes might you make?

Helping Children Learn • Games • *Teaching Elementary Mathematics: A Resource for Field Experiences* © 2009 John Wiley & Sons • **141**

ATTRIBUTE GRID

	1	2	3	4	5	6
6	6 faces	not round anywhere	3 congruent faces	pyramid	6 vertices	0 edges
5	partly slanted	12 edges	0 vertices	5 faces	some rectangular faces	4 congruent faces
4	2 congruent faces	cone	4 faces	4 vertices	18 edges	8 faces
3	0 faces	some square faces	cube	9 edges	some triangular faces	partly round
2	12 vertices	2 faces	6 congruent faces	some circular faces	prism	5 vertices
1	all round	8 vertices	6 edges	cylinder	1 face	some 6-sided faces

GAME BOARD

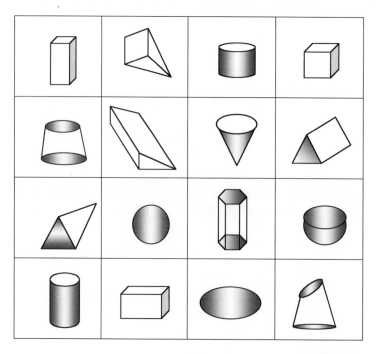

Race to a Yard (or Meter)

Objective: Converting from one measurement unit to another.

Getting Ready: If you are playing Race to a Yard, use one-inch grid paper to prepare 40 1-inch pieces and 4 foot pieces for each player. Organize all of the pieces into a "bank". A pattern for the inch and foot pieces is available on the following page. Each player will also need a yard stick or strip of paper that is one yard long. You'll also need a die. If you are playing *Race to a Meter*, make similar preparations with centimeter paper and a meter stick.

RULES OR PROCEDURES:

Players take turns rolling the die. The number that is rolled determines the number of inch pieces that may be taken.

Players place their pieces along the yard stick. Once they have 12 inches, they must trade it for a foot. A penalty could be imposed if a required trade is not completed or a bonus could be given to the player who discovers an omitted trade.

The winner is the first to trade three feet for a yard.

Gearing Down: Use color tiles or plastic inch worm manipulatives that may be connected together. For Race to a meter, use base ten blocks to trade centimeters, decimeters, and meter.

Gearing Up: Use number cards or dice with fractions on them. For example, you could include ½, ¼, etc.

Try this game with other measurement units. For example, play *Race to a Gallon*. Students could use inch tiles with C for cup, P for pint, Q for quart, and G for Gallon. These could be placed in a place value chart. Two C's would be traded for a P, etc.

Students could draw a line segment, representing what was rolled. For example, if 4 is rolled, draw a four inch line. On each turn, the new line is connected to the one drawn previously.

REFLECTION:

1. After playing this game, what have you learned about the children's understanding of the measurement unit and its equivalent? What experiences would you provide next?

2. How appropriate was this game for the students? Is this something you might like to do some day with your own students? What changes might you make?

One
Foot
One
Foot

One Inch	One Inch	One Inch	One Inch	One Inch	One Inch
One Inch	One Inch	One Inch	One Inch	One Inch	One Inch
One Inch	One Inch	One Inch	One Inch	One Inch	One Inch
One Inch	One Inch	One Inch	One Inch	One Inch	One Inch

Race to 20

Objective: Determining the fairness of a game.

Getting Ready: For each small group of students (2-3 in a group) you'll need a pair of six-sided dice and plain paper or grid paper for recording points.

RULES OR PROCEDURES:

Take turns rolling the two dice and adding the faces to find the sum.
The first player to earn 20 points (or some predetermined number) is the winner.

Version 1

Player A gets a point if the sum is 1, 2, 3, or 4. Player B gets a point if the sum is 5, 6, 7, or 8.
Player C gets a point if the sum is 9, 10, 11, or 12.

Version 2

Player A (the students) gets a point if 2, 3, 4, 10, 11, or 12 is rolled. (6 numbers)
Player B (the teacher) gets a point if 5, 6, 7, 8, or 9 is rolled. (5 numbers)

After each game, discuss the results. Rotate the assignments of A, B, and/or C and play again. Repeat until everyone has had a chance to be A, B, and/or C.
Is each game fair? (No, in each game player B has more ways to score than A and C.)

Gearing Down: If students are unable to determine why the game is unfair, help them list all the ways each number can be obtained with the sum of two dice. Discuss how the sums with more possibilities have a better chance of being rolled. For younger students, simplify the game by using one die. Assign particular numbers for each player.

Gearing Up: Once students agree that the game is not fair, challenge them to change the rules so that it is fair. (Each player should have the same number of opportunities to score.) Try these other versions or have students make up their own versions.

Version 3

Player A gets a point if the sum is even. Player B gets a point if the sum is odd.
Is this game fair? Yes.

Version 4

Player A gets a point if the product is even. Player B gets a point if the product is odd.
Is this game fair? No, Player A has more ways to score than B.

REFLECTION:

1. Were the students able to figure out what made each version fair? Explain.

2. What did you learn about their thinking?

3. How appropriate was this game for the students? Is this something you might like to do some day with your own students? What changes might you make?

*Skunk**

Objective: Using probability to integrate choice and chance.

Getting Ready: This is a whole class game. The teacher will need one pair of dice. Each player makes a score sheet like this:

S	K	U	N	K

RULES OR PROCEDURES:

Each letter of 'skunk' represents a different round. Begin recording in the 'S' column and continue to the 5th and final round in the last 'K' column. The object of 'skunk' is to accumulate the greatest total number of points. The following rules apply to each round.

To accumulate points for each round, a pair of dice is rolled. A player gets the total of the dice and records it in their column, unless a 'one' comes up on either die. If a 'one' comes up, play is over for that round and all the player's points in that column are wiped out. If 'double ones' come up, all points accumulated in prior columns are wiped out. If a 'one' doesn't occur, the player may choose either to try for more points on the next roll or stop and keep what has been accumulated. If a 'one' or 'double ones' occur on the very first roll of a round, then that round is over and the players must take the consequences.

Ask all students to stand to begin the game. Then after each roll of the dice ask all who want to stop and keep their current points for that round to sit down. This makes it clear who is still playing and also builds suspense for each roll. Here is a sample round for Bob. Bob's points for the game: 10 + 6 + 7 = 23

S	K	U	N	K
7	6	4	5	one
3		10	2	
		one		

S—He stayed for two rolls of the dice and earned 10 points.
K—He stayed one roll and stopped with 6 points.
U—He stayed for two rounds but a one occurred on the third roll so he scored 0 points.
N—He stayed for two rolls and earned 7 points.
K—A one occurred on the first roll so he scored 0 points.

This game provides an opportunity to apply probability. For example, "How often will a 'one' occur? How often will 'two ones' occur?" Other questions such as, "When should you risk another roll?" are more personal choices. Have students discuss their strategies.

*Adapted with permission from Dan Brutlag's "Choice and Chance in Life. The Game of Skunk" in *Mathematics Teaching in the Middle School*, April 1994 vol. 1 pp. 28–33.

REFLECTION:

1. What did you learn about the students' thinking?

2. How appropriate was this game for the students? Is this something you might like to do some day with your own students? What changes might you make?

Factor Me Out

▼ Choose a partner and make a chart to play this game:

●	2	3	4	5	6
7	8	9	10	11	12
13	14	15	16	17	18
19	20	21	22	23	24
25	26	27	28	29	30
31	32	33	34	35	36

▼ **Rules:**

- Player 1 chooses a number. He or she gets that many points. The opponent gets points equal to the sum of all the factors.

- Make a table to record scores:

Player 1	Player 2
10	7 (2 + 5)

- Mark out the number and the factors; these cannot be used again.

- Repeat with Player 2 choosing the number.

- Alternate turns until no numbers are left.

The player with the most points wins.

Factor Me Out

Objective: Practice in finding factors.

Getting Ready: You'll need a copy of *Factor Me Out*. Play the game with a friend to make certain that you understand it. Give pairs of students a piece of paper to make the chart and to keep score. You should have the chart on a transparency or on the board if playing with a whole class, or have a large copy so all can see it if you are playing with a small group.

RULES OR PROCEDURES:

Play the game against the small group or whole class to explain the rules (found on *Factor Me Out*). Let students explore their own strategies as they play in pairs to choose numbers.

After the rules are clear, let pairs of children play. Encourage them to analyze who is winning and why. Do the numbers chosen have anything to do with winning?

Gearing Up: Students could use a large set of numbers, say from 2 to 60. Have them analyze more formally whether choosing primes or composites (and if so which composites) is a better strategy.

REFLECTION:

1. Which students used a consistent strategy? Did they do this when they first began playing the game or after they had played several? What happened if they switched partners and that partner was using the same strategy?

2. What mathematics is involved in this game? Of course, you need to be able to find factors of a number, but what else is involved?

3. How appropriate was this game for the students? Is this something you might like to do someday with your own students? What changes might you make?

Helping Children Learn with Technology Content

These technology experiences allow you to examine and try a variety of math activities that use the calculator and computer as an instructional tool and to provide experience presenting an activity to students that integrates technology. This includes planning and carrying out a lesson with a small group or whole class. The technology activities are classified into three grade level bands. Specific grade level suggestions may be found on each lesson plan. "CA" indicates a calculator activity and "CO" indicates a computer activity. We have provided some suggestions for gearing down or up.

Technology by Topic

Key Topics	Technology Activity	K–2	3–5	6–8	Page
1. Issues, Trends					
2. Learning					
3. Teaching, Planning, Adapting	(CO) Reviewing Software	X	X	X	151–152
	(CO) WWW Lesson Plan	X	X	X	153–154
	(CA) Integrating Calculators into a Mathematics Lesson	X	X	X	155–156
4. Assessing, Recording, Reporting					
5. Process Standards	(CO) Problem Solving on the Web	X	X	X	157–158
	(CO) See also pp. 151–154				
6. Problem Solving	(CO) See also pp. 151–154, 157–158				
7. Number Sense, Prenumber	(CA) Counting On and On and On	X	X	X	159–160
	(CA) Skipping Around	X	X		161–162
	(CA) Counting Backward	X			163–164
	(CO) See also pp. 151–154				
8. Place Value	(CO) Base Blocks on the Internet	X	X		165
	(CO) Chip Trading on the Internet	X	X	X	166
	(CA) Hitting Hundreds	X	X		167–168
	(CA) See also p. 107				
	(CO) See also pp. 151–154				

TECHNOLOGY BY TOPIC (continued)

Key Topics	Technology Activity	K–2	3–5	6–8	Page
9. Basic Facts	(CA) Calculator Fact Practice	X	X	X	169
	(CA) Guess My Fact	X	X		170
	(CA) 21 or Bust!	X	X		171–172
	(CA) See also pp. 159–162				
	(CO) See also pp. 151–154				
10. Computational Alternatives	(CA) How Would You Do It? (Whole Numbers)		X	X	173–174
	(CA) How Would You Do It? (Fractions)		X	X	175–176
	(CA) See also pp. 119–120				
	(CO) See also pp. 151–156				
11. Whole Number Operations	(CA) Zeros Count		X	X	177–178
	(CO) See also pp. 151–154				
	(CA) See also pp. 173–174				
12. Fractions, Decimals	(CA) Plug In Puzzles		X	X	179–180
	(CA) Decimal Maze			X	181–182
	(CO) See also pp. 151–154				
	(CA) See also pp. 175–176				
13. Ratio, Proportion, Percent	(CO) See also pp. 151–154				
14. Patterns, Algebra	(CO) Completing Patterns	X	X		183
	(CA) See also pp. 159–162, 187				
	(CO) See also pp. 151–154				
15. Geometry	(CO) Make Me Different	X			184
	(CO) See also pp. 151–154				
16. Measurement	(CO) See also pp. 151–154				
17. Data, Statistics, Probability	(CO) Build a Graph	X	X	X	185
	(CO) Build a Spinner	X	X	X	186
	(CO) See also pp. 151–154				
18. Number Theory	(CA) Divisibility Discovery			X	187–188
	(CO) See also pp. 151–154				

Software Review Form

Title: _____

Subject/Topic: _____ Grade Level(s): _____

Publisher: _____ Copyright Date: _____

Availability: Macintosh _____ PC _____ Apple IIe _____ Other _____

Hardware Requirements: _____

Cost: _____ Catalog: _____

Instructional Type: (Check all that apply)
    _____ Drill and Practice   _____ Tutorial
    _____ Simulation   _____ Game
    _____ Problem Solving   _____ Tool

Possible Educational Objectives:

Description of Program:

RATINGS

Quality	Low				High	
Instructions:	1	2	3	4	5	NA
Support Materials:	1	2	3	4	5	NA
Screen Presentation:	1	2	3	4	5	NA
Ease of Use:	1	2	3	4	5	NA
Appropriate Feedback:	1	2	3	4	5	NA
Developmentally Appropriate:	1	2	3	4	5	NA
Motivation:	1	2	3	4	5	NA
Opportunity for Communication:	1	2	3	4	5	NA
Use of models to support learning:	1	2	3	4	5	NA
Worthwhile Mathematical Tasks:	1	2	3	4	5	NA
Problem Solving/Higher Level Thinking:	1	2	3	4	5	NA
Usefulness for a Wide Range of Abilities:	1	2	3	4	5	NA
Adaptations for Diverse Learners:	1	2	3	4	5	NA
Overall Rating:	1	2	3	4	5	NA

Comments:

(Continued on next page)

Reviewing Software

Examine a piece of software from the school computer lab, from the Internet, from your university computer lab or library, or from some other source. Work your way through the software, trying to think like a child as you try all its features. If possible, watch some children use the software. Think about how you (or they) use it and what your (their) reactions are.

The software review form on the previous page provides several criteria that should be evaluated when considering the use of software with children. The first few criteria focus on the general effectiveness of the software. The last few criteria focus on the mathematical and instructional usefulness of the software.

Complete the form on the previous page to rate the software. Then use the form and the reflection questions below to focus your evaluation.

REFLECTION:

1. What are this software's strengths and weaknesses?

2. How would using this software *add* to a lesson or a classroom? (That is, why use it, rather than just teaching without it?) Explain.

3. Would you use this software with your students? If so, why and how? If not, why not?

4. What additional materials or activities would you use if you were to actually use this software with children?

WWW Lesson Plan

Grades K–8

The purpose of this assignment is for you to use what you know about worthwhile mathematics tasks to adapt and use World Wide Web Resources for teaching mathematics. Specifically, you are to construct a lesson to use with the children in your classroom based on one or more WWW sites. The resource sites can be sites with data or other information that is useful for developing a lesson, or they can be sites that contain actual lessons. In the latter case, you are free to use any lesson materials you can download. Given that you will be assessed on the quality of your lesson rather than where it came from, you will likely to need to adapt what you find to make sure the quality of your tasks meet whatever criteria for worthwhile tasks have been spelled out by the teacher and your instructor.

WWW RESOURCE(S)

Start your plan by providing information about the WWW site(s) used for your lesson. Include the following:

A printout of the home page(s).

The title and URL of the home page(s).

2–3 paragraph description of what resources are available on the home page (you should write this, although you can use information from the home page).

LESSON PLAN

Your lesson should reflect the characteristics of effective lessons. For example, if your instructor has identified tasks, teacher's role, tools, classroom culture, and equity and access as characteristics of effective lessons, your lesson plans should reflect your concern for these elements. Use one of the lesson plan templates to develop your plan. You may or may not get to actually teach this lesson to students. However, once the plan is developed, share it with your teacher. If the whole class is not available, perhaps you could do it with a small group.

GETTING STARTED

Many resources of interest for mathematics educators can be found on the WWW, including software, data bases, interest groups, classroom activities, etc. You are free to use as much as you want from the Web site(s). However, be careful that any activities that you take directly from a site reflect the characteristics of effective lessons outlined by your instructor and are clearly referenced. A list of places to find resources follows on the next page.

REFLECTION

1. What are this site's strengths and weaknesses?

2. How would using this Web site *add* to a lesson or a classroom? (That is, why use it, rather than just teaching without it?) Explain.

3. Would you use this Web site with your own students? If so, why and how? If not, why not?

4. If you taught the lesson, use the *After-Teaching Reflection* form to reflect on it.

Helping Children Learn • Technology • *Teaching Elementary Mathematics: A Resource for Field Experiences* © 2009 John Wiley & Sons • 153

Web Sites

These sites are just suggestions. You are welcome to do your own Web searches if you prefer. The higher the quality of resources you can find, the easier your job will be! (Note that the quality of some activities at the sites below is questionable at best. One of your tasks is to find the better tasks.)

National Council of Teachers of Mathematics Illuminations (http://illuminations.nctm.org and http://standards.nctm.org/document/eexamples/index.htm)

Illuminations contains online investigations, reviewed Web resources, internet-based lesson plans, interactive math applets, and video vignettes. The electronic examples provide electronic lessons that illustrate standards recommendations.

The Math Forum (http://forum.swarthmore.edu/)

The Math Forum is funded by the National Science Foundation as a site for information about mathematics and mathematics teaching at the pre-college level. Numerous resources, including specific lesson plans, can be found.

The MegaMath Project (http://www.c3.lanl.gov/mega-math/index.html)

The MegaMath project is intended to bring unusual and important mathematical ideas to elementary school classrooms so that young people and their teachers can think about them together.

MathMagic K–12 project (http://forum.swarthmore.edu/mathmagic/index.html)

MathMagic is a K–12 telecommunications project developed in El Paso, Texas. It provides strong motivation for students to use computer technology while increasing problem-solving strategies and communications skills. MathMagic posts challenges in each of four categories (K–3, 4–6, 7–9, and 10–12) to trigger each registered team to pair up with another team and engage in a problem-solving dialog. When an agreement has been reached, one solution is posted for every pair.

PBS Teacher Source (http: www.pbs.org/teachersource/siteguide/siteguide_sitemap.shtm)

PBS provides a variety of math lesson plans and mathline video clips with lesson plans for grades K–2, 3–5, and 6–8.

The History of Mathematics Archive (http://www-groups.dcs.st-and.ac.uk:80/~history/)

The History of Mathematics archive is part of the Mathematical MacTutor system developed at the School of Mathematical and Computational Sciences of the University of St. Andrews for learning and experimenting with mathematics. The archive contains the biographies of more than 1000 mathematicians. About 200 of these biographies are fairly detailed and most are accompanied by pictures of the mathematicians themselves.

Textbook Publishers Web Sites

At least three of the elementary textbook publishers have Web sites. They all have supplemental activities to go with their mathematics texts and some activities that can be used without a text and links that help students use the WWW to investigate mathematics questions. Here are several sites:

Silver Burdett Ginn (http://www.sbgmath.com)
Scott Foresman Addison Wesley (http://www.sf.aw.com)
McGraw Hill (http://www.mmhschool.com)

List Other Useful Sites You Found

Integrating Calculators into a Mathematics Lesson

Grades K–8

The purpose of this assignment is for you to use what you know about worthwhile mathematical tasks and to find ways to integrate calculators as instructional tools into mathematics lessons. When calculators are used as instructional tools, they are used for more than just doing computations. They may:

- Facilitate a search for patterns.
- Support concept development.
- Promote number sense.
- Encourage creativity and exploration.

Search the web for sites that provide ideas for integrating calculators into mathematics lessons. Three sites are provided on the following page. Select three calculator activities where the calculator would serve as an instructional tool as described above.

For each activity, list 1) the activity title, 2) website title, and 3) web address. Also, provide a copy of the activity or a short description of the activity including: 4) grade level, 5) mathematics objective addressed by the activity, and 6) a brief description of how you could incorporate this activity into a mathematics lesson. Try out at least one of the activities with children.

1.

2.

3.

REFLECTION:

1. How did the children respond to the calculator activity you shared with them?

2. What are some benefits of integrating calculators into mathematics lessons?

3. How would you rate the quality of calculator resources found on the web?

Calculator Websites

http://education.ti.com/educationportal/sites/US/homePage/index.html
This is the Texas Instruments calculator website. You can find activities under Classroom Activities, Getting Started, and Downloads.

http://edu.casio.com/support/activity/
This is the Casio calculator website. Under Standard Scientific Calculator you will find a variety of calculator activity PDF files, sorted by topic.

http://illuminations.nctm.org/
You can find a variety of math lessons (look under Lessons) and websites (look under Web Links). Several include ideas for integrating calculators.

Problem Solving on the Web

Search the web for sites that could be used to develop or enhance mathematics lessons with a focus on problem solving or using a problem solving approach to developing a mathematics concept. Identify three sites that seem to have good potential.

CHECKING THE WEBSITES:

For each of your three chosen sites, list the website title, web address, and provide a short description of the site, including the following: 1) grade level(s) most appropriate for use of this site, 2) mathematics concepts or aspects of problem solving that could be highlighted through this site, 3) one example of how you might use this site as part of a mathematics lesson (for example, as a lesson launch, as a source of problems, to teach problem-solving strategies). (On the following page, we have provided a short list of additional, interesting problem-solving web resources.) Try out at least one of the sites you selected with some children.

1.

2.

3.

CHECKING THE CLASSROOM:

4. Ask the teacher how he or she uses problem solving in teaching mathematics. Describe briefly.

5. Ask the teacher if he or she uses websites as resources for problem-solving instruction. If so, have the teacher suggest one website and describe how it is used. If not, ask why he or she doesn't.

6. Have you observed any websites being used to teach mathematics? If so, what were they? Did you try out your selected sites? What was the reaction of the children? Were the websites used to develop or enhance problem solving? Explain.

REFLECTION:

1. What do you think are some of the benefits of using a problem-solving approach to mathematics teaching?

2. What do you think are some of the benefits of using the web as a problem-solving resource?

Problem Solving Websites

Tim's Interactive Puzzle Solution Center

http://sakharov.net/puzzle/
Classic mathematical puzzles (e.g., missionaries and cannibals) are solved in interesting ways. Suitable for upper elementary or middle school students.

Pattern Blocks: Exploring Fractions With Shapes

http://arcytech.org/java/patterns/patterns_j.shtml
Provides students with a set of virtual pattern blocks that can be manipulated to solve a variety of conceptual problems associated with basic fraction ideas.

Base Ten Blocks: Exploring Whole Decimal Numbers With Blocks

http://arcytech.org/java/b10blocks/b10blocks.html
Provides students with a set of virtual base ten blocks that can be manipulated to solve a variety of conceptual problems associated with decimal concepts and operations.

Math Problem Solving for Upper Elementary Students With Disabilities

http://www.k8accesscenter.org/training_resources/MathPrblSlving_upperelem.asp
Valuable suggestions for how to engage upper elementary school children with various learning disabilities in mathematical problem solving. The author, Marjorie Montague, is a former president of the Division for Research, Council for Exceptional Children.

Math Word: Computational Problems and Math Worksheets

http://www.cdli.ca/CITE/math_problems.htm
Provides a list of links to word problems, computational sheets and extension and enrichment worksheets written for fifth grade students. Problems have specific foci—for example, helping students attend to relevant information in word problems.

ABCTeach Directory: Problem Solving

http://abcteach.com/directory/basics/math/problem_solving/
Suitable for all elementary grades. Site provides posters for problem-solving strategies, teaching hints, and sets of problems. Members of ABCTeach can access additional resources.

Math Word Problems for Children

http://www.mathstories.com/
Designed to help children in grades 1–6 boost their math problem-solving and critical-thinking skills, this site for teachers, students, and parents has over 15,000 interactive and non-interactive math word problems available in both English and Spanish.

Problem Solving and Word Problem Resources Online

http://www.homeschoolmath.net/online/problem_solving.php
Developed by HomeschoolMath.net, this site provides sets of a variety of math problems for grade 5–12, as well as links to many other interesting math sites.

Counting
On . . . and On . . . and On . . .

▼ Use your [calculator] to count.

• Enter 1 + 1.

• Now press = = = = . . . and count as long as you want.

▼ Time yourself:

• How long did it take to count from 1 to 100? _____

• Guess how long it will take to count from 100 to 200 by ones? _____

• How long did it take to count from 100 to 200 by ones? _____

• Guess how long it will take to count from 1 to 1000 by ones? _____

Counting On and On and On

Objective: Using calculators to count and develop number sense.

Getting Ready: *Counting On and On and On* requires the use of a calculator. Use a calculator that 'counts'. Check this by entering a number and adding 1 and pushing the = key. If you continue to push the equal key, the calculator will show one more each time—so it is counting!

Launch: Ask a child if they can count to 50 or 100 by ones. If yes, ask them to estimate about how long it takes. Record their estimate, and then time them as they count aloud. Compare their estimates with the time required to count.

Investigate: Now, ask them to count with their calculator. Show them (if they don't know already) how to count on their calculator. Start with 1 + 1 as shown on *Counting On and On and On* and begin pressing the = key. Encourage them to watch their display carefully as their calculator counts.

Get ready for a calculator race, by asking them to estimate how long it will take to count to 100 with their calculator. Record their estimates. Before starting the race, make sure they understand to stop counting when their calculator display shows 100. (This encourages children to watch their display carefully as they are pushing the = sign.)

Summarize: Compare their estimates with their calculator counting times.

Gearing Down: Count to a smaller number such as 50.

Gearing Up: You might also do some skip counting with the calculator, by counting by 2's, 3's, or 5's. Repeat the process of estimating the time it will take to count, counting on the calculator, then comparing the estimates with the actual times. After children have counted to 100 with a calculator, ask them to estimate how long it would take to count to 200? a thousand? Did they double or use some multiple of the time it took to count to 100?

REFLECTION:

1. Were the children experienced using the calculators or was it viewed as a novelty?

2. Were the children comfortable making estimates for the counts?

3. Did the children tend to over or underestimate the time for the calculator to count to 100?

4. Was it faster to count to 100 aloud or with a calculator?

5. Describe the level of excitement as the children raced counting with their calculators.

Skipping Around

Can you start at 7 and count by 5's?

Yes, but you decide which of these does it on your

5 + 7 = =
7 + 5 = =

7 12 17 22

▼ Start at 5 every time:

Count by:

9 _14_ ___ ___ ___ ___ ___

10 _15_ ___ ___ ___ ___ ___

49 ___ ___ ___ ___ ___ ___

50 ___ ___ ___ ___ ___ ___

Skipping Around

Objective: Using calculators to practice skip counting.

Getting Ready: *Skipping Around* requires the use of a calculator. Use a calculator that counts. Check this counting feature by entering a number and adding 5 and pushing the = key. If you continue to push the equal key, the calculator will show five more each time—so it is skip counting!

Launch: Ask a child to start at 0, count by 5's and describe patterns. Ask a child to start at 9 and count by 5's. For most children this is much more difficult than counting by ones. They will likely count on 5 at a time, without the use of patterns.

Investigate: Ask them to start at 9 and count by 5's with their calculator. Encourage them to watch their display carefully and say aloud the numbers appearing on their display.
Ask half the class to enter 5 + 9 = = = = = and record their results.
Ask the other half of the class to enter 9 + 5 = = = = = and record their results. Ask them to explain why the results are different. This is a good reminder that the calculator does exactly what it is told.

Encourage children to choose their own beginning number and what number they want to count by. Ask them to write their results for the first 5 counts and to see if a partner can decide what number they counted by. For example, if the first 5 numbers recorded were 7, 16, 25, 34, 43 then they started at 7 and counted on by 9. This provides a nice entry into common differences which promotes algebraic thinking.

Summarize: Have students share their counts and the patterns they discovered.

Gearing Down: Provide a hundred chart students can mark while they count with the calculator.

Gearing Up: *Skipping Around* provides opportunities to count by 5, but you may want to extend this to count by 4, 10, 9, or 100 to provide different patterns for the children to experience.

REFLECTION:

1. What patterns did the children describe when counting by 5's?

2. Were the children comfortable using their calculator to count on from a number?

3. Were the children surprised when 5 + 9 = = = produced different results from 9 + 5 = = = = ?

4. Share some of the counting problems (both start number and counting on number) the children created on their own.

5. Tell how these patterns of constant differences (8, 28, 48, 68, 88) encourage pattern recognition and algebraic thinking.

6. Would starting at zero and skip counting by 4's would help prepare children for multiplication?

Name: _____

Class: _____

Counting Backward

▼ Try these:

15 − 1 = <u>*14*</u> , <u>*13*</u> , _____ , _____ , _____ , _____

20 − 2 = <u>*18*</u> , _____ , _____ , _____ , _____ , _____

35 − 3 = _____ , _____ , _____ , _____ , _____ , _____

Counting Backward

Objective: Using calculators to skip count backward.

Getting Ready: *Counting Backward* requires the use of a calculator. Use a calculator that counts. The three previous activities used the counting on feature by adding. Here the counting backward feature will be used by subtracting. Check the calculator for this counting feature by entering a number and subtracting 1 and pushing the = key. If you continue to push the equal key, the calculator will show one less each time—so it is counting backward!

Launch: Ask a child to count backward from 15 by ones by counting out loud.

Investigate: Now have them enter 15 on the calculator and then press = = = = = and see the results displayed in the calculator.

Consider having some races counting backwards by different numbers. For example, if you start at 100 and count backward by 1 to 0, about how long does it take?

Summarize: Have students share what they learned from this activity.

Gearing Down: Provide counters students can remove each time they push the minus sign.

Gearing Up: Some interesting variations include situations such as: If you start at 100 and count backward by 2 to 0, does it take about half the time? About how much time does it take if you start at 100 and count backward by 4 to 0?

If you are counting backward, what happens when you go beyond zero? How is the negative sign displayed? This provides a nice opportunity to extend the number line and talk about negative numbers.

REFLECTION:

1. Is counting backward or forward easier for children?

2. Ask children to start at 15 and count backward by 1. Observe how they react when they go beyond zero. Do they see the negative sign displayed? Do they notice a pattern?

3. Do you think skip counting backward would help children get ready for division? Tell why.

Base Blocks on the Internet

Objective: Practice composing ten units for 1 ten, ten tens for one hundred, and ten hundreds for one thousand. Also decomposing from one ten to ten ones, and so on.

Getting Ready: Prior work with base ten blocks provides a foundation for composing and decomposing. The National Library of Virtual Manipulatives at http://nlvm.usu.edu/en/nav/index.html created at Utah State University provides a variety of interactive tools. Check the Virtual Library. There are many different tools, but this activity will focus on Base Blocks that is located in Number and Operation in Grades 3-5.

Launch: Show students some Base-ten blocks and review the name of each (ex. flat, long, unit). Have the children use the blocks to show what they already know about representing numbers with the blocks.

Investigate: Go to the Base Blocks manipulative. Decide if the children should focus on 1, 2, 3 or 4 digit numbers and click on that number of columns. You or the children can "Use blocks to represent a number." In this case, click the blocks at the top of each chart column to move pieces to the chart and a number representing the pieces shown appears.

Or you can click on Show a Problem and the caption "Use blocks to show" appears. Then you or children can move the pieces on the Place Value Chart to represent the number. Once the blocks are constructed to show the number—a new problem can be created. Note--there is no built in checking device for this activity, so it is important to monitor the children's work.

Notice that if you move the ten to the ones column and double click it decomposes into 10 ones. Likewise, if you have ten ones in the ones column and enclose them, they recompose into a ten. Likewise for the other pieces. For example, if a hundred is moved to the tens it decomposes into ten tens. This dynamic action provides a visual reminder of the decomposing and recomposing that is frequently occurring as numbers are renamed. Encourage the children to experiment with this feature to use blocks to represent a number in more than one way.

Summarize: Discuss what the manipulative tells us about representing numbers.

Gearing Down: Change the number of places from 2, 3 or 4 places to accommodate your students. Use only base-10 and whole numbers.

Gearing Up: The base for grouping can be changed from 10 to smaller bases, such as 5. You can also provide development and practice with decimals by changing the unit.

REFLECTION:

1. What conclusions did the children draw from this experience? For example, Why were you not allowed to move a ten to the hundreds column?

2. How is 0 shown with the pieces?

Chip Trading on the Internet

Objective: To compose numbers using chip trading.

Getting Ready: You will need a computer with access to the National Library of Virtual Manipulatives for Interactive Mathematics (http://nlvm.usu.edu/en/nav/index.html). Go to the Site Library, Number and Operations, Chip Abacus.

With this manipulative, students can represent place value and exchanges in base 2, base 5, or base 10. Set the desired base with the up and down arrow buttons below the workspace. Chips in columns represent units (1), bases (2, 5, or 10), and base-squared (4, 25, or 100), as indicated by the numbers at the top of each column.

Launch:
Review the following rules for key functions:
- To add a chip, click on the button at the top of a column to add color-coded chips (yellow for units, green for bases, blue for base-squareds).
- Chips can be dragged within a column but not from one column to another.
- To remove a chip, hold down the Shift key and click on it.

Investigate:
Set the base, then have students click to add yellow units and count as they add each unit. When they have enough yellow chips to equal the base (10 in base 10, for example), point out that they can exchange them for a single green chip (representing 10) by clicking on the left-arrow between the columns. Similarly, with enough green chips in the base-column, they could exchange them (using the left-arrow) for a single blue chip in the base-squared column. Note that arrows only become available when an exchange is possible.

Once an exchange is made, have students count or add to be sure the total value of the chips remained the same after the exchange. Discuss the benefit of showing a number with the fewest possible chips. Ex. Easier to count, takes less space, etc.

Let students use chips to represent new starting numbers, count on by ones, and make exchanges. Encourage them to predict when they will be able to make an exchange.

Summarize:
Have students discuss the "rule" for trading chips in a particular base. Ex. In base 10, 10 yellows trade for one green and 10 green trade for one blue.

Gearing Down: Just have students work with the yellow and green chips (2-digit numbers).

Gearing Up: After working with Base 10, challenge students to work with Base 2 or 5, then predict the rule for a different base.

REFLECTION:

1. Which children liked using the computer and chips? Why do you think that they did?

2. What is one advantage of using the chips on the computer? What is a disadvantage?

Name: _____

Class: _____

Hitting Hundreds

▼ Which target will you hit?

Write what your 🖩 *shows.*

Start	Rule	Which target?		Guess	Check
20	+100	(200)	(220)	_____	_____
35	+100	(335)	(500)	_____	_____
41	+100	(410)	(441)	_____	_____
86	+100	(586)	(580)	_____	_____
97	+100	(897)	(970)	_____	_____
169	+100	(469)	(696)	_____	_____
123	+100	(321)	(323)	_____	_____

Hitting Hundreds

Objective: Counting by hundreds to develop place value and pattern recognition.

Getting Ready: *Hitting Hundreds* requires the use of a calculator that counts. Check this counting feature by entering a number, adding 10, and pushing the = key. If you continue to push the equal key, the calculator will show ten more each time—so it is skip counting!

Launch: Ask a child to use the calculator to start at 0, count by 10's and describe patterns.
Ask a child to start at 9 and count by 10's. Ask them to tell the numbers shown on the calculator, display and describe a pattern.
Ask a child to start at 9 and count by 100's. Ask them to tell the numbers shown on the calculator, display and describe a pattern.
Ask them to start at 20, and predict whether the calculator will stop on 200 or 220. Then try it with a calculator.

Investigate: Complete the rest of the target tasks shown on *Hitting Hundreds*.

Summarize: Can the child explain how they know which target they will hit? Discuss.

Gearing Down: Provide a hundreds chart students can mark while they count on the calculator.

Gearing Up: Ask them to start at 220
    Predict the first three numbers displayed if + 100 is keyed three times?
    Predict the first three numbers displayed if + 1000 is keyed three times?
    Predict the first three numbers displayed if + 1100 is keyed three times?

REFLECTION:

1. Do you think this activity helps develop place value? Tell why.

2. Do you think this activity helps develop mental computation? Tell why?

3. Describe how you would modify this activity to subtract 100 rather than add 100?

4. Suppose a colleague said, "We can do this activity without a calculator." What would you say?

Calculator Fact Practice

Objective: To practice basic addition or multiplication facts.

Getting Ready: For each student you will need a calculator and a score sheet. Most calculators have a repeat feature. Students can use this to practice their basic facts. For example, have students enter + 5 = . Adding 5 is now "locked in" to the calculator. When a student now enters 6 = the calculator will show 11. He or she can then enter 7 = and the calculator will show 12. For multiplication facts, a similar series of keystrokes can be used (e.g., x 5 =).

Launch: Have the students begin the activity by writing the number that they will practice adding at the top of their sheet.

Investigate: Have them enter the number they will add to the top number and say the sum (or product) to themselves before pressing the equal sign. They next try a different number, and so on.

Variations of this activity include using a blank recording sheet with a die or spinner to generate the numbers to add on or to multiply by, or having students practice their facts in pairs (they take turns naming a number for the other student to add on or to multiply by).

Summarize: Students can then use the score sheets to keep track of which basic facts they know and which they need to practice. Watch the students as they do the activity. Talk with students about their approach. Pay attention to who has facts memorized and who needs more help learning thinking strategies. See if you can determine what strategies, if any, students are using to derive the sums or products.

Gearing Down: Have students work on just the basic facts up to 5 + 5.

Gearing Up: Challenge students to design a score sheet for practicing their basic subtraction or division facts.

REFLECTION:

1. How appropriate was this activity for the students? Is this something you might like to do someday with your own students? Would you make any changes?

2. What were you able to learn about the students' knowledge of basic facts? About their use of strategies?

Guess My Fact

Objective: Practicing basic facts and identifying multiple representations of a number.

Getting Ready: For each pair of students, you'll need a calculator and paper and pencil.

Launch: Tell students that today they are going to be math fact sleuths and their challenge will be to find the mystery fact. Begin by demonstrating the procedure for the class. Without showing the students, select a basic fact (such as 3 + 6), enter it into your calculator and press equals. Then display the result on the calculator screen (9) and write it on the paper as the target number. Challenge students to guess the fact you entered. For each guess, record the number sentence and whether it is the mystery fact you entered (yes or no). For example:

Target: 9	
2 + 7	No
10 − 1	No
3 × 3	No
6 + 3	Yes (6 + 3 may be counted as the same as 3 + 6)

If one of the players thinks a number sentence guessed does not match the target number, the calculator may be used to check. If a fact is guessed and recorded that does not correctly match the target number, then it should be crossed out. If you like, you may have students keep track of the number of guesses it takes to "Guess My Fact." In this example, four guesses would be a score of 4.

Investigate: Have students pair up and take turns entering a mystery math fact and guessing. Some students may need to write down their fact on a hidden piece of paper so they don't forget what they entered. Each pair's recording sheets can be assessed for correctness of guesses for the target number.

Summarize: Bring everyone together and discuss strategies they used when guessing the fact. What was the highest number of guesses? The lowest?

Gearing down: You can limit or identify the operations to be used at the beginning of the activity or round. For example, rather than guessing any operation, they may be limited to addition facts only. You can also limit the size of the target numbers. Provide counters to help students determine possible math facts as needed.

Gearing up: Challenge students to reduce the number of guesses they must make to "Guess My Fact." Use larger target numbers. Students may also be allowed to make up sentences with more than 2 numbers and/or operations such as 1 + 12 − 4 = 9.

REFLECTION:

1. How fluent were the children with their basic facts? Was this a good way to practice?

2. Were some operations used more frequently than others? What strategies were used?

3. What role did the calculator play? Would the activity have been as effective without it?

Name: _____

Class: _____

21 or Bust!

▼ Play this game with a partner:

- Enter 1, 2, 3, 4, or 5 in your .

- Give the to your opponent, who adds

  1, 2, 3, 4, or 5 to the displayed number.

- Take turns adding 1, 2, 3, 4, or 5 to the total. The first player to reach 21 wins! If you go over 21 you "bust," or lose!

What next?

21 or Bust

Objective: Using a game to develop logical reasoning and to practice addition

Getting Ready: Each pair of students needs a calculator. Copies of the *21 or Bust* game sheet are optional since they essentially just define the rules of the game. You could introduce the rules of the game orally.

Launch: Choose a student to play against you as the class observes and a second student to work the calculator as you play. Explain the rules of the game. Each player should announce what number he/she is choosing to add, and the sum, before checking the sum with the calculator. Play once through and win! Challenge another student to play against you.

Investigate: Let students explore their own strategies as they play in pairs. They should take turns choosing a number to add on, predicting the sum, then checking with the calculator.

Summarize: Bring the class back together and ask if anyone has discovered a way to avoid going "bust." If someone volunteers, ask him/her to keep the rule a secret at first. Let him/her challenge others in the class to play. Ask the class to raise their thumbs at the point in the game when they are sure who will win, and challenge them to explain why.

Gearing Down: Change the game rules, so that you choose to add just 1 or 2 each time. The target number can also be changed. Counters could also be provided as needed.

Gearing Up: Challenge students to identify a strategy that ensures you can always win if you go first. (The strategy involves finding all the "key" numbers that a winning player would need to "hit" to ensure a win and knowing what first number to choose.)

REFLECTION:

1. Which students used a consistent strategy and which simply played randomly? How many games did it take for various students to discover patterns that helped them win? Did anyone discover a strategy for winning consistently? If so, how did he/she explain it?

2. What mathematics is involved in this game? Of course, you need to be able to add on using numbers up to 5, but what else is involved?

3. How appropriate was this game for the students? Is this something you might like to do someday with your own students? How might this game be used differently with primary aged students or with older students?

Name: _____

Class: _____

How Would You Do It?

	In your head	With a calculator	With paper/pencil
60×60	☐	☐	☐
945×1000	☐	☐	☐
450×45	☐	☐	☐
$24 \times 5 \times 2$	☐	☐	☐
$2000\overline{)16000}$	☐	☐	☐
$45\overline{)450}$	☐	☐	☐
4×15	☐	☐	☐
$50 \times 17 \times 2$	☐	☐	☐

Follow Up

▼ Write a computation YOU would solve with a calculator _____

▼ Write a computation YOU would solve mentally _____

▼ Write a computation YOU would solve with paper/pencil _____

How would you do it? (Whole Numbers)

Objective: Encourage wise use of computational alternatives.

Getting Ready: *How would you do it? (Whole Numbers)* encourages students to think about doing computations mentally and to reflect on appropriate computational alternatives. You may make a copy of *How would you do it? (Whole Numbers)* for each child, or make a transparency and use it to guide a group activity. We prefer to engage students in discussions on "How would you do it?" and learn why they decided to choose a particular approach. Calculators and paper and pencil may also be available.

Launch: Make sure children recognize the choices, namely—mental (in your head), calculator or written (paper and pencil).

Instruct: Reveal one computation at a time and ask students to tell the strategy they would use. Ask them to explain why they chose that strategy. Skip any computations that you think are inappropriate for your children—such as division.

Focus attention on the notion that the numbers and operations involved influence the choice. For example, while 450 x 45 is difficult to do mentally—if it had been 450 + 45 the choice of computation would likely be different.

Encourage children to tell how they would do the computation, as their approaches may be different. For example, one child may compute 25 x 5 x 2 mentally by thinking 5 x 2 is 10 and then multiplying that times 25. Another child may not have seen that approach and therefore choose a calculator or paper/pencil.

Summarize: After completing this list and discussing the computational alternatives, ask children to write two different computations that would be easy to do in their head. Ask them why they are easy. Write two that would require a calculator or paper/pencil. Have them explain.

Gearing Up: After selecting the computational tool, have students actually compute the answer. Sometimes they will change their tool selection once they get started. Make note of any changes they make.

REFLECTION:

1. Give examples to demonstrate the wide range of ability to mentally compute among these children.

2. Were there any computations that everyone agreed on using the same approach? If so, which ones?

3. Which computations did some people chose to do mentally while others chose a different approach? If so, which ones?

4. Make a list of the 'easy' mental computations that the children constructed. Was there a wide range of difficulty? If so, explain.

How Would You Do It?

	In your head	With a calculator	With paper/pencil
$\frac{1}{2} + \frac{1}{4}$	☐	☐	☐
$1 - \frac{1}{3}$	☐	☐	☐
$\frac{3}{4} + \frac{3}{4}$	☐	☐	☐
$\frac{1}{5} + \frac{1}{6}$	☐	☐	☐
$\frac{1}{2} + \frac{5}{6}$	☐	☐	☐
$1\frac{1}{2} + 2\frac{3}{4}$	☐	☐	☐
$2 - \frac{3}{4}$	☐	☐	☐
$\frac{1}{2} - \frac{1}{3}$	☐	☐	☐

Follow Up

▼ Write a computation YOU would solve with a calculator _____

▼ Write a computation YOU would solve mentally _____

▼ Write a computation YOU would solve with paper/pencil _____

How would you do it? (Fractions)

Objective: Encourage wise use of computational alternatives.

GETTING READY:

How would you do it? (Fractions) parallels *How would you do it? (Whole numbers)*. It encourages students to think about doing computations with computations mentally and to reflect on appropriate computational alternatives. You may make a copy for each child, or make a transparency and use it to guide a group activity. We prefer to engage students in discussions on "How would you do it?" and learn why they decided to choose a particular approach. Calculators and paper and pencil may also be available.

Launch: Make sure children recognize the choices, namely—mental (in your head), calculator or written (paper and pencil).

Instruct: Reveal one computation at a time and ask students to tell the strategy they would use. Ask them to explain why they chose that strategy. Skip any fractional computations that you think are inappropriate for your children.

Encourage children to tell how not only what computational approach but how they would do the computation, as their approaches may be different. For example, we have found some students have a visual model of 1 – 1/3 (a whole pizza with one-third missing) and conclude the result is 2/3.

Summarize: After completing this list and discussing the computational alternatives, ask children to write two different computations with fractions that would be easy to do in their head. Ask them why they are easy. Write two that would require a calculator or paper/pencil. Have them explain.

Gearing Up: After selecting the computational tool, have students actually compute the answer. Sometimes they will change their tool selection once they get started. Make note of any changes they make.

REFLECTION:

1. We have found that very rarely do children choose to use a calculator to compute fractions. Did any of the children choose to use a calculator?

2. Were there any computations that everyone agreed on using the same approach? If so, which ones?

3. Which computations did some people chose to do mentally while others chose a different approach? If so, which ones?

4. Make a list of the fractional computations that the children constructed to do mentally. Was there a wide range of difficulty? If so, which do you think would be easy? difficult?

Name: _____

Class: _____

Zeros Count

▼ Use your to find the product:

8 × 10 = _____

- How many 0's in 10? _____
- How many 0's in the product? _____

36 × 100 = _____

- How many 0's in 100? _____
- How many 0's in the product? _____

290 × 1000 = _____

- How many 0's in 1000? _____
- How many 0's in the product? _____ Why?

▼ Complete this multiplication table. Use your to check your answers.

×	10	100	1000
7			
14		1400	
28			28000
240			
989			

Zeros Count

Objective: Discover the patterns that result when multiples of ten are multiplied (that we can state a rule: ignore trailing zeros, then affix them later).

GETTING READY:

Have copies of *Zeros Count* and calculators for the students. Of course, students do not actually need calculators. They could discover these patterns by doing paper and pencil multiplication repeatedly. But you want them to concentrate on the patterns and not be too involved in the procedure of multiplying.

The purpose of this activity is for you to work closely with some students to observe how they approach a guided discovery activity. It is better if they do not already know the rule for multiplying multiples of ten (otherwise there is nothing to discover).

Launch: Tell the students there is a short way (other than using a calculator) to find the product of two numbers when one or more is a multiple of ten. For example, you can quickly look at 320 x 100 and know that it is 32 000. (Let the students find this product on their calculators to verify the answer.) Challenge them by asking for two other numbers that both end in trailing zeros and showing that you know the product. Their job is to solve problems to discover the pattern in the answers that reveals the shortcut.

Investigate: Have the students do the page and encourage them to talk aloud with each other and with you as they do it. Encourage them to set additional problems for each other as they work down the page (one student states a problem, the second student predicts the answer, and the first student checks by using a calculator). Also, encourage them to explain their thinking as they predict each product. Although students may believe they've found the pattern after just the first two exercises, they may find they were wrong when they try 290 x 1000 because this problem requires noticing the zeros on both factors, rather than just one.

Summarize: See if the students can state the rule in their own words. Let them check their conjecture with some other numbers.

Gearing Down: Work only with single digit (or two-digit) numbers times a multiple of ten (e.g., 3 x 100, 5 x 1000, 23 x 100).

Gearing Up: Encourage students to find a rule for multiplying when *both numbers* have trailing zeros, but neither number is 10, 100, or 1000, etc. (For example, 340 x 20, 180 x 200, etc.)

REFLECTION:

1. What do you think students would have done without the structure of this sheet?

2. Can you think of other rules that children could discover by similar guidance?

3. Did the students "prove the rule" or were they convinced by examples only?

Name: _____

Class: _____

Plug-in Puzzles

▼ Use these decimal fractions to fill in the blanks.

8.3	4.2	5.5	3.1	7.6	6.7

Do each multiplication or division. In the division problems, divide to the hundredths place. Sum the four answers.

____ × ____ = ☐

____ ÷ 5 = ☐

____ × ____ = ☐

____ ÷ 3 = ☐

Total ☐

- Can you get a total greater than 50?
- Can you get one greater than 100?
- What is the largest total you can get?

▼ Arrange these four decimals in the blanks so that the sentence is true. (Remember to do the parts in the parentheses first.)

5.13	4.24	3.84	3.16

$$\left(\underline{} \times 5\right) + \underline{} = \left(4 \times \underline{}\right) + \underline{}$$

▼ Pick the two decimals from those listed that will make the sentence true.

21.21	42.42	36.36	63.63	27.27

$$\left(\underline{} \div 7\right) \times 8 = \left(\underline{} \div 9\right) \times 6$$

Objective: Develop decimal number sense.

GETTING READY:

Prepare a copy of *Plug in Puzzles* for each student (or each pair of students) and provide additional paper for computation and recording purposes. If students work in pairs, they should talk with each other about their strategies for arranging the numbers and they are likely to place numbers more thoughtfully. You could give students a pile of 1-inch paper squares on which the numbers for the challenge can be written. Then they can try various arrangements of the numbers on the sheet without erasing and rewriting. You may choose to have students use a calculator with this worksheet. Then they can focus all their attention on estimating, predicting, and problem solving rather than on laboriously calculating and recalculating.

Launch: Explain that the goal of the sheet is to figure out how to predict what numbers should go in certain spots. Encourage students to "avoid work" by thinking hard, rather than computing hard! Also, point out that keeping track of the arrangements you try, and their result, may be an important key to observing patterns and identifying a "winning strategy."

Investigate: Circulate as students are working. Encourage them to talk about their thinking and to explain their rationale for placing numbers in certain places. Remind them to keep records of what they try and to use earlier guesses to help improve their later choices.

Summarize: Bring the class back together and ask students to report back. Encourage talk not only about the "answers" to the exercises, but (more importantly) about observations that students made. Emphasize explaining "why."

Gearing Down: Using a calculator helps bring these problems within reach of more students.

Gearing Up: Encourage students to generalize. What strategies could a player use in the first problem, no matter what decimals were involved, in order to create the largest (or smallest) possible sum? Challenge students to make up their own puzzles of this type and to exchange with others.

REFLECTION:

1. Which students were able to use estimation skills successfully? Which students seemed to work randomly, simply using trial and error?

2. What did you learn about students' thinking from observing and talking with them and from their reporting back?

3. How appropriate was this sheet for the students? Is this something you might use someday with your own students? How might you modify it?

Decimal Maze

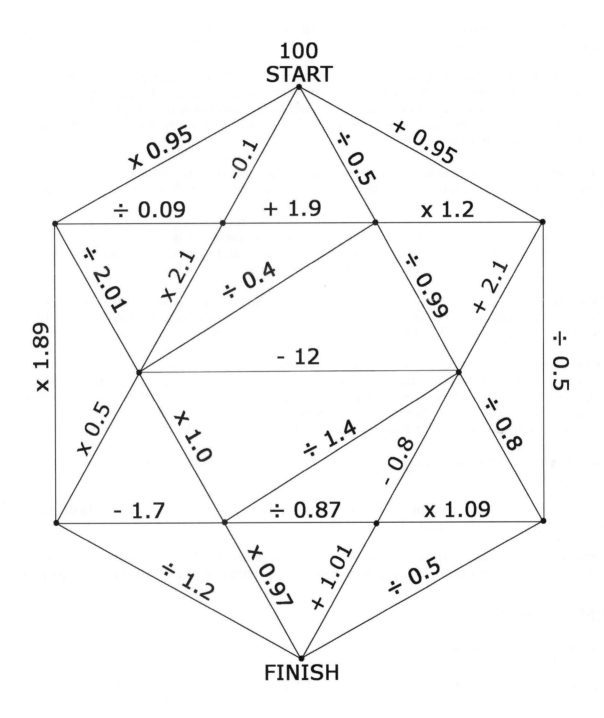

100
START

× 0.95   − 0.1   ÷ 0.5   + 0.95

÷ 0.09   + 1.9   × 1.2

÷ 2.01   × 2.1   ÷ 0.4   ÷ 0.99   + 2.1

× 1.89   − 12   ÷ 0.5

× 0.5   × 1.0   ÷ 1.4   − 0.8   ÷ 0.8

− 1.7   ÷ 0.87   × 1.09

÷ 1.2   × 0.97   + 1.01   ÷ 0.5

FINISH

Decimal Maze

Objective: Use estimation to make initial decisions and then use a calculator when it is helpful to determine a final exact result.

Getting Ready: Students will need a calculator, pencil, and *Decimal Maze* sheet. Students need to be fluent with basic facts. It is also important for students to recognize how factors between 0 and 1 as well as different addends impact results. For example, if a number N is multiplied by 0.9 how will that result compare to the result when 0.9 is added to N? In other words, how does 0.9N compare to 0.9 + N? (See launch below.)

Launch: Review with students what happens when you add, subtract, multiply, or divide by a decimal. Have the students solve the following examples, mentally or with a calculator, then generalize the results.

10 + 0.5 = 10.5	When adding a decimal, the result is larger.
10 – 0.5 = 9.5	When subtracting a decimal, the result is smaller.
10 x 0.5 = 5	When multiplying by a decimal, the result is smaller
10 ÷ 0.5 = 20	When dividing by a decimal, the result is larger.

Investigate: The goal is to trace a path from the Start to the Finish and produce the highest result that you can. Start with 100 and decide whether to multiply it by 0.95, subtract 0.1, divide by 0.5 or add 0.95. The path can NOT be retraced and you must always move in a horizontal or downward path.

Once a path is started, ask students to either mentally compute or estimate a result each time they come to a decision point. Then trace an entire path that yields the greatest result. After an entire path has been traced on the Maze, have them use a calculator when necessary to determine an exact result for the path that was traced. As students determine results ask them to tell how they decided what to do. There are at least 4 different decision points in moving from the Start to the Finish.

Summarize: Have students share strategies and final results. See if they can determine the greatest possible result.

Gearing Down: Have students work in pairs to complete the activity. Ask them to decide which decision points were the easiest. The hardest?

Gearing Up: Instead of trying to get the largest results at the Finish, ask students to choose a different target number and decide which path will produce a result closest to their chosen target number.

REFLECTION:

1. What kind of strategies did the students use?

2. Why did both the operation and the number need to be considered when making a decision?

Completing Patterns

Objective: Complete patterns using colors or numbers.

Getting Ready: The National Library of Virtual Manipulatives at http://nlvm.usu.edu/en/nav/index.html created at Utah State University provides a variety of interactive tools. Check the Virtual Library. There are many different tools, but this activity will focus on Color Patterns or Number Patterns that are located under Algebra and Number and Operations in Grades PK-2. A calculator, paper, and crayons may be necessary when working with Color or Number Patterns.

Launch:
Review the definition of a pattern and have students share examples of patterns they can see in the room.

Investigate:
Have students open either the Color Pattern manipulative or the Number Pattern manipulative. Click on Create a New Pattern. Students should use words to describe the pattern, then complete the pattern. Once they are satisfied, they can click Check Answer to see if they are correct.

Summarize:
Encourage children to label each pattern with the "rule". Ex. Red, red, blue (AAB); multiply by 9.

Gearing Down: Use only Color Patterns. Provide prompts if the pattern completion is incorrect and the students can't figure out what is wrong.

Gearing Up: Use both Color Patterns and Number Patterns. Encourage students to use paper and crayons to make another pattern with the same rule as one on the screen.

REFLECTION:

1. How did the children like completing patterns on the computer?

2. What is one advantage of completing patterns on the computer? What is one disadvantage?

MAKE ME DIFFERENT

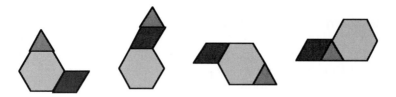

Objective: To make different shapes from the same pieces.

Getting Ready: You will need a computer with access to the National Library of Virtual Manipulatives for Interactive Mathematics (http://nlvm.usu.edu/en/nav/index.html). Go to the Virtual Library, Geometry in Grades PK-2, Pattern Blocks. After children have used pattern blocks, let them use the virtual ones. First, let children freely make designs or pictures. In so doing they need to become familiar with sliding and rotating the shapes, and putting two shapes next to each other.

Launch: Model one of the activities with the children and then let them work.

Investigate:
Activity One (for pairs of children).
One child should make a "picture" using two shapes. The second child should then copy that shape. Then the second child can add a shape to his or her picture and the first child should do the same. Have the children tell what their picture looks like.
Activity Two (for pairs of children).
The first child makes a "picture" using two shapes but doesn't show it to the second child. Instead, the first child tells the other child which two shapes were used. The second child uses these two shapes to make a "picture." Then, they look to see if they made the same or different pictures.
Activity Three (for individual child).
See how many different "pictures" a child can make using two shapes. Since there are an infinite number, you may want to impose some rules such as sides must match. Then, try three shapes.

Summarize: Since children may be working on this at different times (depending upon how many computers are available), you will want to talk with the pairs to have them tell what they did. You may want to print the work of the individual children in Activity Three, especially as they work on three or more shapes. You could post the results with a heading like, "Look what I made with these three shapes."

REFLECTION:

1. Which children liked using the computer and pattern blocks? Why do you think that they did? What is one advantage of using the pattern blocks on the computer? What is a disadvantage?

2. Can you think of questions to ask children as they are working with the pattern blocks? What questions would help them extend their geometric knowledge? What questions could you ask to encourage a child?

Build a Graph

Grades K–8

Objective: Using graphing software to examine the shape of data.

Getting Ready: You will need a piece of graphing software. Several are available that are designed specifically for elementary and middle school students. For example, *The Graph Club*, by Tom Snyder Productions is appropriate for elementary students. It allows students to enter data and display them using a bar, picture, or circle graph.

Launch: Have students think of a question that can be answered by collecting data and collect it. For ideas, see *Let's Find Out*, with In the Classroom Lessons.

Investigate: Have students enter the data into the computer. Then have them use the software to display and print that same data in a variety of ways. For example, change from a picture graph to a circle graph or change the scale on the bar graph or picture graph. Print a variety of graphic displays for students to examine.

Summarize: Have students analyze the various graphic displays and discuss the shape of data. Point out how some representations better communicate or display trends in the data than others. Encourage students to select a particular display and explain why it is effective or ineffective.

Gearing Down: Keep your number of data categories small (2 or 3). Have students compare just two representations.

Gearing Up: Have students also create graphs by hand and compare them with the ones created with the software.

REFLECTION:

1. What insights did students gain about graphs after participating in this activity? Were any misconceptions evident? What experiences would you provide next for these students?

2. How did the use of the computer software enhance or improve the activity?

Build a Spinner

Objective: Determining the likelihood of events.

Getting Ready: You will need a probability simulator. For example, the software program, *Probability Toolkit,* is published by Ventura Educational Systems, Grover Beach, California. This program simulates the flipping of two-color counters, rolling dice, drawing marbles from a jar, drawing cards, drawing random numbers, and spinning spinners. It also can graph the results. If simulation software is not available, a simple spinner simulator may be found at the following Web site: http://www.shodor.org/interactivate/activities/spinner/index.html

Launch: Use the technology available to display a spinner that is divided into four equal parts. Talk about the possible outcomes and have students predict which outcome will occur most. Encouraging students to explain their predictions will allow you to assess their prior knowledge concerning probability.

Investigate: Have students spin the four-part spinner 20 times. Examine the results displayed on the computer. Compare their predictions with the actual results. Repeat the experiment, spinning 50 or 100 times. Discuss those results. Build a spinner that is not divided into equal parts. For example, it could be divided into two-fourths and one-half. Repeat the predicting and experimenting used with the first spinner.

Summarize: Ask: If these spinners were used in a game, which ones would be fair to each player? Why or why not? Do students notice that unless the spinner is divided into equal parts, it is not fair? Do students notice the actual results are closer to the theoretical probability when there is a larger number of trials?

Gearing Down: Use a spinner divided into halves or thirds. When designing an unfair spinner, make one part much larger than the others. Limit the activity to simply predicting, experimenting, and examining results.

Gearing Up: Students in grades 5–8 can calculate the theoretical probability before conducting each experiment, then compare to the actual results. Introduce the concept that the more trials that occur, the closer the actual results will be to the theoretical probability. Have students design their own spinners and experiments. Have students develop and conduct another simulation using materials other than spinners.

REFLECTION:

1. What insights did students gain about probability after participating in this activity? Were any misconceptions evident? What experiences would you provide next for these students?

2. How did the use of the computer simulation enhance or improve the activity?

Name: _____

Class: _____

Divisibility Discovery

▼ Use your [calculator]. Fill in the chart and look for patterns.

Number	Divisible by 3?	Divisible by 9?	Sum of digits	Sum divisible by 3?	Sum divisible by 9?
456	yes	no	4 + 5 + 6 = 15	yes	no
891					
892					
514					
37					
78					
79					
1357					
1358					
1359					
1360					
1361					
1362					

▼ What do you think?

- A number is divisible by 3.
  Is it always divisible by 9?

- A number is divisible by 9.
  Is it always divisible by 3?

- What does the sum of the digits tell you?

- What did you notice about the sequence of
  numbers 1357, 1358, 1359, . . . 1362?

Divisibility Discovery

Objective: Discover divisibility rules for 3 and 9.

Getting Ready: Have copies of *Divisibility Discovery* and calculators for the students. Calculators with integer division work best because whole number remainders are given. Of course, students do not need calculators. They could do the division by paper or pencil, but you want them to concentrate on the patterns and not be too involved in the procedure of dividing.

The purpose of this activity for you is to work closely with a couple of students to observe how they approach a guided discovery activity. You should try it first, thinking about what you did and why it is set up as it is. Choose two or three students to do this so you can observe and talk with them. It is better if they do not know the divisibility test for 3 and 9 (otherwise, there is nothing to discover).

Launch: Tell the students that there is a short way (other than using a calculator) to find out whether a number is divisible by 9. For example, you can quickly look at 2,346,587 (practice a few of these) and know it is not divisible by 9. Their task is to make a conjecture about the rule for 9 and for 3 so they can also do this.

Investigate: Have the students do the page, discuss what patterns they see in the chart. If the students have not seen patterns, give them a few more numbers to add to the chart. The questions at the end may also give hints about the conjectures.

Summarize: See if the students can make a conjecture in their own words. Let them check their conjectures with some other numbers.

Gearing down: Only work with nines.

Gearing up: Have students model numbers with base-ten blocks to see if they can justify the rule. Have the students explore divisibility by 11.

REFLECTION:

1. What do you think students would have done without the structure of this sheet?

2. Can you think of other rules that children could discover by similar guidance?

3. Did the students "prove the rule" or were they convinced by examples only?

Helping Children Learn: In the Classroom Lessons Content

These lesson experiences allow you to teach mathematics lessons to individuals, small groups, or a whole class of students. This includes planning, teaching, and reflecting on the lessons. The lessons are classified into three grade level bands. Specific grade level suggestions may be found on each lesson plan. You will need to be responsive to the children's level of ability. Suggestions for gearing the lessons up and down are provided.

You may use the Lesson Plan Cover Sheet and one of the Lesson Plan Templates found at the beginning of this section to create your lesson plan. An After-Teaching Reflection Page is included at the beginning of this section. You may copy it and use the questions to reflect on your own performance after using one of these lessons.

In the Classroom Lessons by Topic

Key Topics	Lesson	K–2	3–5	6–8	Page
Lesson Plan Materials	Lesson Plan Cover Sheet	X	X	X	192
	Lesson Participant Summary	X	X	X	193
	Investigative Lesson Template	X	X	X	194
	Direct Instruction Lesson Template	X	X	X	195
	Exploration Lesson Template	X	X	X	196
	After-Teaching Reflection Sheet	X	X	X	197
	After-Teaching Feedback Sheet	X	X	X	198
1. Issues, Trends, Principles					
2. Learning	Different Kinds of Four-Sided Figures		X		199–200
	Patterns with Blocks		X		201–202
3. Teaching, Planning, Adapting					
4. Assessing, Recording, Reporting	See also pp. 67–68	X			
5. Process Standards					
6. Problem Solving	Composing Fractions		X		203–204
7. Number Sense, Prenumber	Who am I?	X	X		205–206
	Alike-and-Difference Trains	X	X		207–208
	Hunting for Numbers	X	X		209–210
	Skip Counting	X	X		211–212
	See also pp. 159–164				

IN THE CLASSROOM LESSONS BY TOPIC (continued)

Key Topics	Lesson	K–2	3–5	6–8	Page
7. Number Sense, Prenumber	Decide If It's Up or Down See also pp. 159–164	X	X		213–214
8. Place Value	Counting on a Hundreds Chart Finding Tens The Power of 10 on the Thousand Chart Thousands Chart See also pp. 165–168	X X	X X X	X	215–216 217–218 219–220 221
9. Basic Facts	Literature Context for Facts Dot Sticks Rectangles and More Rectangles See also pp. 159–162, 211–212, 273–274	X X X	X X	X X	222 223–224 225–226
10. Computational Alternatives	Finding 100 How Could It Happen? Sorting Products See also pp. 173–176, 209–210, 235–237	X	X X	X	227–228 229–230 231–232
11. Whole Number Operations	Number Net Look for Patterns See also pp. 173–174	 X	X	X	233–234 235–237
12. Fractions, Decimals	Fraction Strips Comparing Models See also pp. 175–176, 203–204	 X	X X	X	238–240 241–242
13. Ratio, Proportion, Percent	Know Your Coins		X	X	243–244
14. Patterns, Algebra	Balance Me In-Out Machine ✓ See also pp. 187–188, 201, 211–212, 215–216, 219–220, 235–237, 243–244	X	X X		245–246 247–248
15. Geometry	Solid Activities ✗ Gumdrops and Toothpicks ✓ Show My Sides ✓ See also pp. 199–200	X	X X	X X X	249–250 251–252 253–254

16. Measurement	Measuring Length with Arbitrary Units
	Comparing Height and Circumference
	How are We Alike? Different?
	Make Two of Me!
	What is the Connection Between
	  Volume and Surface Area?
	What is the Connection Between
	  Perimeter and Height?
	See also pp. 201–202, 243–244
		X	
			X
				
				X
				X
				X
				
				X
					255–256
					257–258
					259–260
					261–262
					263–264
					
					265–266

IN THE CLASSROOM LESSONS BY TOPIC (continued)

Key Topics	Lesson	K–2	3–5	6–8	Page
17. Data, Statistics, Probability	Let's Find Out	X	X	X	267–268
	Peanuts			X	269–270
	What are the Chances?	X	X		271–272
	Rolling and Recording	X	X		273–274
	Can You Make Predictions?		X	X	275–276
18. Number Theory	What Do You See in Me?		X	X	277–278
	Do You Believe That?			X	279–280

Lesson Plan Cover Sheet

Name_____

School   Grade   Cooperating Teacher

Lesson Topic/Title/Theme

Date to be Taught   Estimated Time (minutes)

Lesson Type: (Check one) ____ Investigative ____ Direct Instruction ____ Exploration

Lesson Prerequisites and Preassessment of students:

Lesson Objective(s):

District Outcome(s) and/or State/National Standard(s):

Assessment:

Adaptations:

    Gearing Up:

    Gearing Down:

Materials/Special arrangements:

References:

Lesson Participant Summary

Provide a brief description of the students you taught. To maintain confidentiality, use only first names if you refer to specific children.

1. How many students participated in your lesson?

2. Describe the grade level, average age, and developmental characteristics of the students as a group.

3. Discuss the diversity of the group. For example, describe the number of students by gender, SES, ability, ethnicity, language, special needs, or any other characteristic that may impact participation in your lesson.

4. How did the student characteristics described above affect the planning and delivery of your lesson? What adaptations did you make? What else could you have done?

Investigative Lesson Plan Outline

I. Launch

II. Investigate

III. Summarize

Direct Instruction Lesson Plan Outline

I. Launch

II. Instruct

III. Summarize

Exploration Lesson Plan Outline

I. Launch

II. Explore

III. Summarize

After-Teaching Reflection

Respond to the following after teaching the lesson but, *before* conferencing with the classroom teacher or supervisor.

1. Describe at least two things that went well during the lesson.

2. Describe one thing that went "differently" than you expected (if applicable).

3. How successful were students in achieving the objectives of the lesson? How do you know? Include data to support your conclusion.

4. Describe any changes you'd consider if you were to teach this again.

5. As a result of teaching this lesson, and feedback you received from the teacher and/or students, what have you learned that will help you?

After-Teaching Feedback

This form may be completed by a cooperating teacher or supervisor who observes a lesson.

Person Teaching Lesson: _____ Date: _____

Person Observing Lesson: _____

Please mark an assessment of each characteristic of the lesson as:
4 = Excellent   3 = Satisfactory   2 = Needs Improvement   1 = Unsatisfactory   NA = Not Observed

1. The student showed <u>independence in planning</u> this lesson.

   Comments:

                                              4 3 2 1 NA

2. The student was <u>well prepared</u>. They had all materials ready on time and put them away at the end. Materials were effectively used and managed.

   Comments:

                                              4 3 2 1 NA

3. The student used <u>effective pacing</u> and made efficient use of the time given.

   Comments:

                                              4 3 2 1 NA

4. The student provided <u>clear directions</u> and clear and accurate instruction.

   Comments:

                                              4 3 2 1 NA

5. The student <u>interacted with</u> and <u>managed</u> the <u>class</u> confidently and effectively.

   Comments:

                                              4 3 2 1 NA

6. Overall Rating of the Lesson   4 3 2 1 NA

Please attach additional comments regarding strengths of the lesson or goals for improvement.

Name: _____

Class: _____

Different Kinds of Four-sided Figures

Objective: To classify four-sided figures.

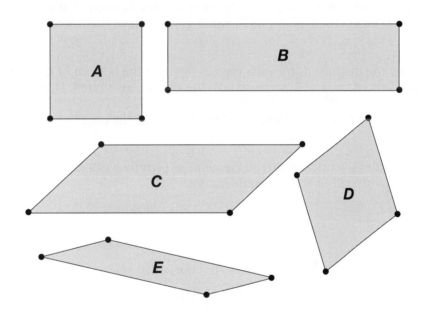

▼ Write the letters of the figures that are:

- Squares _____

- Rectangles _____

- Parallelograms _____

- Regular polygons _____

- Equilateral quadrilaterals _____

Different Kinds of Four-sided Figures

Objective: To classify four-sided figures.

Getting Ready: You will need a copy of *Different Kinds of Four-sided Figures* for each student. A resource book or mathematics textbook that includes definitions and illustrations for the five types of figures on the page would be helpful to have available.

Launch: Begin by directing the students' attention to the five figures on the sheet. Ask students to name any of the figures they can. Hopefully, more than one name will be used. Ask students if any of the figures can have more than one name. Ask them to give some examples.

Investigate: Give students time to individually complete the bottom of the page. Then have them compare answers and discuss their solutions in small groups. Have them work through any disagreements.

Summarize: Review the definitions for each type of figure at the bottom of the page. Ask students if they wish to change any of their answers, based on the definitions shared. Discuss final results.

Gearing Down: Begin by reviewing the terms at the bottom of the page before having students complete their sheets.

Gearing Up: Have students work together to create their own four-sided figures and have them challenge other pairs to identify all of their possible names.

REFLECTION:

1. How accurate were the students the first time they completed their sheets? Which terms did they understand and which ones needed clarification?

2. How appropriate was this activity for the students? Is this something you might like to do some day with your own students? Would you make any changes?

Patterns with Blocks

▼ Each of these boxes holds 16 blocks. Record the length, width, height, and volume (number of blocks) in the table.

 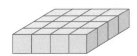  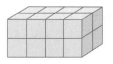

Length	Width	Height	Volume

▼ Take 24 blocks. Estimate how many different boxes you can make. _____

▼ Make as many different boxes as you can. Record the length, width, height, and volume in the table. How many different boxes did you make? _____

Length	Width	Height	Volume

▼ You have four piles of blocks. You must use all the blocks in a pile to make boxes.

Pile A has 16 blocks.   Pile B has 25 blocks.

Pile C has 36 blocks.   Pile D has 50 blocks.

   • Which pile of blocks would let you build the most different boxes. Why?

   • Which pile would let you build the fewest different boxes? Why?

▼ Build the boxes, fill in a table, and see if you are right. What did you find out?

▼ What patterns do you see in your tables?

Patterns with Blocks

Grades: 3–5

Objective: Finding volume of solids and realizing that different dimensions can produce the same volume.

Getting Ready: You'll need a copy of *Patterns with Blocks* and about 30 blocks per group.

Launch: Ask a child to use exactly 16 cubes to 'build' a box.

Investigate: After their box is built, ask if they can build a different box with 16 other cubes. Ask them to make a list of the dimensions (length, width, and height) of all the boxes that are built for a given number of cubes. If they have not built at least 4 different boxes, show them the *Patterns with Blocks* for some clues. Repeat activity with 24 cubes.

Summarize: Examine the list of dimensions for the various boxes. See if the students can identify the formula of length x width x height = volume. Discuss whether 16, 25, 36, or 50 blocks would make the most boxes. Encourage students to predict, then build to find out.

Gearing Down: Guide students to build a box by building one layer at a time. Provide some small rectangular prism containers and have students fill the boxes with cubes.

Gearing Up: Ask students to make a drawing of their box(es) with isometric paper. Then have them give their drawing to another child and see if that child can use the drawing to make the same box.

REFLECTION:

1. Did you notice any pattern in the boxes being built? (i.e., Was a three dimension box (2 x 2 x 4) built before a two dimensional (1 x 4 x 4 or 1 x 2 x 8) box?)

2. Did children realize that two of the pictured boxes are the same box, just in a different position? Tell why it is important for children to recognize the same figure in different positions.

3. Would it make 'sense' to try this activity with children if blocks were not available? Tell why?

4. When children decided which pile (A, B, C, or D) would build the most (fewest) different, did any of them connect multiplication (factors) to their answer? Explain.

Composing Fractions

Player 2

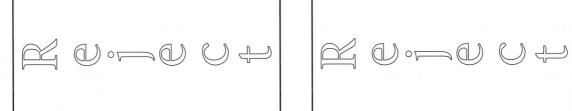

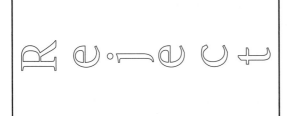

Player 1

Composing Fractions

Objective: Use logical reasoning to construct a fraction larger than that of your opponent.

Getting ready: Two people play this game. For each pair of opponents you need two game boards (on the following page), and two sets of 1-9 numeral cards (Appendix A). A calculator and fraction strips (see Fraction Strips Lesson) should be available to help compare the fractions.

RULES AND PROCEDURES:

You may choose to play this game for a given period of time, or until you have played a given number of rounds (for example, 10 rounds). Decide this before starting.

Players take turns drawing four cards. Each time s/he draws, s/he places the card that is drawn on one of his/her four boxes, according to the following rules:

- Once you place a number in a box, you may not remove it.
- The numbers in the two boxes that are aligned in fraction form will represent a fraction.
- The extra two boxes are reject boxes. They are places where you can place numbers that you don't want to use for your fraction.
- When you have each placed your numbers (after each player has had 4 draws), you will compare your fractions. The larger fraction wins the round.

Gearing Down: Have dice (or a simple spinner) available so that the students can play with smaller and fewer numbers (1-6) to compose their fractions. You might also provide students with fraction strips they can use to visually compare the size of their fractions. They can use a calculator to divide the numerator by the denominator, then compare the decimals, or you could help them to draw pictures to help with comparisons.

Gearing Up: Require students to predict which fraction is largest and explain their thinking before using a calculator or fraction strips. Require students to draw a picture of each of their fractions, using a specified shape (circle, rectangle, square) as the whole. Require the students to write a number sentence for each round, using inequality signs to compare their fractions.

REFLECTION:

1. What logical reasoning did the students use in deciding on a winning strategy?

2. What difficulties did students have in comparing or representing fractions? Were they able to draw and shade regions that were accurate representations of fractions?

3. How appropriate was this game for this level of students?

Who Am I?

■ LBS	■ SBS	▼ LBT	▲ SBT
□ LWS	□ SWS	△ LWT	△ SWT
■ LGS	■ SGS	▲ LGT	▲ SGT
⬟ LBP	⬟ SBP	● LBC	● SBC
⬠ LWP	⬠ SWP	○ LWC	○ SWC
⬟ LGP	⬟ SGP	● LGC	● SGC

▼ Match me with the attribute blocks shown here:

A. I have three sides.
I am black.
I am large.

Who am I? _____

B. I am black or white.
I have three sides.
I am not large.

Who am I? _____

C. I am not black.
I am not white.
I have five sides.
I am small.

Who am I? _____

D. I am not large.
I have more than
four sides.
I am gray.

Who am I? _____

• Which clues describe more than one piece? _____

• Which clues describe only one piece? _____

▼ Your turn:

Play "Who Am I?" with a partner.

Who am I?

Objective: Using attribute pieces to develop classification and reasoning.

Getting Ready: *Who am I?* requires the use of attribute or logic pieces. A master for the attribute pieces is provided in Appendix A. Use the master to copy the pieces on heavy paper and cut them out. This set of 20 pieces will serve one child or a group of 2–4 children. If you laminate the heavy paper before cutting out the pieces, the set will last much longer. Store in zip-lock bag. If you use a commercial set of attribute pieces, you will need to change the color attributes described on *Who am I?*.

Launch: Ask a child to choose a piece and describe it to you, or to other members of the group. Is their description complete? (i.e., Did they characterize the shape, color and size?) Once vocabulary is established to describe the pieces (i.e., pentagon [or five sided piece], square and circle), then you are ready for *Who am I?*. The vocabulary can be refined during the activity, so the main focus at this stage is to begin developing the language through oral communication.

Investigate: Ask children to try each of the activities, A, B, C, and D. Help a child distinguish between "AND" and "OR" by asking for a piece to that is "black and square" and later for a piece that is "black or square."

Summarize: Often young children associate only numbers with mathematics. Yet logical thinking and classification are essential in learning about numbers. As you wrap up the lesson, ask the children whether they thought they were doing mathematics when they were working with the attribute pieces.

Gearing Down: Narrow your set of attribute pieces to two attributes by using only the large pieces or the small pieces. Children will describe each piece by its shape and color.

Gearing Up: Play *Who am I?* where one child chooses a piece (but does NOT touch or remove it from the set of attribute pieces) to describe to a partner. The partner has to use the clues given to find the piece that was chosen.

REFLECTION:

1. Were there any patterns in the children's descriptions of attributes? i.e. Did the children omit any attributes? Did they focus on a particular attribute, such as color first? Were they equally fluent with the geometric names of square, circle and pentagon?

2. Were the statements "I am large." and "I am not large." equally understood? If not, describe how you helped children clarify this idea. Did the child seem to understand the use of "AND" when describing characteristics of an attribute piece? Was the term "OR" understood?

3. If they provided some clues about what they think is mathematics, describe. If they did not think they were doing mathematics, discuss how you could help them broaden their idea of what mathematics includes.

Alike-and-Difference Trains?

Each car in a train is like the car it follows in two ways, *or* it is different from the car it follows in two ways.

▼ Find the alike-and-difference pattern in each train, and describe the missing car:

Train A   ▲   ▲   ▲   ▼   △   ___

Train B   ▲   ⬟   ⬠   ●   ○   ___

Train C   •   ○   ___   ▼   ●   ⬠

Train D   •   △   ⬠   ●   ○   ___

- Which of these are one-difference trains? _____

- Which of these are two-difference trains? _____

▼ Your turn:

- Begin with ■. Make a train (with at least six cars) in which each car has exactly one attribute different from the car it follows. Compare your train with someone's train. Are they the same?

- Begin with ■. Make a train (with at least six cars) in which each car has exactly one attribute the same as the car it follows. Compare your train with a classmate's train. Tell how they are alike.

Alike-and-Difference Trains

Objective: Using attribute pieces to recognize patterns and identify relationships.

Getting Ready: *Alike-and-Difference Trains* requires the use of attribute or logic pieces. A master for this activity is provided in Appendix A. Use the master to copy the pieces on heavy paper and cut them out. This set of 20 pieces will serve one child or a group of 2-4 children. If you laminate the heavy paper before cutting out the pieces, the set will last much longer. Store in zip-lock bag. If you use a commercial set of attribute pieces, you will need to change the color attributes described on *Alike-and-Difference Trains*.

Launch: Do *Who am I?* first. You may need to model thinking aloud about the attributes to help children understand the activity. They need to be know that shape, color and size are involved and be able to use each of these attributes to describe any piece.

Investigate: The alike and difference patterns challenge students to decide exactly how many attributes are changing from one car to another. These trains provide visual patterns to promote logical thinking. Focus on one train (Train A) and ask a child to decide what car goes next, and to explain their thinking. As children find the next car in the train they may realize that more than one 'right' answer exists. If this doesn't happen, ask "Can you find another car that could go here?"

Summarize: Discuss the trains built by the children. Have them share which were easiest and most difficult.

Gearing Down: To help children who have difficulty with so many pieces, use a reduced set of pieces (i.e., no gray or omit one shape).

Gearing Up: Use the 'Your turn' to encourage children to build a train with at least six cars that has a constant number of differences.

REFLECTION:

1. How many different correct solutions did children find for Train A? Train B?

2. Did students feel comfortable knowing that more than one correct answer exists? Why do you think some children (even adults) feel more than one right answer is unacceptable in mathematics class?

3. Did your children find one-difference trains to be the same difficulty as two-difference trains?

4. Which did your children find more difficult: Building their own train or working with a predetermined train?

Hunting for Numbers

▼ Look at this chart:

1	2	3	4	5	6	7	8	9	10
11	12	13	14	15	16	17	18	19	20
21	22	23	24	25	26	27	28	29	30
31	32	33	34	35	36	37	38	39	40
41	42	■	44	45	46	47	48	49	50
51	52	53	54	55	56	57	58	59	60
61	62	63	64	65	66	67	68	69	70
71	72	73	74	75	76	77	78	79	80
81	82	83	84	85	86	87	88	89	90
91	92	93	94	95	96	97	98	99	100

- What is hidden by the ■?
- What number is after ■?
- What number is before the ■?

▼ Put a ● on any number.
   - Begin at ●: Count forward five.
   - Begin at ● again: Count backward five.

▼ Put a ▲ on a different number.
   - Begin at ▲: Count forward five.
   - Begin at ▲ again: Count backward five.

▼ Tell about any patterns you see.

Hunting for Numbers

Objective: Using a hundred chart to recognize patterns and identify relationships.

Getting Ready: *Hunting for Numbers* requires the use of a hundred chart. The hundred chart shown goes from 1 to 100. Other charts start at 0 and go to 99. One advantage of the latter chart is that the ten digit in each row is constant, whereas in the 1 to 100 chart the tens digit always changes in the last column. Choose one of the hundred chart masters provided in Appendix A or make one from grid paper. Use this master to make at least one copy for each child and encourage children to mark on their hundred chart.

Launch: Ask a child to answer the questions regarding the number hidden by the box, after the box and before the box. Cover another number on the chart and ask similar questions, including "How did you figure out the number?"

Investigate: Have a child to choose a start number on the hundred chart and then count five forward. Ask them to count five backward from the same start number. Ask them to describe a pattern between these two numbers. When children are successful using the hundred chart to find 5 or 10 more, ask them to find 9 more or 11 more and observe their solutions. Extension questions can lead to powerful and useful patterns. For example, "What number is 10 more? Where is it located on the hundred chart? How can you find a number 10 more? 10 less?"

Summarize: Have students describe the patterns they found on the chart and explain how those patterns can be used to find numbers more or less than the original number.

Gearing Down: Cover the bottom half of the chart and use only 1–50. Work with only 1 or 10 more or less.

Gearing Up: Encourage students to continue the activity using a more difficult chart from Appendix B such as the triangular chart, the thousandths chart, or the thousands chart.

REFLECTION:

1. What was easier for a child to find: the missing number that was covered on the hundred chart, the number before, or the number after?

2. At first when asked to find a number 10 more, children will start at the covered number and count ten more. After doing this a few times, they will find shortcuts to find numbers 10 more. Try this with a child and report how many times they count 10 more before finding a shortcut. Describe what happened.

3. Describe some of the strategies children used to find numbers on the chart.

Skip Counting

▼ Use your calculator and a hundred chart to count.

1	2	3	4	5	6	7	8	9	10
11	12	13	14	15	16	17	18	19	20
21	22	23	24	25	26	27	28	29	30
31	32	33	34	35	36	37	38	39	40
41	42	43	44	45	46	47	48	49	50
51	52	53	54	55	56	57	58	59	60
61	62	63	64	65	66	67	68	69	70
71	72	73	74	75	76	77	78	79	80
81	82	83	84	85	86	87	88	89	90
91	92	93	94	95	96	97	98	99	100

- Start at 3 and count by 3s.

- Circle every number you counted.

- Describe a pattern.

▼ Which of these numbers would be counted?

13, 51, 61, 62, 63, 100, 113

Skip Counting

Grades K–5

Objective: Using a hundred chart to skip count and identify resulting patterns.

Getting Ready: *Skip Counting* requires the use of a hundred chart. Choose one of the hundred chart masters provided in Appendix A or make one from grid paper. Use this master to make at least one copy for each child. Encourage children to write on the hundred chart as they record their skip counting.

Launch: Ask a child to count by 3's aloud. If they can do this easily, then this activity may not contribute much (besides some additional practice) to their counting skills. You could select a more difficult number.

If the child counts aloud slowly or makes errors, ask them to count by threes on the chart, and to circle or cross out each number they count, beginning with 3, 6 . . . Encourage them to look for patterns and describe any they see. For example, they may recognize the diagonal pattern. They may observe some relationships between digits, such as the far left diagonal (3, 12, 21) and notice the digits add to three (i.e., 12 => 1 + 2 = 3). After the chart is complete, encourage children to count by 3's by reading from their chart. Reading from the chart helps develop confidence and speed in counting.

Investigate: Ask children to count by 2's, 4's, or 5's, and to circle or cross out each number counted. Encourage them to look for and describe patterns that they see. Also ask them to count by a particular number by reading from their chart and visualize the patterns from the chart.

Summarize: Have children display their charts, discuss the patterns, and explain which were easiest or most difficult.

Gearing Down: Cover the lower half of the chart and use 1–50. Have the child use a marker and "jump" the marker to find the next number in the pattern.

Gearing Up: This chart goes to 100, however it could be extended. Ask children to think about where some numbers greater than 100, such as 102, 113, would go. Then ask them what column, numbers such as 161 and 201 would be found. You might also build onto *Skip Counting* with *Hunting for Numbers*, and ask them to count by ten (i.e., 83 count 10 is 93; 93 count 10 is 103, etc.).

REFLECTION:

1. Was it easier for children to count by 2, 3, 4, or 5 on the hundred chart? Explain what you observed. How many numbers did children actually count (when circling or crossing out) before they begin to observe and rely on a pattern to decide what to mark?

2. Were the patterns in the columns of the hundred-chart strong enough to support conjectures as to where column 113 goes? If not, did counting 10 more help? Were the children able to decide which of the numbers (100, 113, 161, 201) would be counted when counting by threes? Did they use the hundred chart to decide? Tell how they decided.

Decide If It's 👍 Up or 👎 Down

- Circle the 👍 if the number of dots is *more than* the number symbol.

- Circle the 👎 if the number of dots is *less than* the number symbol.

20

100

20

100

Decide If It's Up or Down

Objective: Comparing quantities with specific benchmarks.

Getting Ready: This activity doesn't focus on counting, so it is not expected or recommended that children count. A transparency can be made of *Decide If It's Up or Down* or the activity can be modeled with counters.

Launch: Place several counters (pennies, beans, or whatever) under a piece of paper or on an overhead projector but do NOT allow children to see the counters. Tell them you are going to remove the cover—allow them to see the counters—then cover them again.

"Ready, I am going to count to three and then remove the cover:

If you think there were more than 5, hold your thumb up. (Give a thumbs up signal)

If you think there were less than 5, hold your thumb down." (Give a thumbs down signal)

Now uncover the counters (or turn on the overhead) for several seconds. (You should experiment to find the optimal time to allow children to see the counters, as this will vary by grade and the number of counters displayed.) Allow children time to briefly see the counters but not long enough for the children to count, and then cover them (or turn off overhead). Ask children to show thumbs up or down. You may want to check on their ability to subsitize (instantly see how many) with small quantities, however the focus of this activity is using benchmarks to decide whether it is more or less than the benchmark number shown.

Instruct: *Decide If It's Up or Down* has four squares each containing some dots. Cover them all, and then unmask each square one at a time. Use the number beside the square as the benchmark and ask children to show thumbs up or down.

Summarize: Discuss the strategies the children used to decide if the objects were more or less than the benchmark number.

Gearing Down: Use fewer objects or counters and use the benchmarks 5 and 10.

Gearing Up: Use more objects or counters and use the benchmarks 50 and 100.

REFLECTION:

1. Did some children miss the uncovering because they were doing something else and forgot to watch when you said "Ready, 1, 2, 3"? If so, did they pay closer attention the next time when you told them you were going to uncover another square?

2. Observe to see if some children wait to show their thumb until they get clues from other children. Tell how you handled this situation.

3. If the focus is on benchmarks, why it is critical to not count but to try and grasp the 'big' number picture?

4. Name some numerical benchmarks you think are important for children to develop?

Name: _____

Class: _____

Counting on a Hundred Chart

Objective: Using a hundred chart to explore place value and pattern.

1	2	3	4	5	6	7	8	9	10
11	12	13	14	15	16	17	18	19	20
21	22	23	24	25	26	27	28	29	30
31	32	33	34	35	36	37	38	39	40
41	42	43	44	45	46	47	48	49	50
51	52	53	54	55	56	57	58	59	60
61	62	63	64	65	66	67	68	69	70
71	72	73	74	75	76	77	78	79	80
81	82	83	84	85	86	87	88	89	90
91	92	93	94	95	96	97	98	99	100

↑ Fifth column

0	1	2	3	4	5	6	7	8	9
10	11	12	13	14	15	16	17	18	19
20	21	22	23	24	25	26	27	28	29
30	31	32	33	34	35	36	37	38	39
40	41	42	43	44	45	46	47	48	49
50	51	52	53	54	55	56	57	58	59
60	61	62	63	64	65	66	67	68	69
70	71	72	73	74	75	76	77	78	79
80	81	82	83	84	85	86	87	88	89
90	91	92	93	94	95	96	97	98	99

▼ Use the hundred charts to answer these questions:
- What is alike for all the numbers in the fifth column?
- How are the numbers in the fourth and sixth columns alike? Different?
- Tell where you stop, if you start on any square in the first three rows and count forward 10 more squares.
- Start on a different square in the first three rows and count forward 10 more squares. Where did you stop?
- After you have done this several times, tell about a pattern that you found.

▼ Cut out a piece like this ⌐ and lay it on the chart.
- What numbers are covered? Tell how you found them.
- Move the piece to a different place, and tell what numbers are covered.
- Do it again with different shapes like ▭ and ▢ .

▼ Here is only a part of a hundred chart:
- Use what you know about a hundred chart to:
- Find A _____ B _____ C _____ D _____
- Tell two different ways to find C.
- Suppose 46 is replaced by N.
- Find A _____ B _____ C _____ D _____

	A
	46
B	
C	D

Counting on a Hundred Chart

Objectives: To recognize patterns.
To develop powerful counting strategies.

Getting Ready: Use either of the 100 charts shown on *In the Classroom* 8–1 (See Appendix A). Have different counters available that can be placed on the chart.

Launch: Ask children to place a counter on any number in the fifth column.
Ask them to move five places to the right.
Ask "What column is your counter in now?"

Repeat this activity—i.e., have children place their counter on the same column and everyone move the same number of spaces to the left or right. Make connections to addition or subtraction.

Ask children to place a counter on any number in the second row.
Ask them to move ten places.
Ask "Where is your counter now?"

Summarize: The first question looks for patterns involving five and ten. Since there are ten columns, and we started in the fifth column, everyone should end in the tenth column. Having children describe where they started—(25 + 5 = 30; or 35 + 5 = 40, . . .) reinforces the idea that five plus five is ten. In a similar manner, the second activity adds ten to each number, so they should end up in the cell directly below the cell they started. Thus 12 + 10 = 22 and 16 + 10 = 26, so counting on ten more is moving down one row. Recognizing and discussing these patterns can facilitate mental computations involving 5 and 10.

Gearing Down: Ask children to move their counter two places to the right. If they start on an even number, where will they land? If they start on an odd number, where will they land?

Gearing Up: Ask children to move their counter two or three rows down, and describe where they are and how much has been added. Ask children to place their counter in the fifth row, and move their counter up two or three rows. Then ask them to describe where they are and how much has been subtracted.

REFLECTION:

1. Were students able to count accurately? Did they utilize the patterns for counting by fives or tens? Describe.

2. Which chart (starting with 0 or 1) did you like best? Tell why.

3. Which chart (starting with 0 or 1) did the children prefer to use? Could you determine why?

Name: _____

Class: _____

Finding Tens

▼ Provide a pile of beans or counters.

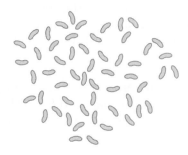

▼ Provide a pile of interlocking cubes.

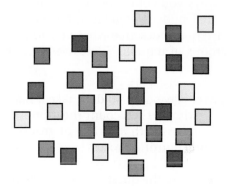

▼ Ask children to group by ten.

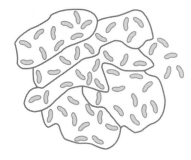

▼ Ask children to build trains with ten cubes in a train.

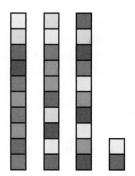

▼ Some questions to ask:
- How many beans in each group?
- How many groups of ten?
- How many beans left over?
- Which pile is easier to count?

- How many cubes in each train?
- How many trains of ten?
- How many cubes left over?
- Which group is easier to count?

Developing Representation

▼ Some questions to ask:

- How many groups (trains) do you have? _____

- How many beans (cubes) are left over? _____

Finding Tens

Objective: Group objects into groups of ten.

Getting Ready: You'll need one copy of *Finding Tens* for yourself. For each student, provide 50–99 of two kinds of counters (such as beans and connecting cubes) and paper or a chalkboard for recording results.

Launch: Show students the containers of counters and ask them to estimate how many counters are in each. Record their estimates. Take a handful of counters, estimate how many you have, and discuss different ways you could count them to find out how many. For example, you could count by ones, twos, etc. Tell students you know an even faster way to find out how many. Arrange the counters into groups of ten and describe what you found. For example, if you had 37 counters, you would say, "I have 3 groups of ten and 7 left over." Count the counters, "ten, twenty, thirty, thirty-one … thirty-seven."

Investigate: Have each student take a handful of counters and repeat the process you just modeled. Have them estimate then count the groups of ten and leftovers to find out how many. Students should repeat this process with a variety of groups. Combine the counters into a larger group and repeat the grouping and counting process.

Summarize: Use the questions on the *Finding Tens* worksheet to guide the discussion. Talk about how grouping into tens helps us quickly find out how many when we have large numbers.

Gearing Down: Reduce the number of counters students will group. Have students work together to group and count their counters.

Gearing Up: Increase the number of counters counted. If students seem to be ready, introduce a two-column place value chart with the headings tens and ones. Once the counters have been grouped, place them on the chart and write the symbols as well. If there were three groups of ten with seven left over, write a 3 in the tens column and 7 in the ones column to represent 37.

REFLECTION:

1. Were the students able to accurately count and group the counters? Describe strategies they used.

2. How comfortable were the students with making an estimate? Did the students' estimates improve as the activity was repeated?

3. What should students do next to help them develop more number sense with two-digit numbers?

The Power of 10 on the Thousand Chart

10	20	30	40	50	60	70	80	90	100
110	120	130	140	150	160	170	180	190	200
210	220	230	240	250	260	270	280	290	300
310	320	330	340	350	360	370	380	390	400
410	420	430	440	450	460	470	480	490	500
510	520	530	540	550	560	570	580	590	600
610	620	630	640	650	660	670	680	690	700
710	720	730	740	750	760	770	780	790	800
810	820	830	840	850	860	870	880	890	900
910	920	930	940	950	960	970	980	990	1000

▼ Count by 10:

- Start on any square in the first three rows.
- Count forward 10 squares, and tell where you stopped.
- Start at a different square, and count forward 10 squares.
- After you have done this several times, tell about a pattern that you found.
- Describe a quick way to count "a hundred more" on this thousand chart.

▼ Count by 100:

- Tell how you could use the thousand chart to add 300 to 240.
- Tell how you could use the thousand chart to add 290 to 240.

▼ Connect the charts:

- Tell how using the hundred chart helps you use the thousand chart.

The Power of 10 on the Thousand Chart

Objective: Using a thousand-chart to identify patterns and skip count by tens and hundreds.

Getting Ready: You will need *The Power of 10 on the Thousand Chart*. This activity extends the hundred-chart to make a thousand-chart. Instead of counting by one and ten as was done on the hundred chart, this chart facilitates counting by 10 and 100—both of which are important skills for mental computation. If you use this activity with more than one student, make a copy of the thousand-chart for each child. A master of the thousand chart may be found on the following page.

Launch: This chart is rich in patterns. Allow children some time to look at the chart and mentally explore its contents. Then ask, "Look at this chart and tell about a pattern you see." After a pattern has been described, ask, "Do you see another pattern? Tell me about it."
Continue exploring additional patterns until several have been identified and described.

Investigate: Now try the 'Count by 10' and 'Count by 100' tasks that are shown on the page.

Summarize: Ask student to describe how to find 130 more on the thousand chart. Ask, "What are the easiest numbers to add 130 to with the chart? What makes them easy? What are the hardest numbers to add 130 to with the chart? What makes them harder?"

Gearing Down: Have students color or cover the squares to keep track of their moves.

Gearing Up: Ask the students to picture the chart in their mind—but don't look at the chart. Suppose you start at 240.
    Where would you be if you went down three rows?
    Where would you be if you went two columns to the right?
    Where would you be if you went down three rows and then two columns to the right?
Try other start numbers and movements on the thousand-chart.

REFLECTION:

1. What was the first pattern the child described? Was it a pattern that you had also seen?

2. Do you think practice on the thousand-chart helps students improve their ability to mentally compute? Tell why.

3. If you asked children to find 130 more with the chart, describe some of their strategies. Summarize what they said about what makes them 'easy' and what makes them 'harder'."

Thousand Chart

10	20	30	40	50	60	70	80	90	100
110	120	130	140	150	160	170	180	190	200
210	220	230	240	250	260	270	280	290	300
310	320	330	340	350	360	370	380	390	400
410	420	430	440	450	460	470	480	490	500
510	520	530	540	550	560	570	580	590	600
610	620	630	640	650	660	670	680	690	700
710	720	730	740	750	760	770	780	790	800
810	820	830	840	850	860	870	880	890	900
910	920	930	940	950	960	970	980	990	1000

Literature Context for Facts

Objective: Use children's literature as a context for problem solving with basic operations.

Getting Ready: Find a popular trade book that would be useful as a motivator for a problem-based lesson revolving around one of the four basic operations (addition, subtraction, multiplication, or division). Identify the operation the story evokes and write a problem that you will challenge students to work on after hearing the story. Try to pose a problem that has more than one answer or several different ways to arrive at the answer. (For example, if the story is about sharing cookies such as *The Doorbell Rang* by Pat Hutchins, a good problem might be "What different sizes of groups of kids can share 12 cookies, if each kid must get the same number of cookies and no cookies can be broken or cut?")

Launch: Concentrate first on the story itself, by reading the book aloud to the students and taking time to enjoy the story. Let the children respond personally to what was read, by asking them questions like "What kinds of cookies do you like best?" Then discuss some of the mathematics in the story, turning back to specific pages as needed. (For example,"How many cookies were there? How many cookies did each person get when there were six children?")

Investigate: Next, present your problem to the students, and have them work on solving it. Encourage the students to think about more than one way to solve the problem, and to use multiple representations for their ideas.

Summarize: After students have worked on the problem, engage the whole group in a discussion where students present their thinking and their solutions, and encourage them to react to each others' ideas. Talk about what has been learned from the problem. After completing the lesson, collect the students' written work and analyze it for evidence of understanding of the basic operation involved in the story.

Gearing Down: Start with a simpler version of the problem.

Gearing Up: Encourage students to come up with as many solutions as they can. Students can also be asked to write their own problems using the basic operation.

REFLECTION:

1. Include the following information, along with a brief description of your lesson, with your summary of this activity in the classroom: (1.) Bibliographic information (author, date, title, publisher) for the book, (2.) Brief overview of the story, (3.) Basic operations involved in the story, and (4.) The problems you chose for the students to work on.

2. How appropriate was the book for the activity you did? How well do you think the problems you presented worked? Was it too easy or too hard? Were the children able to demonstrate what they know about the basic operations involved?

3. Describe what you learned about each student's understanding of the operations involved. What, if anything, might you do differently if you use this book again?

Name: _____

Class: _____

Dot Sticks

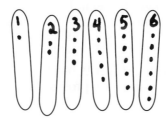

▼ Ask children to pick up 4 dots. (Most children will pick up the 4 stick.)

  • Is there another way to pick up 4 dots?

▼ Now ask them to pick up 6 dots.
  • How many ways can you do it?
  • Can you pick up 6 dots using 3 sticks?

▼ Ask for 11 dots.
  • Can you do it with 2 sticks?
  • 3 sticks?
  • 4 sticks?

▼ Ask for 8 dots using only 3 sticks.

▼ Ask how many different ways you can pick up 10 dots: List them on the chalkboard.

▼ Follow up with individual worksheets.

Dot Sticks

Objective: Provide multiple representations of numbers using addition.

Getting Ready: Prepare dot sticks for each student to match the illustration on the *Dot Sticks* worksheet. You can do so by gluing beans on tongue depressors or Popsicle sticks, then writing the numeral with a permanent marker. There is some educational value in having the students help you make the sticks. You can create a Dot Stick Factory in your classroom. Students will receive practice counting the beans and writing the numerals.

Launch: Use the questions on *Dot Sticks* as a guide. Begin by asking to children to pick up 4 dots. See if they can find more than one way to do it. If not, show them 1 + 3 and see if they can find 2 + 2. List the possibilities as number sentences.

Instruct: Continue with the number six. Once students have found 6, 1 + 5, 2 + 4, and 3 + 3, challenge them to show six using three sticks. Continue the process for 11, 8, and 10. Have students think of other numbers to represent.

Summarize: Have the students talk about why it is good to be able to show a number in more than one way. See if they can give a real-life example for one of the problems listed on the board. For example, I have 6 candies. I have 1 red and 5 yellow.

Gearing Down: Help the students count the dots if needed. Limit the number sentences to combinations with only two sticks.

Gearing Up: Create more dot sticks for the numerals 0, and 7–9 and provide each child with two sets of sticks 0–9. Increase the size of the target numbers.

REFLECTION:

1. Which solutions were the easiest for the students to find? Which were the hardest? Why do you think that was the case?

2. What strategies did the students use to find combinations?

3. How comfortable were the students representing the combinations with number sentences?

4. After this lesson, what will you have students do next?

Name: _____

Class: _____

Rectangles and More Rectangles

▼ How many ways can you make a rectangle with this many tiles? Draw pictures. The first one is done for you.

▼ List the ways:

6 tiles

$\underline{1 \times 6}$ or $\underline{6 \times 1}$

$\underline{2 \times 3}$ or $\underline{3 \times 2}$

4 tiles

_____ or _____

_____

3 tiles

_____ or _____

8 tiles

_____ or _____

_____ or _____

9 tiles

_____ or _____

_____

2 tiles

_____ or _____

10 tiles

_____ or _____

_____ or _____

Rectangles and More Rectangles

Objective: Building rectangles with tiles to develop visual representations for multiplication facts.

Getting Ready: Each student will need a copy of *Rectangles and More Rectangles*, tiles, a piece of grid paper (Appendix A), paper, and pencil.

Launch: Begin by demonstrating the activity using 6 tiles to build rectangles as shown on the *Rectangles and More Rectangles* sheet. Show how to arrange the tiles, draw the rectangles on the grid paper and record the number sentences. Discuss how a 1 by 6 and a 6 by 1 could be considered different rectangles. Tell students they will use a multiplication sign (x) to show the dimensions of the rectangles. For example a 1 tile by 6 tile rectangle would be recorded 1 x 6. Also introduce the term, factor. Factors of 6 include 1, 2, 3, and 6. These are the whole numbers we can multiply together to get 6.

Investigate: Have students work together to build and record rectangles for the rest of the sheet. If they are ready for more challenge, have them repeat the process for the numbers 11–20. Ask children to decide which number of tiles between 10 and 20 has the most rectangular arrangements (and therefore the most factors). (Answer: 12—1 x 12; 12 x 1; 2 x 6; 6 x 2; 3 x 4; 4 x 3, so 12 has the factors 1, 12, 2, 6, 3, 4) As a follow up, students could investigate similar questions for the numbers 20 to 30, and 30 to 40.

Summarize: After students have worked on the problems, ask them to share their thinking and the patterns they found. Discuss which rectangles had the most arrangements (and therefore the most factors) and which had the fewest. You may introduce the terms prime number (only one rectangle that has dimensions 1 and the number itself, so just these 2 factors) and composite number (more than one rectangle possible, and thus more than 2 factors).

Gearing Down: Reduce the numbers being represented. Have students trace and cut out grid-paper rectangles and glue the various arrangements for each number on a page for display.

Gearing Up: After students have completed *Rectangles and More Rectangles*, ask them to use between 10 and 20 tiles. Ask them to decide which number of tiles can be arranged only in one long row (prime number—11, 13, 17, 19), and which can be arranged in only rectangles but not squares (composite numbers—10, 12, 14, 15, 18, 20) and which can be arranged in rectangles, including squares (composite number—16).

REFLECTION:

1. Describe any patterns the students observed as they moved these tiles into different arrangements.

2. Explain how this rectangle activity provides good readiness for learning basic multiplication facts and area and volume.

Finding 100

Find pairs that add to 100.

8	18	82	30	70	96	4	99
91	92	88	80	66	86	87	7
9	51	12	20	34	13	14	93
50	49	64	36	21	79	46	54
50	19	81	83	26	18	29	73
2	98	17	91	74	71	92	27
45	55	25	9	36	64	5	95
60	40	75	35	65	15	85	1

Finding 100

Grades 1-4

Objective: Finding pairs of whole numbers that total 100.

Getting Ready: Each student will need a Finding 100 sheet and crayons or markers. Students need to be fluent with the addition facts, and aware of pairs of numbers that total ten. Experience with missing addend problems of the form.

$25 + \square = 100$ or $\square + 10 = 100$.

Launch: Ask children to look for number pairs that total 100. Shade pairs as you find them. Encourage to find pairs by inspection rather than recording their computation.

Investigate: Give students time to locate pairs. Have them record the pairs on the back of the sheet.

Summarize: After children search for number pairs, ask them to list the 5 easiest pairs to find. Why were they the easiest? Ask them to list the 5 hardest pairs to find. Why do you think they were hard? Have children compare their list of hard (easy) pairs and discuss patterns.

Gearing Down: Provide a 10 x 10 grid to assist them in finding pairs. Ask students to search find just 10 pairs of numbers that total 100. Make a new chart with pairs of numbers that total 50.

Gearing Up: Ask students to make a list of 5 pairs of whole number that total 100 but are not on the chart. Tell how work with this equation $\lozenge + \square = 100$ would be helpful here.

REFLECTION:

1. What kind of strategies did the children use to identify pairs?

2. How many different pairs that total 100 could be in the 8 x 8 chart? Tell why.

3. How many different pairs that total 100 could be in a 10 x 10 chart?

How Could It Happen?

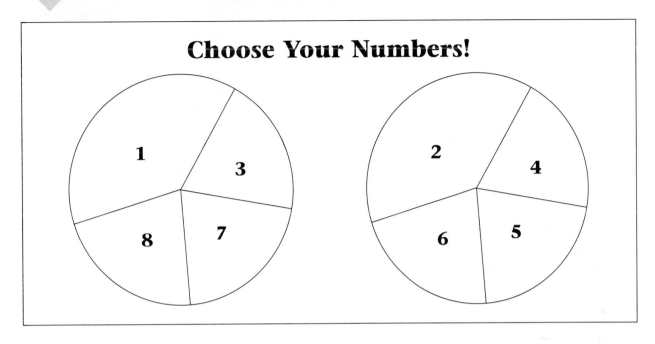

Choose Your Numbers!

(Circle 1: 1, 3, 7, 8)   (Circle 2: 2, 4, 5, 6)

To play: Choose one number from each circle and add or multiply them.

How could this happen?

1. List 5 different results for this game.

2. Kara chose two numbers and got 10. What numbers could she have picked from each circle?

3. Whitney chose two numbers and got 3. What could she have picked from each circle?

4. How many different ways can you make 5?

5. What is the smallest whole number that can NOT be made? Tell how you decided.

6. Pretend the circles are spinners. What number would you expect to come up most often on each spinner? What sum would come up most often? Product?

How Could It Happen?

Objective: Choosing different numbers and operations to hit a target.

Getting Ready: Make a copy of the *How Could it Happen?* gameboard for the children.

Launch: As a warm-up, ask children for different ways to make 10—such as 5 x 2, 50/5, 12 – 2 and 6 + 4. Create a list of different possibilities.

Instruct: Distribute the gameboard. For each question, list the solutions that are proposed and discuss how each was found. A point could be awarded for each correct answer. Possible answers:
1. 24 – 12, 3 + 9, 6 x 2. Actually we found 14 ways to make 12.
2. We found 7 ways to make 20.
3. No, 16 – 15 is one way to make 1.
4. Answers will vary.
5. Answers will vary, but 49 is the largest.
6. 1 and 2, Sum–3, Product–2

Summarize: Discuss the strategies children used to solve the problems.

Gearing Down: Just use addition.

Gearing Up: Allow division as an operation and have children explore the implications for each question. Ask children to pretend that the circles are spinners. What sum would they expect to come up most often? What product?

REFLECTION:

1. Which of the 5 questions was the <u>easiest</u> for your children? Why do you think it was easy?

2. Which of the 5 questions was the <u>most difficult</u> for your children? What do you think made it difficult?

3. Do you think this was a problem solving or skill activity or both? Explain.

Name: _____

Class: _____

Sorting Products

1. Decide in which box each letter should be placed. Explain your decisions.

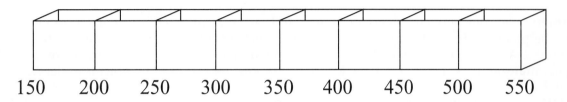

| 150 | 200 | 250 | 300 | 350 | 400 | 450 | 500 | 550 |

P = 800 x 0.6   A = 6000 x 0.06   E = 600 x 0.4

B = 0.82 x 200   H = 4000 x 0.08   P = 6000 x 0.07

Y = 0.9 x 600

2. Decide in which box each letter should be placed. Explain your decisions.

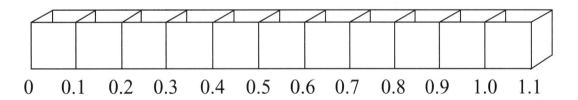

| 0 | 0.1 | 0.2 | 0.3 | 0.4 | 0.5 | 0.6 | 0.7 | 0.8 | 0.9 | 1.0 | 1.1 |

T = 0.30 x 2.1   L = 0.6 x 0.60   E = 2.0 x 0.24

O = 0.80 x 0.90   Y = 2.1 x 0.50   M = 1.8 x 0.10

D = 0.42 x 2.0   A = 9.2 x 0.10   I = 0.5 x 0.5

S = 9.2 x 0.01

Sorting Products

Grades 6–8

Objective: Mentally compute and estimate products involving decimals and to recognize how a product is influenced by a factor between 0 and 1.

Getting Ready: Provide each student with a *Sorting Products* sheet. Student need to be fluent with basic multiplication facts, and have experience in patterns associated with multiplication of decimals. Students should realize that when one factor is between 0 and 1, the product will always be less than the other factor. Further, students should recognize how factors close to 0 and close to 1 influence the product.

Launch: Select one of the problems under Activity 1. Ask students to either mentally compute or estimate the product. Then place that product in the appropriate box. Only one number should go in each box. Also ask them to write the letter corresponding to that equation on the front of the box. Discuss strategies they used to estimate. Repeat the process for one of the problems under Activity 2.

Investigate: Give students time to work on the sheet.

Summarize: After students determine products, ask them to decide which they mentally computed and produced an exact answer and which were estimates. Ask them to tell how they decided what to do. Have students check the message on the faces of the box to confirm their solution is correct.

Gearing Down: Have students work in pairs to complete the activity. Ask them to decide which were the easiest numbers to sort. The hardest?

Gearing Up: Ask students to make an activity similar to this one. Have them decide the bounds for the boxes and tell how they established these bounds.

REFLECTION:

1. What kind of strategies did the children use to estimate the products?

2. How many products reflected exact computation?

3. What products were the most difficult to make?

Number Net

▼ Work with a partner or in a small group to determine the missing values:

Dividend	Divisor	Quotient	Integral Remainder
632	73	_____	_____
345	_____	_____	45
_____	34	_____	27
_____	_____	_____	18
_____	746	89	_____
7439	_____	274	_____
_____	_____	56	73

▼ If the solutions are not unique, explain why not.
If no solution is possible, explain why.

- Which combination result in unique solutions?

- Given any two numbers in a row, can a solution always be found? Why or why not?

- Given only one number in a row, can a solution always be found? Why or why not?

- Which combinations make finding a solution easy? Difficult? Why?

Number Net

Objective: Working with others to develop logical reasoning and number sense involving division.

Getting Ready: Each pair or small group of students will need a copy of *Number Net* and paper, and pencils. You also may want to have calculators available.

Launch: Present a problem such as the following to the students: Ms. Pastry baked donuts for 17 restaurants. One day, she decided to try a new chocolate chip donut recipe. One batch of dough produced 334 donuts. If each restaurant gets the same amount, how many chocolate chip donuts would each restaurant get?

Ask the students how they might solve the problem. Do they know what the dividend will be? the divisor? the quotient? the remainder? How do they know? Ask them to work in pairs to find what the missing numbers would be. Also challenge them to determine if this is the only solution to the problem. When they are ready, have the students discuss their thinking and the solutions that they found for the problem.

Next, ask the students if they could have found the divisor if they had known what the quotient was. How would this have changed the problem?

Investigate: Have the students work in pairs or small groups to find the missing numbers and to answer the questions on *Number Net*. Observe and listen to students as they work on the problems. See if you can determine who is struggling with the concepts and who understands the division that they are working on.

Summarize: After students have worked on the problems, engage the whole group in a discussion where students present their thinking and the answers that they found for the division problems and for the questions below, and encourage them to react to each others' ideas. After completing the lesson, collect the students' written work and analyze it for evidence of understanding of the division.

Gearing Down: Begin with problems that have two-digit dividends.

Gearing Up: Have students write word problems to go with problems from the page.

REFLECTION:

1. How appropriate was this activity for the students? Is this something you might like to do someday with your own students? Would you make any changes?

2. What did you learn about the students' knowledge of division?

Name: _____

Class: _____

Look for Patterns

▼ Complete the sums in these addition problems:

Find a pattern in the answers!

$3 + 6 = \;\; 9$

$13 + 6 = 19$

$23 + 6 = 29$

$53 + 6 = \;\Box$

$83 + 6 = \;\Box$

▼ How does 4 + 8 help you to add 14 + 8?

$$\begin{array}{r} 4 \\ + 8 \\ \hline 12 \end{array} \qquad \begin{array}{r} 14 \\ + 8 \\ \hline 22 \end{array}$$

▼ Your turn:

$$\begin{array}{r} 9 \\ + 5 \\ \hline \end{array} \quad \begin{array}{r} 19 \\ + 5 \\ \hline \end{array} \quad \begin{array}{r} 29 \\ + 5 \\ \hline \end{array} \quad \begin{array}{r} 39 \\ + 5 \\ \hline \end{array} \quad \begin{array}{r} 79 \\ + 5 \\ \hline \end{array} \quad \begin{array}{r} 89 \\ + 5 \\ \hline \end{array}$$

$$\begin{array}{r} 7 \\ + 3 \\ \hline \end{array} \quad \begin{array}{r} 17 \\ + 3 \\ \hline \end{array} \quad \begin{array}{r} 27 \\ + 3 \\ \hline \end{array} \quad \begin{array}{r} 37 \\ + 3 \\ \hline \end{array} \quad \begin{array}{r} 47 \\ + 3 \\ \hline \end{array} \quad \begin{array}{r} 87 \\ + 3 \\ \hline \end{array}$$

Look for Patterns

Grades K–2

Objective: Use observed patterns to develop mental computation skills with addition.

Getting Ready: Each student will need a copy of *Look for Patterns*, paper, and a pencil. You'll need the variation on the following page if you want to do subtraction.

Launch: Have the students look at the first group of addition problems on *Look for Patterns* and find the missing sums. Ask them questions like: "What is alike about each problem?", "What is alike about the sums?", and "What patterns are there in these problems?", and "How does knowing this pattern help you to add 73 + 6 ?"Ask the children to use the patterns to mentally compute the sums to some more examples, such as 93 + 6, 43 + 6, and 63 + 6.

Investigate: Have the students talk about the next question on *Look for Patterns*, "How does 4 + 8 help you to add 14 + 8 ?" Have students talk about some other __4 + 8 addition problems and the corresponding patterns. Next, have them work on the rest of the addition problems on the page independently or in pairs, and encourage them to continue looking for patterns.

Summarize: After students have worked on the problems, engage the whole group in a discussion where students present their thinking and the patterns they found, and encourage them to react to each others' ideas.

Gearing Down: Have students begin looking for the patterns by finding all of the problems in a series. For example, 3 + 6, 13 + 6, 23 + 6, 33 + 6, . . . 73 + 6, 83 + 6, and 93 + 6. Do the same for 4 + 8, 14 + 8, etc. For more practice use 5 + 7, 15 + 7, etc.

Gearing Up: Have students look for patterns in problems in which both of the addends are two-digit numbers. Also, have students look for patterns in subtraction problems. (See the following *Looking for Patterns* Activity Sheet for subtraction.)

REFLECTION:

After completing the lesson, collect the students' written work and analyze it for evidence of understanding of the patterns and the addition skills needed.

1. How appropriate was this activity for the students? Is this something you might like to do someday with your own students? Would you make any changes?

2. What did you learn about the students' knowledge of addition?

Variation on Look for Patterns (Subtraction)

Write the answer to the last problem in this group:

16	26	46	56	36
− 4	− 4	− 4	− 4	− 4
12	22	42	52	

Try these:

18	28	48	38	68	58	98
− 2	− 2	− 2	− 2	− 2	− 2	− 2

18	28	68	38	48	78	58
− 9	− 9	− 9	− 9	− 9	− 9	− 9

Complete these subtraction problems:

60	60	60	60
− 27	− 47	− 17	− 57

- What is alike about each example?

- What is alike about each answer?

- Use the pattern to do these mentally:

  $60 - 37 = $ _____ $60 - 7 = $ _____

Now try these:

$43 - 13 = $ _____ $153 - 13 = $ _____

$73 - 13 = $ _____ $123 - 13 = $ _____

$93 - 13 = $ _____ $273 - 13 = $ _____

Fraction Strips

one	1										
halves	$\frac{1}{2}$					$\frac{2}{2}$					
thirds	$\frac{1}{3}$			$\frac{2}{3}$			$\frac{3}{3}$				
fourths	$\frac{1}{4}$		$\frac{2}{4}$		$\frac{3}{4}$			$\frac{4}{4}$			
fifths	$\frac{1}{5}$	$\frac{2}{5}$		$\frac{3}{5}$		$\frac{4}{5}$		$\frac{5}{5}$			
sixths	$\frac{1}{6}$	$\frac{2}{6}$		$\frac{3}{6}$		$\frac{4}{6}$		$\frac{5}{6}$		$\frac{6}{6}$	
eighths	$\frac{1}{8}$	$\frac{2}{8}$	$\frac{3}{8}$	$\frac{4}{8}$	$\frac{5}{8}$	$\frac{6}{8}$	$\frac{7}{8}$	$\frac{8}{8}$			
ninths	$\frac{1}{9}$	$\frac{2}{9}$	$\frac{3}{9}$	$\frac{4}{9}$	$\frac{5}{9}$	$\frac{6}{9}$	$\frac{7}{9}$	$\frac{8}{9}$	$\frac{9}{9}$		
tenths	$\frac{1}{10}$	$\frac{2}{10}$	$\frac{3}{10}$	$\frac{4}{10}$	$\frac{5}{10}$	$\frac{6}{10}$	$\frac{7}{10}$	$\frac{8}{10}$	$\frac{9}{10}$	$\frac{10}{10}$	
twelfths	$\frac{1}{12}$	$\frac{2}{12}$	$\frac{3}{12}$	$\frac{4}{12}$	$\frac{5}{12}$	$\frac{6}{12}$	$\frac{7}{12}$	$\frac{8}{12}$	$\frac{9}{12}$	$\frac{10}{12}$	$\frac{11}{12}$	$\frac{12}{12}$

Fraction Strips

Objective: To help children understand and use the region model to represent, compare and order fractions.

Getting Ready: Prepare strips of construction paper (3 inches by 9 inches) for each student. Use one color for each fraction. For example, use black for the whole, yellow for halves, blue for thirds, and green for fourths. (For older children also make sixths and eighths.) Have some extra thirds because children have difficulty folding thirds. Be ready to help them after they have tried on their own. You may also use the fraction strips found on the previous page.

Launch: Pretend that the strips are candy bars (children like to give them fanciful names like "lemonut") that you will share with other children. Ask the children how they could share the yellow candy bar with two children. Introduce vocabulary, if necessary, and have the children label their strips as shown below.

	halves		thirds		

As you make each strip, take some time to have children tell about the strip, and count the parts. Ask how many halves, thirds, fourths it takes to make a whole (the same amount as the black strip). Ask children if they would trade three-fourths for a whole. How about six-sixths? See if they can generalize what it takes to make a whole, but do not force the generalization.

Have children count how many, say thirds that they have all together—one-third, two-thirds, three-thirds, four-thirds, and so fourth. Have the children show on their own candy bar fractional parts such as two-thirds or three-fourths. Don't forget four-fourths.

Investigate: Develop a series of about 10 appropriate tasks that children, in pairs or as a group, can investigate with their strips such as the following:
> Which is larger? Three-fourths or two-thirds?
> What fractions are larger than one-half?
> Show that 1 2/3 is equivalent to 5/3.
Be certain that you asked children to explain or justify their answers.

Summarize: Ask children how they would explain to someone else how to make a strip to show a given fraction.

Gearing Down: Only ask children to make the strips and count fractional parts to identify the representation of fractions.

Gearing Up: Have the group investigate the relationship between mixed numbers and improper fractions. Have them show 15/4 and find how many wholes and how many extra parts. Also begin with a mixed number and have them find the equivalent improper fraction using the strips.

(Continued on next page)

1. Did you find that children were engaged in the task? What did they appear to understand? (Representing a given fraction with a strip, counting parts with the correct language, comparing fractions, seeing the equivalence of fractions.) What difficulties did they encounter?

2. What advantages and disadvantages do you see to using the strips?

3. If you did the gearing up part, did children find short cuts—that is, did they establish a rule for themselves that did not depend on using the strips? For example, if asked to find the equivalent mixed number for 17/3, did they say "I need to know how many threes in 17; there are 5 and 2 left over. This would be 5 wholes and 2/3 of another."

4. Could you use these strips to help children with adding and subtracting fractions?

Name: _____

Class: _____

Comparing Models

Materials needed: Pattern blocks

The four basic shapes of the pattern blocks that you will use are the hexagon, triangle, rhombus, and trapezoid. Each child or pair of children will need multiple copies of each shape.

Let children have a chance to explore by making designs and seeing how they could make the hexagon with the other pieces.

Idea One: Use the hexagon as the whole. What is the size of each of the other pieces? Use the pieces to show that

$$\frac{2}{6} = \frac{1}{3} \qquad \frac{3}{3} = 1 \qquad \frac{3}{6} = \frac{1}{2} \qquad \frac{2}{3} > \frac{1}{2} \qquad 2\frac{2}{3} = \frac{8}{3}$$

Idea Two: Use the figure made from two hexagons as the whole.

Use ◢ to cover the shape above. How many does it take? What fractional part of the whole is the rhombus? What fractional part of the whole is the trapezoid?

Use the shape to show that $\frac{3}{4}$ is greater than $\frac{2}{3}$.

Idea Three: Given the shape of a fractional part and have children construct the whole.

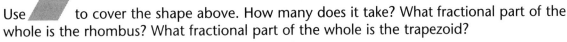

If ◢ is $\frac{2}{3}$, what is the whole?

If ▼ is $\frac{3}{4}$, make the whole.

If ▲ is $\frac{1}{5}$, make the whole.

If ▲ is $\frac{2}{5}$, draw the whole.

Comparing Models

Objective: Use pattern blocks to compare and model fractional parts of a whole and equivalent fractions.

Getting Ready: For each student or group you'll need a copy of *Comparing Models* and 6-12 each of the following pattern block pieces: yellow hexagon, green triangle, blue rhombus, and red trapezoid.

Launch: Begin by distributing the pattern blocks and letting children explore with them. Encourage them to make designs and to see if they can make the hexagon using the other pieces. Tell students that today they are going to use fractions to represent the pattern block relationships they found. Have them use their pattern blocks to find out that it takes 6 triangles, 3 rhombuses, and 2 trapezoids to make a hexagon. Using fractions, if the hexagon is one whole, the triangle is 1/6 of the hexagon, the rhombus is 1/3 of the hexagon, and the trapezoid is 1/2 of the hexagon. Review how to write the fraction symbols. Also define (using 1/2): the numerator (1) shows the number of parts of the whole and the denominator (2) shows the number of equal parts into which the whole has been divided.

Investigate: Have the students use their pattern blocks to model the number sentences under *Idea One* on the *Comparing Models* sheet. Discuss their results. Introduce the term equivalent. Two fractions are equivalent if they have the same size or area. 2/6 is equivalent to 1/3. They cover the same area. If students understand *Idea One*, have them complete *Idea Two* where the whole is TWO hexagons. The rhombus is now 1/6 of the whole and the trapezoid is 1/4 of the whole.

Summarize: Review key fractional ideas the students discovered. For example, you have to know what is one whole before you can identify the fractional parts. The fractional parts must be equal. An amount can be represented in more than one way using equivalent fractions.

Gearing Down: Just work with *Idea One*. After those problems have been completed, make up more problems to solve using the hexagon as one whole.

Gearing Up: For those students ready for the challenge, have them try *Idea Three* on the *Comparing Models* sheet. If they are unable to do it independently, work it out together. You may also have students figure out how to add and subtract fractions using their pattern blocks.

REFLECTION:

1. What was most difficult for the students? How did the pattern blocks help students understand the fraction concepts?

2. What fraction experience would you provide next for these students?

Know Your Coins

Objective: Using value of coins in a ratio table to develop patterns and proportions and to examine algebraic relationships.

▼ Use a ratio table to help complete these patterns:

Number of Quarters	1	2		4	5	6
Number of Nickels	5	10	15	20		30
Number of Pennies	25	50	75		125	150

▼ Answer these questions and fill in the blank:
- Describe a pattern you found in each row.
- Write a ratio for the number of quarters to nickels. _____
- Write a ratio for the number of nickels to pennies. _____
- Write a ratio for the number of quarters to pennies. _____

▼ Try these:
- How many nickels will be needed for 8 quarters? _____
  Tell two different ways to decide.
- How many pennies will be needed for 10 quarters? _____
  Tell two different ways to decide.
- Give three numbers (not shown in the table) that could go
  in the nickels row. _____
  in the pennies row. _____
- Give three numbers that could *not* go
  in the nickels row. _____
  in the pennies row. _____
- How many quarters would you have when the number of quarters plus the number of nickels plus the number of pennies (all in one column of the ratio table) first exceeds $30? _____

Know Your Coins

Objective: Using the value of coins to develop patterns and proportions and to examine algebraic relationships.

Getting Ready: This activity encourages students to find and discuss patterns involving ratios. You may want to have some coins to model several parts of the table. You may also want to make a copy of *Know your Coins* for each child, or make a transparency and use it to guide a group activity.

Launch: Ask children to decide answers to these questions, and show them how to write the ratio:

How many pennies are equivalent to a nickel? *[Ratio 5/1; 5 — 1; or 5 to 1; or 5:1]*

How many nickels are equivalent to 5 pennies? *[Ratio 1/5; 1 — 5; or 1 to 5; or 1:5]*

Make sure children see that the order of the values of the ratio is related to the question asked.

Investigate: Ask children to complete the table on *Know your Coins*. Then ask them (either individually or in groups) to complete the bulleted tasks.

The final bullet challenges students to think about an expression with three variables. Ask them to tell how they would decide when the sum of $30 is exceeded.

Q + N + P = $30

When each of these equals $10, (40 quarters, 200 nickels and 1000 pennies) the sum of $30 is reached. So anything more than 40 quarters will exceed the $30.

Summarize: Have students discuss their solution strategies.

Gearing Down: Provide coins so students can "act out" their solutions.

Gearing Up: The final bullet may be used as a more challenging problem.

REFLECTION:

1. Did the children prefer to write a particular form of ratio? If so, what was the form of preference (x/y; x—y; x to y; or x:y)?

2. Summarize at least two strategies the students used in solving Q + N + P = $30.

3. Describe another real world example of ratio that you think would be of interest to your students and provide an opportunity to discuss and write different ratios.

Balance Me

MATERIALS

Weights (1-10 ounces or 1-10 washers), or
Labeled containers weighing 1-10 units (2 of each)
(Note: You can fill containers with unifix cubes to make weights.)

Balance scale

QUESTIONS TO ASK STUDENTS

A. I am going to put some weights on each side of the balance. Which will balance?

Left side	Right side
4	4
3	8
2 and 3	5
3 and 4	6
1, 2, and 3	6

B. If I put a 5 weight on the left side, what could I put on the right side to balance it?

C. If I put a 3 weight on one side and a 7 weight on the other side, what would I need to add to the side with the 3 weight to make the scale balance?

D. If I put a 8 weight on the left side and a 2 weight on the right side, can I balance the scale by adding a 6 weight to the left side?

E. I have the scale balanced with a 6 weight on each side. What could I add to each side to keep it balanced?

F. I only have four weights, 3, 4, 5, and 7. Could I put all or some of the weights on the scale to have it balance?

G. Could I balance the scale by using one of each of the 10 different weights?

◆ *Balance Me*

Objective: To explore equality on a balance scale.

Getting Ready: You will need the following materials: Balance Me sheet with questions A-G, balance scale, weights (1-10 ounces or 1-10 washers), or labeled containers weighing 1-10 units (2 of each). Note: You can fill containers with connecting cubes to make weights of various amounts.

If you set up a station for children to investigate on their own, you will need to make cards with questions C-F and similar questions with other numbers. It would also be helpful to have a recording sheet.

Launch: What makes a balance scale balance? After discussing the answers, ask question A and B.

Investigate: Either proceed with a large group discussion of the other questions or set up a station for pairs of students to investigate the questions.

Summarize: Ask what we learned about the weights that will balance. Ask if they can think of two ways to change a scale that has a 2 weight on one side and an 8 weight on the other by changing only one side at a time.

Gearing Down: Let children experiment with balancing the scale with different weights and record the different ways they can balance the scale. For example, if they find that weights of 2 and 4 on one side balance a weight of 6, they could write $2 + 4 = 6$.

Gearing Up: Have children use the balance to solve open sentences such as the following:

$2 + \underline{\quad} = 6$ $\qquad$ $5 = \underline{\quad} = 3$ $\qquad$ $8 = 2 + \underline{\quad}$

$7 = 9 - \underline{\quad}$ $\qquad$ $\underline{\quad} + 3 = 7$ $\qquad$ $\underline{\quad} - 5 = 4$

REFLECTION:

1. Did young children understand what is meant by "to balance" the scale? Or did you have to illustrate this concept? Did they know which was heavier by looking at the balance scale or did some children think if the arm was higher that meant the contents of that size were heavier? What would you do if they held this misconception?

2. How do activities like this lead to algebraic thinking? In particular, what meaning of equality is stressed?

3. How did children approach Question G? Did they do it the same way that you would do it?

Name: _____

Class: _____

In-Out Machine

Dr. de Zine invented an in–out machine. The machine adds, subtracts, multiplies or divides markings on animals as they go through it. He has kept a record of what happened each day as animals went in and came out of the machine. Your job is to fill in the blanks in his record and to figure out how the machine worked each day.

	IN	**OUT**
M O N	skunk with 3 stripes	skunk now has 12 stripes
	leopard with 12 spots	leopard now has 48 spots
	zebra with 5 stripes	zebra now has _____ stripes
T U E S	dog with 5 spots	dog now has 15 spots
	cat with 2 stars	cat now has 12 stars
	rabbit with 3 marks	rabbit now has _____ marks
W E D	horse with 12 lines	horse now has 6 lines
	pig with 8 spots	pig now has 4 spots
	cow with 0 spots	cow now has _____ spots
T H U R	elephant with 32 stars	elephant now has 16 stars
	rhino with 24 diamonds	rhino now has 8 diamonds
	hippo with 41 spots	hippo now has _____ spots
F R I	frog with 4 spots	frog now has 11 spots
	toad with 3 spots	toad now has 9 spots
	salamander with _____ stripes	salamander now has 15 stripes

In-Out Machine

Objective: To analyze the actions of a function machine.

Getting Ready: Have copies of the *In-Out Machine* sheet for each child.

Launch: Dr. de Zine invented an in-out machine. The machine adds, subtracts, multiplies, or divides markings on animals as they go through it. He has kept a record of what happened each day as animals went in and came out of the machine. Your job is to fill in the blanks in his record and to figure out how the machine worked each day. Let's talk about what the machine did on Monday.

Investigate: Have students work on the other days. When they have finished one day, have them check with their partner and discuss the answers.

Summarize: When students have completed the five days, discuss their rules for each day. You should expect different rules. Have students justify their rules (show that it works for each case.) To see if students understand the rule, you might give an example of another input for that day (for example, a hamster with 3 spots-what happens each day?

Gearing Down: Give the rule and the input to children and have them tell the output. After they are familiar with this, then give the input and output which is one simple operation, like add 3 or double.

Gearing Up: Give inputs and outputs that require a two-step rule like the one on Friday. Have them make up their own in-out puzzle.

REFLECTION:

1. Do children need more examples before they determine a rule?

2. Do children want to say the rule after one example?

3. How do activities like this help children determine a functional rule given a table of values?

4. Can children make up their own in-out puzzles? What types do they make? Are they easier or harder than the ones in this activity?

Solid Activities

Objective: To describe and classify three-dimensional objects.

Getting Ready: Choose and prepare one of the activities described below that is appropriate for the students with whom you are working. Write your plan in the lesson plan template.

BEGINNING ACTIVITIES

1. *Who am I?* Show three objects such as a ball (sphere), cone, and box (rectangular prism). Describe one of them (it is round all over, it is flat on the bottom, its faces are all flat) and have the children guess which one you are stacking.
2. *Who Stacks?* Have children decide which solids stack. A more sophisticated activity requires children to sort the solids into three categories: those that will stack no matter how placed, those that will stack only if placed in certain ways, and those that will not stack.
4. *How Are We Alike?* Hold up two solids and ask children how they are alike and how they are different. Or put out three solids and ask children which is different from the other two (look for any answer but a plausible justification).

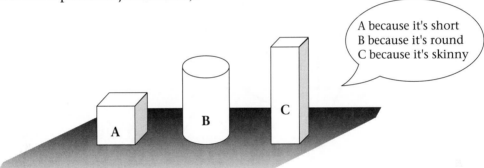

A because it's short
B because it's round
C because it's skinny

INTERMEDIATE ACTIVITIES

1. *Riddles involving edges, vertices, and faces.* Make up simple riddles about the number of edges, vertices, or faces of a solid. Some may have more than one answer. For example, "I am a solid with 8 edges."
2. *Classifying solids.* Have students sort a set of solids and explain their sorting or ask other students to see if they can tell how they sorted the solids. This is a good way to introduce the names of solids, and begin to help children describe the defining attributes (what makes a prism, a pyramid).
3. *Searching for solids.* This is a variation of the riddles, but concentrate on length of edges and shapes of faces rather just the number. For example, find a solid whose faces are all congruent, or a solid who has four congruent faces and one that is different.

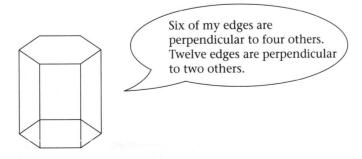

Six of my edges are perpendicular to four others. Twelve edges are perpendicular to two others.

ADVANCED ACTIVITIES

1. *Parallel faces.* Ask students why three-dimensional objects in the real world have certain characteristics. For example, why are the top and bottom of soup cans parallel? Why are roofs of house in cold climates not parallel to the ground. Why are bookshelves parallel? Have them find examples of objects with non-parallel faces.

2. *Perpendicular edges.* Have children make models of three-dimensional objects to solve a mystery. After giving a few examples, students can make up their own mini-mystery. For example, the clue that will solve the mystery is found in a "box" that has each edge perpendicular to each of four other edges.

4. *Right prisms.* Right prisms are named by their top and bottom faces. What solid could you make if you placed two identical right triangular prisms face to face? Can you make a rectangular prism? Another triangular prism? Explore other prisms such as equilateral triangular prisms.

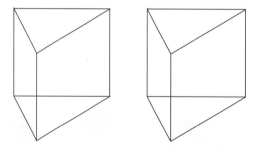

REFLECTION:

1. What vocabulary do students naturally use? Do you notice confusion between the two-dimensional vocabulary (square, circle, sides) and the three-dimensional vocabulary (cube, sphere, edges)? How can you help students to build vocabulary?

2. Explain why you chose the activity you did. How did students react? What did you learn?

Name: _____

Class: _____

Gumdrops and Toothpicks

Materials: Gumdrops and toothpicks (about twenty of each for each child). Clay can be substituted for gumdrops.

Directions: Explore making three-dimensional shapes with the gumdrops and toothpicks. Here are a few examples. How many gumdrops and toothpicks did each take?

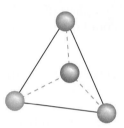 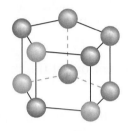 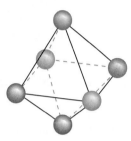

Now, try some with the given number of gumdrops and toothpicks.

Three rules to follow:

1. Two gumdrops can be used on each toothpick, one at each end.

2. Toothpicks should only be used to make the outline of a face (no extra ones stuck across the face).

3. The figure should be closed. Imagine it is a container with a hole in one face—you could fill it.

Some of these are not possible. See if you can figure out which ones and why. If you can make a shape, tell whether it is a prism, a pyramid, or another shape.

Letter	Gumdrops	Toothpicks	Can Make? (yes or no)	Name of shape
A	6	9		
B	5	8		
C	8	5		
D	6	10		
E	7	12		
F	8	12		
G	10	15		
H	12	18		
I	8	14		
J	10	3		
K	6	12		
L	5	9		

1. What is your conjecture about the ones that could not be made?

2. Which ones make pyramids? What is the relationship of the numbers? Using the models, explain why.

3. Which ones make prisms? What is the relationship of the numbers? Using the models, explain why.

Gumdrops and Toothpicks

Objective: To construct three-dimensional figures with given number of edges and faces.

Getting Ready: Gather the materials you need (gumdrops and toothpicks or clay and toothpicks, *Gumdrops and Toothpicks*). Try some of the shapes. Make the chart on the board or a transparency.

Launch: Show the children one of the models you have made. Ask them how many toothpicks (edges) and how many gumdrops (vertices) you used? Ask them if they thought you followed any other rules. (See if you can pull out the three rules listed.)

Investigate: Give each child one of the shapes (A–L) to make. You may have two children making the same shape. It would help if they labeled their shape (make a flag with a piece of masking tape to fly on the shape). Collect the information about which shapes could and could not be made. See if the children can see any patterns in the chart.

See if the children can answer the questions at the bottom of the sheet. Have them test their conjectures with other numbers.

Summarize: See if children always made the same shape, given the same pair of numbers. See if children can tell why you always need at least as many toothpicks as gum drops.

Gearing Down: Have children make any three-dimensional shape and then count the number of edges and vertices.

Gearing Up: See if students can explain why the ratio of edges to vertices is always 3 to 2 for prisms.

REFLECTION:

1. Do children get frustrated when they cannot make the shape specified? Why? What do you need to do about this?

2. Are children able to take a lot of data like in this chart and make sense of it? If not, how can you help them organize that information.

Show My Sides

▼ Use a geoboard to show these figures:

1. Can you make a 4-sided figure with exactly two equal sides?

2. Can you make a 12-sided figure with all sides equal?

3. Can you make a 3-sided figure with three equal sides?

4. Can you make an 8-sided figure with four sides of one length and the other four of another length?

5. Can you make a 5-sided figure with exactly four equal sides?

6. Can you make a 4-sided figure with two pairs of equal sides that is not a parallelogram?

7. Can you make a 3-sided figure with two equal sides?

8. Can you make a 7-sided figure with no equal sides?

Objective: Making shapes with a specified number of sides and congruent sides.

Getting Ready: You'll need geoboards, rubber bands, geoboard paper, and a copy of the puzzles on *Show My Sides*. Geoboard Recording paper may be found in Appendix A.

Launch: Display the geoboards and rubber bands. Review behavior expectations for using the materials. Challenge the children to make the shapes described on *Show My Sides*.

Investigate: Let the students investigate the different challenges on *Show My Sides*, working alone or with a partner. Have them record their findings on the geoboard recording paper.

Summarize: Have students discuss their findings, sharing examples of the shapes they make.

Gearing Down: Have students make shapes and describe the number of sides and the relationships between sides.

Gearing Up: Have students make up their own puzzles.

REFLECTION:

1. Which shapes were impossible? Are they also impossible on geoboards, but not impossible to make?

2. Which students seem to enjoy challenges such as these? Is there a way to help others become more persistent in doing such puzzles?

3. What mathematics is involved in doing these puzzles? Look at the process standards of *Principles and Standards for School Mathematics* (NCTM 2000) available on the World Wide Web (www.standards.nctm.org). Do any involve these standards?

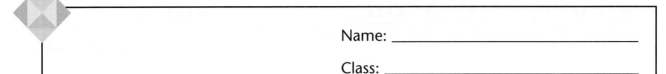

Name: _____

Class: _____

Measuring Length with Arbitrary Units

Materials: Erasers, paper clips, books, boxes, and other objects that can be used as arbitrary units of measure.

Description:

▼ Give each pair of children an arbitrary unit and the name of what they are to measure.

▼ Have the children record their measurements at a place everyone can see. Observe to see whether they record the unit (if they do not, it will lead to the discussion below).

▼ Ask children to use the information about the lengths to compare the lengths of the different objects.

▼ Ask children why the unit is necessary. Ask the children which comparisons are easy to make (ones measured with the same unit) and what they can tell about those made with different units.

Measuring Length with Arbitrary Units

Grades K–2

Objective: To measure lengths with different arbitrary units; to compare those measurements.

Getting Ready: Read the outline of a lesson on *Measuring Length with Arbitrary Units*. Develop a complete lesson plan for the class you are working with or for a small group of children. Decide what in the room the children will measure, what units you will use, and how you will give directions. You will need to fill in the Launch, Investigate, Summarize parts of the plan below. Also describe here what else you need to get ready:

Launch:

Investigate:

Summarize:

REFLECTION:

1. Describe what happened when you taught the lesson. What would you change the next time that you tried it?

2. Which of the following ideas about the unit of measurement did children seem to handle? Which were not included in the lesson? Give evidence.
   a. a measurement must contain both a number and a unit
   b. two measurements may be easily compared if the same unit is used
   c. one unit may be a more appropriate size than another
   d. there is an inverse relationship between the number of units and the size of the unit
   e. a smaller unit will give a more exact measurement

Comparing Height
and Circumference

MATERIALS: Cans of various sizes (at least one for each pair of students) and string. Label the cans and make a recording sheet as suggested below. (If you cannot find cans, roll construction paper to represent cans of various sizes.)

A   B   C   D   E

LAUNCH: Ask students, showing them a can, which they think is longer: The distance around the can or the height of the can. Students are often surprised about the comparison. Have them verify their conjecture by using string to mark each of the distances.

ACTIVITY: Have pairs of children work together. They should first decide which is longer (the distance around or the height) by looking and then verify their guess by measuring each with a piece of string. Have them record their guesses and verification on a chart like the following:

Can	My Eyes Said	The String Showed
A	height	distance around
B		
C		
D		

DISCUSSION: Which cans were obvious? Which cans fooled your eyes?

Comparing Height and Circumference

Objective: Compare the distance around an object with its height.

Getting Ready: Develop a complete lesson plan for a class or small group with whom you are working. The outline for such a lesson is on the previous page.

Launch:

Investigate:

Summarize:

Gearing Down: If students are having difficulty estimating whether the height or distance around is longer, have them measure both dimensions on several cylinders. Then, ask them to decide by looking which is longer.

Gearing Up: Challenge students to make cylinders from construction paper (rolling it and connecting two opposite edges) that is

> taller than the distance around,
> shorter than the distance around
> the same height as the distance around.

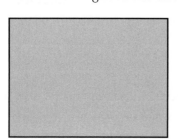
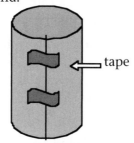
tape

REFLECTION:

1. Which cans were very easy for students to make the decision? Why?

2. Did you notice students who had difficulty measuring? What were those difficulties? How did you help them?

3. Could you describe the type of rectangular paper needed to make each of the cylinders described in the Gearing Up activity?

4. What would the size of the rectangular paper that would make a cylinder that is twice as tall as it is around?

5. What visualization skill is being developed as students make cylinders by rolling a piece of paper as described in Gearing Up.

Name: _____

Class: _____

How Are We Alike? Different?

Materials: Ruler, scissors, and tape.

Directions: Cut out each of the figures at the bottom of the page. See if you can pair a nonrectangular parallelogram with a rectangle of the same area. Cut the nonrectangular parallelogram to show that it has the same area as its pair counterpart-tape. Fill in the table below.

Letters of Pairs	Base	Altitude	Area

Cut out these shapes:

A

B

C

D

E

F

How Are We Alike? Different?

Grades 6–8

Objective: Explore the connection between the area of a rectangle and the area of a parallelogram.

Getting Ready: Have scissors, tape and a copy of *How Are We Alike? Different?* for each pair of students. Have a large model of a rectangle and parallelogram that is not a rectangle that have the same area.

Launch: Ask the students if they know how to find the area of a rectangle. (If children do not know that why the area is the base times the altitude and what that means, you need to postpone this lesson and investigate the area of a rectangle in a meaningful way.) Ask them if they know how to find the area of a parallelogram. See if they can suggest a way to cut the parallelogram to make it a rectangle.

Investigate: Have the children cut out the shapes and see if they can cut each of the parallelograms D-F to make one of the rectangles A-C. Then they should measure the base and the altitude of each and find the area.

Summarize: See if students have discovered that they can always cut the parallelogram on an internal altitude to make the transformation. They may look at this line as a line perpendicular to the base. See if the students generalize to how they could find the area without cutting the parallelogram, or if they see the area is also the base times the altitude.

Gearing Down: If children are not ready for this, they may need not only to revisit area of a rectangle, but they may not understand altitude. Design a lesson to have students investigate the altitude of parallelograms.

Gearing Up: Challenge students to see if they can discover how to find the area of any triangle.

REFLECTION:

1. Are three examples enough to generalize to a rule? What else would you do before you expect students to understand how to find the area of a parallelogram?

2. Did your students really understand what an altitude of a parallelogram is? How would you help them understand this? Does it have any connection to the altitude of a mountain?

Make Two of Me!

Materials: Scissors, ruler, and tape.

Directions: Work with a partner. Cut out the triangles below from each of your sheets. Tape them together to make a parallelogram. Use what you know about finding the area of a parallelogram to find the area.

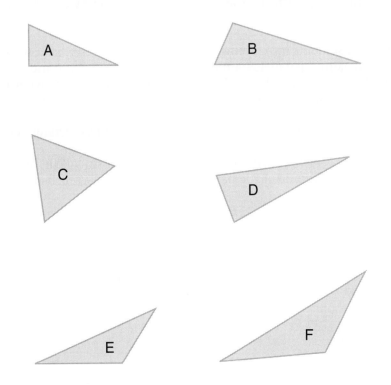

	Base	Altitude	Area of parallelogram	Area of triangle
A				
B				
C				
D				
E				
F				

▼ Describe how you found the area of a triangle.

Make Two of Me!

Objective: Investigate how to find the area of a triangle.

Getting Ready: Check to see that the students you are working with understand how to find the area of a parallelogram, to identify and measure a base and altitude of a triangle. If the triangles on *Make Two of Me!* are not large enough for students to handle easily, make larger versions. Have scissors, tape and two copies of *Make Two of Me!* for each pair of students.

Launch: Ask the students how to find the area of a parallelogram (this lesson depends on this; if they do not know how then do the previous lesson *How Are We Alike? Different?*). Ask the students what shapes they can make from two copies of a triangle.

Investigate: Have the students investigate the triangles on the sheet by cutting out pairs of triangles and filling in the table.

Summarize: Discuss what students have found. See if students can describe in words how to find the area of a triangle by first making a parallelogram and measuring the altitude and base. See if they then describe that the triangle's area is half of this. Then, see if they can describe what they need to measure to find area without first making a parallelogram.

Gearing Down: Investigate finding the area of simpler figures such as rectangles or parallelograms.

Gearing Up: See if students can find ways to cut a triangle with a single cut, and rearrange to make a parallelogram. How does the altitude of the parallelogram compare with the altitude of the original triangle?

REFLECTION:

1. Did the students see the connection between the area of the parallelogram and the area of the triangle? Were they able to see how to use this to find the area of any triangle?

2. What do students really need to understand before this activity can make sense to them? How would you find out if they understand these concepts?

What Is the Connection Between Volume and Surface Area?

Materials: Construction paper (9 in. by 12 in.), tape, and dry filler.

▼ Use construction paper to make two tubes:

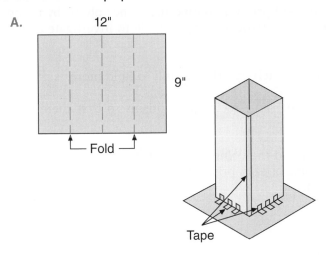

A.   12"

9"

└─ Fold ─┘

Tape

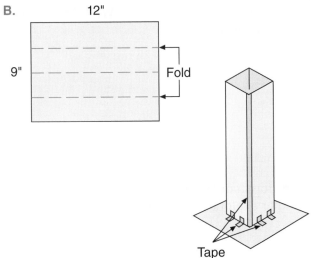

B.   12"

9"   Fold

Tape

▼ Guess which tube holds more, or do they hold the same? _____

▼ Fill and see.

▼ Try the same with triangular prisms, hexagonal prisms, octagonal prisms, and cylinders.

▼ Do you have a conjecture about which shape, the shorter or the taller of each pair, will hold the most?

What is the Connection Between Volume and Surface Area?

Grades 6–8

Objective: Exploring the volume of prisms and cylinders with the same lateral area.

Getting Ready: Gather the materials including dry filler such as rice or cereal and a copy of *What is the Connection Between Volume and Surface Area?*

Launch: Pose the problem. Which prism, made of the construction paper, will hold more—the one folded lengthwise or the one folded sidewise, or do they hold the same amount? Show the students the two prisms (see *What is the Connection Between Volume and Surface Area?*).

Investigate: Let pairs of children make pairs of prisms and investigate the volume by filling. You may want some pairs to start with half a sheet of construction paper, some to investigate cylinders, triangular prisms, or hexagonal prisms.

Summarize: Have the students tell which of each pair they found to hold more.

Gearing Down: Have all students make the same rectangular prisms so that there will not be so much variations.

Gearing Up: Even older children who can find the volume of a rectangular prism are often surprised at the result. Have them compute the volume of each prism. Students could also investigate which of all the prisms and cylinders hold the most.

REFLECTION:

1. Reflect on your own answer to this question when you first read it. What two attributes are people confusing that think they will hold the same amount?

2. Why are explorations like this important for students? Would you expect all students to understand after this one experience? What other explorations would you plan for your students?

What Is the Connection Between Perimeter and Height?

Materials: Stiff paper such as file folders.

▼ Cut 6 strips (2 cm by 21 cm) from stiff paper.

▼ Fold one strip into thirds, and tape together to make a fence triangle:

Tape

▼ Fold the other strips into fourths, fifths, sixths, sevenths, and eighths to make additional fences.

▼ Fill it in the chart:

Number of sides	Length of each side in mm	Height (stand it on one side and see how tall)
3	_____ mm	_____ mm
4	_____	_____
5	_____	_____
6	_____	_____
7	_____	_____
8	_____	_____

- Which has the largest area?
- Which has the smallest area?

What is the Connection between Perimeter and Height?

Grades 6–8

Objective: Explore the relationship between polygons with the same perimeter and their height.

Getting Ready: Gather the materials that you need including a copy of *What is the Connection between Perimeter and Height?* Cut the strips from stiff paper such as file folders. Have rulers available so students can mark sevenths or fifths. The others they can make if they fold carefully.

Launch: Pose the problem. What do you think will happen to the height of a regular polygon if we keep the perimeter constant as the sides increase? Show the students a triangle and a square made of the same size strip (as shown).

Investigate: Have each small group make a set of regular polygons (triangles, squares, pentagons, hexagons, heptagons, and octagons), and measure the altitudes. Have students investigate the area of the polygons by filling one layer with dry filler and measuring the amount in a graduated cylinder, or put the figures inside of each other.

Summarize: See what the students found and if they explain the pattern. See if they can predict which would be "taller"—an 11-sided regular polygon or a 12-sided regular polygon if each had the same perimeter.

REFLECTION:

1. What did you expect to happen to the heights? Is the conjecture about the area of these figures easier to justify than the one about the heights?

2. Think of other shapes activities you could do with the strips of papers. How could you explore the Pythagorean Theorem?

Let's Find Out

Steps:

1. Think of a question you would like to answer. Here are some ideas to get you started.

   - **Questions about ourselves:** Who can tie our shoes? How far can we throw a softball? What is our class's typical height, eye color, shoe size, number in family, amount of allowance, pets . . . ?

   - **Questions about opinions or feelings:** How do you feel about fractions? Does life exist on other planets? What should be done about pollution? What country do you want to study in social studies? What is your favorite television show, song, book, sport, color, food . . . ?

   - **Questions about the world:** Which month has the most birthdays? What is the most popular color of car in the school parking lot? Which brand of cookie has the most chocolate chips? How many paper towels do we use in one day? What is the effect of fertilizer on bean plant growth? What type of paper airplane will fly the farthest?

My Question: _____

_____

2. Plan the survey by answering these questions.
   a. Where or from whom will I collect the data?
   b. How will I collect the data?
   c. How much data will I collect?
   d. When will I collect the data?
   e. How will I record the data as I collect them?
   f. What else do I need to do before I start collecting data?

3. Collect your data!

Let's Find Out

Grades: K-8

Objective: Planning and conducting a survey.

Getting Ready: All you'll need for this lesson is *Let's Find Out*, lined paper, graph paper (Appendix A), pencils or markers.

Launch: Talk with the students about surveys and why people conduct them. Tell them today they will be conducting their own survey. Share some of the sample survey ideas found on *Let's Find Out*. Together brainstorm other ideas they might like to investigate for each of the three categories. Allow individuals or small groups to select one idea they would like to investigate and write it as a question.

Investigate: Help students get organized to collect their data by discussing questions A–F on *Let's Find Out*. Have students collect their data. Once it is collected, they may organize it in a chart or graph.

Summarize: Have students display and discuss their results.

Gearing Down: Simplify this activity by increasing the amount of guidance you provide with questions A–F and making some or all of the decisions for the students. You could also help them write the question and provide a chart or table for recording the data.

Gearing Up: Challenge students to select a question that requires conducting a larger, more complex survey. Once data have been collected, have students display the data in a graph and present their results.

REFLECTION:

1. What types of survey questions were the students most interested in? Why do you think students have those types of interests at this age?

2. When planning their survey, which details were the most difficult for students to decide?

3. How successful and engaged were the students in conducting a survey? What would you do differently if you were to do this again with this age level?

Name: _____

Class: _____

Peanuts

Suppose you have opened some Nutty Bars to check the company's claim of an "average" of 8 peanuts per bar. Here is what you found after opening ten bars.

Bar	1st	2nd	3rd	4th	5th	6th	7th	8th	9th	10th
Number of Peanuts	5	8	8	8	11	7	8	6	6	6

▼ Create some different sketch graphs so you can examine the shape of the data. Which graph would the company probably use to promote their product? Why?

▼ Calculate the averages. You may use counters such as beans and grid paper to represent the peanuts if you wish.

- What is the mean number of nuts?

- What is the median number of nuts?

- What is the modal number of nuts?

- Which average did the company probably use? Why?

▼ Write at least three questions that can be answered by your graphs and statistics.

1. _____

2. _____

3. _____

◆ *Peanuts*

Objective: Choosing the best average.

Getting Ready: You need a copy of *Peanuts*, counters or grid paper (Appendix A), paper, pencil, or a calculator.

Launch: Display the peanut problem and data on *Peanuts*. Work with the students to complete some quick sketch graphs so they can examine the shape of the data. For example you might make towers with connecting cubes, use self-stick notes in columns, make a line plot or a stem-and-leaf plot, or use computer software to generate several types of graphs. Discuss which graph would probably be used by the company president.

Instruct: Explain that statistics are used to describe or summarize data. Demonstrate with counters or grid paper how to find mean, median, mode, and range for the peanut data. First concretely model each of the numbers in the data set (ex. 5 counters or grid squares to represent 5) and place them in order them from smallest to largest (5, 6, 6, 6, 7, 8, 8, 8, 8, 11).

> Range is a measure of variation in a data set or how spread out the data are. Visually compare the largest (tallest) number in the set (11) with the smallest (shortest) number (5). Eleven is 6 units taller than five. The range or spread is 6.
>
> Median, mode, and mean are all measures of central tendency or averages. Median is the middle of an ordered data set. To find this value, start with the outside numbers (5 and 11) then count in from each side until you reach the middle value. In this set of data there are two numbers in the middle (7 and 8). The middle of 7 and 8 is 7.5. This can also be calculated by finding the mean or average of 7 and 8. The median or middle is 7.5.
>
> Mode is the value that occurs most frequently in a set of data. In examining our ordered data we see that there are more eights (4) than any other number. The mode is 8.
>
> Mean is arithmetic average because to find it we add all the values and divide by the number of addends. One conceptual approach to the mean is to think of it as equally sharing or evening out the data. For example, if we had 73 candies and wanted to share them among 10 children...To model this, join or add each of the numbers (counters) in the set then divide the total number of counters (73) into groups of 10 (the number of items in the data set). You will have 7 full groups with 3 out of 10 counters left (7.3). The mean is 7.3.

Summarize: Have students discuss which statistic might be used by the company president to promote his or her product. Also have them generate questions that could be answered.

Gearing Down: Consistently use concrete materials to find the statistics. Eliminate mean.

Gearing Up: Challenge students to translate the concrete models into numbers.

REFLECTION:

1. How did the use of concrete models promote conceptual understanding?

2. What experiences will the students need next?

What Are the Chances?

▼ Sort these statements into the best box.

Impossible	Unlikely	Likely	Certain

A. The sun will rise in the west.

B. The cafeteria will serve chocolate milk.

C. A boy in our class will be 2 meters tall.

D. Everyone in this room is alive.

E. Most people in our class have brown eyes.

F. There are more right-handed people in this room than left-handed.

G. The price of gas will be higher next year.

H. It will rain today.

▼ Write more statements to be sorted in the boxes. Explain your reasons for each.

What Are the Chances?

Grades: K–5

Objective: Identifying the likelihood of an event.

Getting Ready: Write the statements from *What Are the Chances?* on strips of paper or make a copy of the card and cut the statements apart into strips. Prepare four "boxes" or pieces of paper with the labels Impossible, Unlikely, Likely, and Certain. Also have some blank paper strips prepared so students may create their own statements to be sorted.

Launch: Begin by discussing how probability is a branch of mathematics which helps us predict the chance of something happening. Also display your boxes and define the following terms:
　　Impossible—an event will never happen
　　Unlikely—an event probably won't happen
　　Likely—an event might happen
　　Certain—an event will always happen

Instruct: Take each statement (A–H) and discuss with the students which box best describes it. Have them place the statement in the correct box. Below are possible responses, although as noted, some depend on the setting.
　　Impossible—A, C (2 meters is approximately 6 feet 6 inches)
　　Unlikely—H (depends on the weather for the day)
　　Likely—E (depends on the classroom), F, G
　　Certain—B (depends on school food service), D

Summarize: Give students some blank paper strips and have them write at least one statement for each box. Share and discuss the statements they created.

Gearing Down: Narrow the four categories to two, Impossible and Certain OR Unlikely and Likely. Prepare and discuss additional real-world statements that will help students understand the categories.

Gearing Up: Divide a number line into four sections, corresponding to the four categories. Assign the value 0 to Impossible, and 1 to Certain. The center of the line should be .5 or 1/2. Challenge students to assign numeric values to their statements. Also provide statements from probability experiments that could be assigned a specific value by making a ratio of the possible outcomes to the total number of outcomes. For example, use a 6-sided die. The chance of rolling 1, 2, 3, 4, 5, or 6—(6/6 or 1). The chance of rolling an even number—(3/6 or 1/2). The chance of rolling a 1 or 2—(2/6 or 1/3). The chance of rolling 1, 2, 3, or 4—(4/6 or 2/3). The chance of rolling a 7—(0/6 or 0).

REFLECTION:

1. Which categories were the easiest for the students? Which were the most difficult?

2. What experiences will the students need next to further develop their understanding of probability?

Rolling and Recording

▼ Try this:

1. Choose a partner, and each of you make a chart like the one shown. Predict which sum of two dice will come up most often.

2. Each of you take turns rolling two dice.

3. On a turn, find the sum of the spots on the two dice, and place a tally mark in that column on you chart.

4. Continue rolling and recording until one of you has 10 tally marks in one column. Compare your prediction with the actual result.

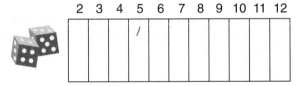

Putting it together:

• Why doesn't the chart need a ones column? A thirteens column?

• In which column did you or your partner reach 10?

• Compare your results, and tell how they are similar. Different.

• Tell why you would expect more sums of 7 than 2.

• Complete the following: "I would expect about the same number of sums of 4 as . . . . "

• Would you expect to get about the same number of even sums as odd sums? Tell why.

Extending this activity:

Suppose you multiplied the numbers on the dice instead of adding them.

• How would the values along the top of the chart change?

• How many values (that is, different products) would be needed?

• Which values would be least likely?

• Would you expect to get about the same number of even values as odd values? Tell why.

Rolling and Recording

Objective: Conducting a probability experiment.

Getting Ready: For each student or group of students, you'll need two six-sided dice and a copy of *Rolling and Recording* for recording the results from rolling and summing the dice.

Launch: Show students the two dice and have them list all the possible sums that can be obtained from rolling the dice and adding the faces. Have students predict which sum will occur most and explain why they chose that sum. (Item 1 on *Rolling and Recording*)

Investigate: Have students conduct the experiment. (Items 2–4)

Summarize: Discuss and compare their initial predictions and actual results. Talk about the "Putting it Together" questions.

Gearing Down: Help students construct a table which lists all the ways the dice can land to get the possible sums. Point out the sums that have the most combinations and those that have the least. Talk about how the more combinations that are possible, the more often that sum will occur.

Gearing Up: Have students try the Extending this activity suggestions at the bottom of *Rolling and Recording*. Can they accurately predict that which product will occur the most? Have them construct a chart to "prove" their theory. Then have them collect data.

REFLECTION:

1. How did students initially predict which sum would occur most?

2. While conducting the experiment, did any students begin to notice particular sums were occurring more often? How did they explain what was occurring?

3. If students didn't see why particular sums were occurring more often, what did you do to guide them in that direction?

Can You Make Predictions?

▼ Roll a die six times and record the results:

1 2 3 4 5 6

- Did each face appear once? _____

- Does knowing what happened on the first roll help predict

  the second? _____

  the third? _____

▼ Roll a die 24 times and record the results.

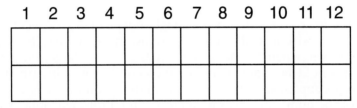

1   2   3   4   5   6   7   8   9   10 11 12

13 14 15 16 17 18 19 20 21 22 23 24

- Did each face appear once? _____

- The same number of times? _____

- What face appeared most? _____

- Does this mean the die is unfair? _____

- Does this record tell you what will occur on the next roll? _____

Can You Make Predictions?

Objective: Identifying independence of events.

Getting Ready: For each student or group of students you'll need a six-sided die and copies of *Can You Make Predictions?* so students may record the results from rolling the die.

Launch: Show the six-sided die. Ask students to tell you all of the possible numbers that might show if you roll the die. Review the following terms:
<u>outcome or event</u>—What could happen in a given situation, 6 outcomes-could roll 1, 2, 3, 4, 5, or 6?
<u>sample space</u>—All possible outcomes. For example, on a six-sided die, the sample space has six possible outcomes include rolling 1, 2, 3, 4, 5, or 6.
<u>random</u>—Each outcome has an equal chance of occurring. The order outcomes occur cannot be pre-determined.
<u>fair</u>—If a die is fair, you have an equal chance of randomly landing on each face. If something is unfair, the outcomes may not occur randomly. For example, sliding the die rather than rolling it may favor a particular number.

Investigate: Have students complete *Can You Make Predictions?*

Summarize: Discuss the results. Emphasize that the die is fair. Because of randomness, we cannot predict what will occur next. Discuss independence of events. If two events are independent, one event does not affect the outcome of the other. Rolling a 2 on the die, four times in a row, does not influence the chance of getting a 2 on the next roll. Each time the die is rolled, there is still a one out of six chance of getting a 2. The rolls of a die are independent of one another.

Gearing Down: Have students flip a coin or two-color counter (only two outcomes) instead of rolling a die.

Gearing Up: Introduce the concept that even though independence of events gives each outcome an equal chance of occurring, with a small number of trials, the actual results may not match the theoretical probability. However, when the number of trials gets very large, the ratio of a particular outcome to the total number of trials approaches the theoretical probability (the ratio of the outcome to the sample space). For example the theoretical probability of rolling a 2 is 1/6. When many trials are completed the ratio of the number of twos rolled to the total rolls will approach 1/6.

REFLECTION:

1. As you introduced the probability terms, which ones were already familiar to the students?

2. Did any misconceptions emerge from this lesson? What experiences could you provide to help eliminate those misconceptions?

Name: _____

Class: _____

What Do You See in Me?

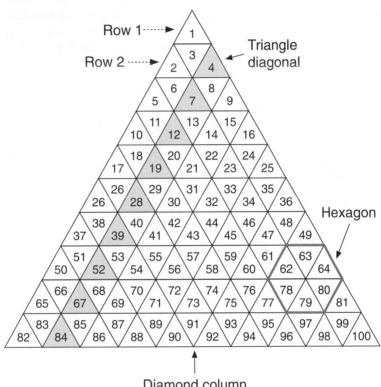

- Do you see the perfect squares?

- Where are the odd numbers?

- Find the sum of the numbers in each row. See if you can find a shortcut.

- Take any hexagon like the one outlined. What is its sum? Can you find a shortcut?

- Take any two adjacent numbers in a triangle diagonal (for example, 4 and 7). Find their product. Where is it?

What Do You See in Me?

Objective: Identify number patterns.

Getting Ready: Give each student a copy of *What Do You See in Me?*, crayons or colored pencils, and a calculator.

Launch: Give each student a copy of *What Do You See in Me?* and have them look at the triangle for patterns. Challenge them to find as many patterns as they can. If they have difficulty getting started, suggest they look at how each row is changing or how the sums of the numbers in successive "diamonds" are growing or how the sums of the rows are changing. Show how you can generalize the sums of rows pattern. Row K has a sum of K times the middle number. Have them share the other patterns they found.

Investigate: Review that perfect squares are products such as 2×2, 3×3, 4×4, etc. Have students work together to answer the questions on the sheet. Have them use crayons to shade what they find. Remind them that you did the third bullet with them during the launch.

Summarize: Discuss the patterns identified and whenever possible, have the students write an expression to represent each pattern.

Gearing Down: Identify and shade the patterns on the triangle together.

Gearing Up: Have students use reference materials to learn more about the mathematician Pascal and patterns found on Pascal's triangle.

REFLECTION:

1. Were students able to find patterns without much teacher direction? What strategies did they use?

2. How can the use of pattern activities like this one encourage problem solving and critical thinking by students?

3. Based on your experience with this activity, what would you recommend these students do next as a pattern activity?

Name: _____

Class: _____

Do You Believe That?

▼ Try one of these conjectures about positive whole numbers.
See if you can find examples that disprove each.

- *Tinbach's Conjecture:* Every number can be expressed as the difference
of two primes.

    Examples: $14 = 17 - 3$ $5 = 7 - 2$ $28 = 31 - 3$

- *Zinbach's Conjecture:* Every number can be expressed as the sum of
3 squares (0 is permitted).

    Examples: $3 = 1^2 + 1^2 + 1^2$ $14 = 1^2 + 2^2 + 3^2$
    $9 = 3^2 + 0^2 + 0^2$

- *Aluminumbach's Conjecture:* Every odd number can be expressed as the
sum of 3 primes.

    Examples: $15 = 5 + 5 + 5$ $11 = 3 + 3 + 5$

- *Brassbach's Conjecture:* Every square number has exactly
3 divisors.

    Example: $2^2 = 4$, 4 has 3 divisors 1, 2, and 4

- *Copperbach's Conjecture:* The product of any number of primes is odd.

    Examples: $5 \times 3 \times 7 = 105$ (3 primes)
    $7 \times 3 \times 3 \times 5 = 315$ (4 primes)

Do You Believe That?

Grades 6–8

Objective: To explore conjectures about positive whole numbers.

Getting Ready: You'll need a copy of *Do You Believe That?* Be familiar with Goldbach's conjecture that any even number greater than 2 can be written as the sum of two primes. This conjecture has never been proved or disproved. These are variations on this and other number theory conjectures. None of them, as written, are true. Several can be disproved through counterexamples. Some of them may seem true for numbers of a given size. Try one yourself to see that if the conjecture is reasonable.

Launch: Try this first with one or two students who need a challenge. Then, you may broaden the investigation to others. All students at this level could contribute to a class investigation if you build the interest in the problem. You may want to read a little about Goldbach to the class.

Investigate: Choose one, or let the children choose one of the conjectures. Challenge them to disprove the conjecture or to modify it so it seems more reasonable.

Gearing Down: Work together as a class.

Gearing Up: Have students make up their own conjectures.

REFLECTION:

1. Which conjecture did you chose? Why?

2. What conjectures did students want to investigate?

3. Were students more willing to work with a conjecture that soon produced a contradiction or with one that they could not disprove?

Appendix A:
Blackline Masters

A-1   Base-Ten Blocks

A-2   0-9 Numeral Cards

A-3   0-9 Dot Cards

A-4   Attribute Pieces

A-5   Hundreds Charts

A-6   Geoboard Recording Paper

A-7   Centimeter Grid Paper

A-8   Inch Grid Paper

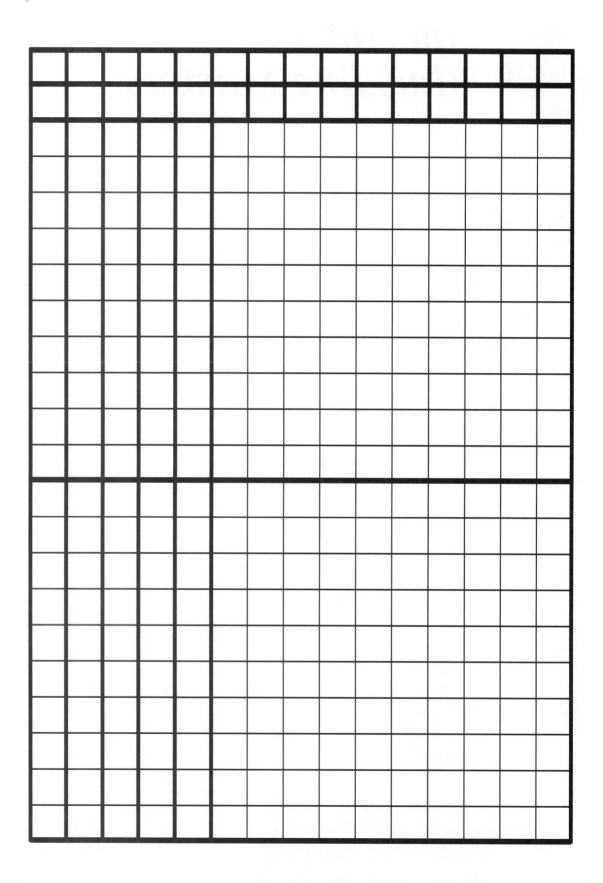

4	9
3	8
2	7
1	6
0	5

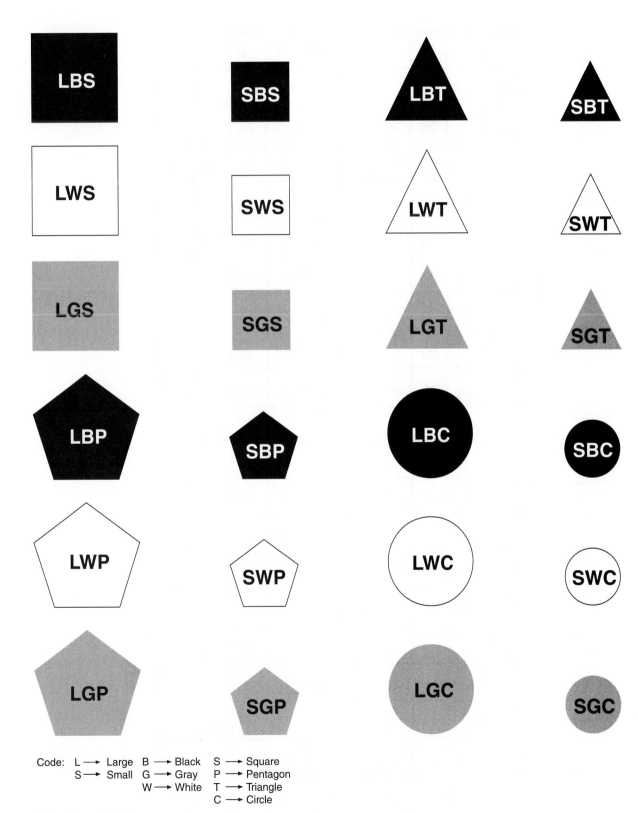

Code: L ⟶ Large B ⟶ Black S ⟶ Square
       S ⟶ Small G ⟶ Gray   P ⟶ Pentagon
                  W ⟶ White   T ⟶ Triangle
                              C ⟶ Circle

LBS = Large Black Square

1	2	3	4	5	6	7	8	9	10
11	12	13	14	15	16	17	18	19	20
21	22	23	24	25	26	27	28	29	30
31	32	33	34	35	36	37	38	39	40
41	42	43	44	45	46	47	48	49	50
51	52	53	54	55	56	57	58	59	60
61	62	63	64	65	66	67	68	69	70
71	72	73	74	75	76	77	78	79	80
81	82	83	84	85	86	87	88	89	90
91	92	93	94	95	96	97	98	99	100

0	1	2	3	4	5	6	7	8	9
10	11	12	13	14	15	16	17	18	19
20	21	22	23	24	25	26	27	28	29
30	31	32	33	34	35	36	37	38	39
40	41	42	43	44	45	46	47	48	49
50	51	52	53	54	55	56	57	58	59
60	61	62	63	64	65	66	67	68	69
70	71	72	73	74	75	76	77	78	79
80	81	82	83	84	85	86	87	88	89
90	91	92	93	94	95	96	97	98	99

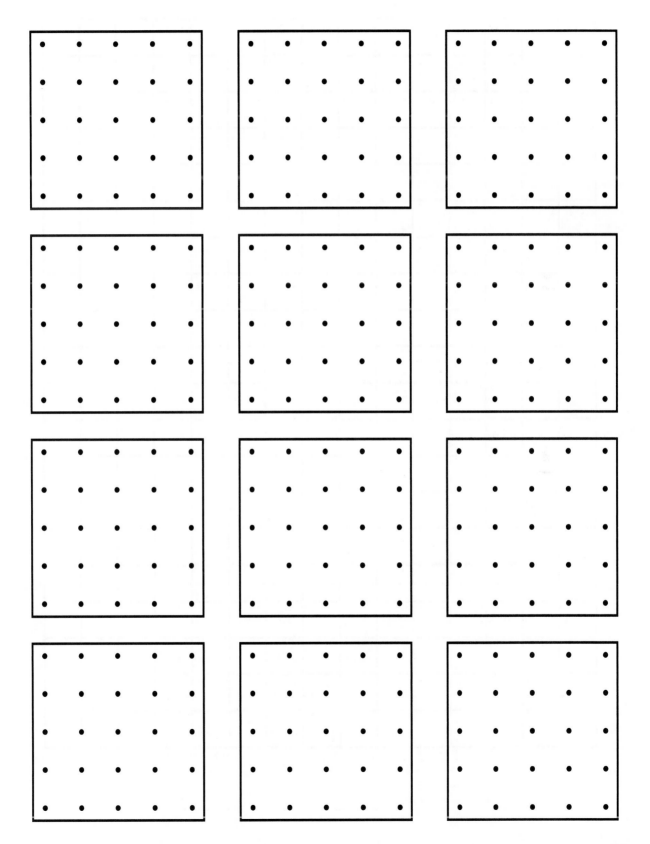

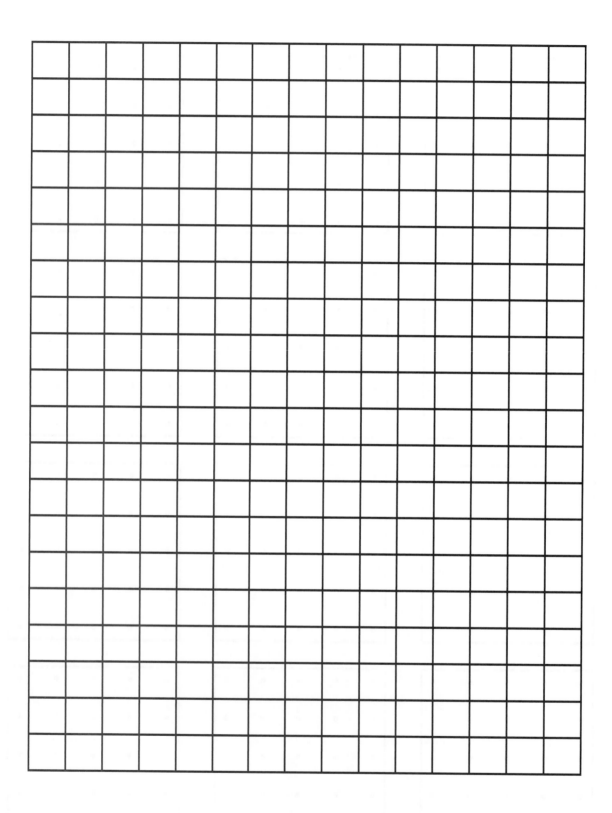